AF559592

Managing Qualities Services in Library and Information Sciences

Managing Qualities Services in Library and Information Sciences

Utpal Sharma

RANDOM PUBLICATIONS
NEW DELHI (INDIA)

Managing Qualities Services in Library and Information Sciences

ISBN 978-93-5111-566-3

Published in 2015 in India by

RANDOM PUBLICATIONS

4376-A/4B, Gali Murari Lal, Ansari Road
New Delhi-110 002
Phone : +9111-43580356, 011-23289044, 011-43142548
e-mail: sales@randompublications.com,
info@randompublications.com, randomexports@gmail.com

Reprinted, 2021

Type Setting by : Friends Media, Delhi-110089
Digitally Printed at : Replika Press Pvt. Ltd.

Preface

The library is an organization to offer reference and information services to its users. Library service is the combination of the services-process and its delivery. In a library, the service offered from acquisition section, technical section, maintenance section etc. are the processes carried out there and thereafter delivered to the users.

The quality should start from the acquisition section, which should be carried uniformly to circulation section. A user who had an unpleasant experience from the library will tell it to many people, but a good experience will be told to very few. Therefore it is very necessary for librarian to understand the users, what they want, how they want, and when they want the documents and information.

Library and information services are fundamental to the goals of creating, disseminating, optimally utilising and preserving knowledge. They are instrumental in transforming an unequal society into an egalitarian, progressive knowledge-based society. It is well known that in India most of the libraries function in the government sector.

New information technology can potentially support a range of traditional and Non-traditional library services. Most of the library services generated using information technology resemble closely to those generated manually with improvements and modifications to suit the requirements of automated services.

Librarians are also creating Web sites, answer archives, and links to answers to "frequently asked questions" all designed to anticipate user questions and help people find information independently. Traditional reference desk service continues to be highly valued by library users in many settings, but the newer forms continue to grow in popularity. Consequently, it is all the more important that librarians understand the range of enquiries that can be expected, allowing them to provide a full and ready answer, regardless of the form in which the query arises.

The book is suppose to be useful for the practicing librarians, information scientists, teachers and students of library and information services.

I would like to thank my team for standing beside me throughout my career and writing this book. My special thanks go to "Random Publications" who have published the book.

–Utpal Sharma

Contents

Preface .... *v-vi*

1. Service Quality in Library 1

Background 1
Role of Libraries 2
Measuring Library Quality 6
Customer Satisfaction and Service Quality 8
Methodology of Library Quality Services 13
Data Analysis 16
Library Quality Assessment 18
Value of Library Services in Development 21

2. Managing Quality of Academic and Research Library 34

Market-Driven Collaboration 34
Academic Libraries in India: A Historical Study 36
Academic Library Structures 54
Technology-Enhanced Library Services 70
CD-ROM and Electronic Databases 71
Digital Libraries 73
The Impact of Information Technology on Academic Libraries 75

3. Multimedia Trends in Library and Information Services 88

Introduction 88
Applications of Multimedia 89
Multimedia Library information Kiosks/Walk-Through Programmes 91
Limitations of Multimedia 100
Basic Architecture of Multimedia Catalogue 101
Information Sources in the Library/Internet 107

4. Management Information Systems 119

Introduction 119
Management Information System vs. Decision Support System 123
Changes in Library and Information Centre Management 124
Change Management Standards 134

Library Skills and Managerial Challenges 148
Information Technology use in Library Management System 153
Library Movement and Issues in Indian Digital Libraries 156

5. Quality Concept in Library Services 160

How to Improve the Quality in Library Services 160
Kinds of Information Service 162
Measuring Qualities of Library Services 165
Use of Public Library Services 168
Technological Innovations in Improving
Library Services 183

6. Quality Management Approaches

in Library Services 189
Introduction 189
Information Service System 192
Quality Management Approaches 195
Quality by Design 197
Management of Digital Library Education 199
Managing Library Technology: Planning for the Future 217

7. Management in Library Information Service 222

Where should Libraries Focus their IT Resources 222
Resources for Web Based Library Services 226
Library Services: Challenges and Opportunities 229
The Successful Virtual Library 233
Saving Libraries with Technology 235
Metadata at Digital-Informative Era 237
New Information Technology in Special Libraries 243

8. Role of Information Technology in Managing Organisation 254

The Evolution of Information Technology 254
IT's Role in Managing Organisational Change 265
Impact of Information and Communications Technology 269
Authoritative and Validated Information 276
Impact of Information Technology on Information Professionals 278

***Bibliography* 300**

***Index* 302**

1

Service Quality in Library

BACKGROUND

Libraries exist to collect the record of human experience and to provide intellectual and physical access to that record. For academic libraries in particular, there is a responsibility to preserve scholarly communications as well as the primary resources upon which scholarship often depends.

During the past two decades, myriad challenges and opportunities for libraries have been presented as a result of the rapid development and deployment of information technologies. This environment has spurred librarians to reconsider and redefine collections, services, organizational structure, the skill sets required of library staff, and the attributes of library facilities. A task force of the University of California Libraries recognized this state of change in libraries.

- The continuing proliferation of formats, tools, services, and technologies has upended how we arrange, retrieve, and present our holdings. Our users expect simplicity and immediate reward and Amazon, Google, and iTunes are the standards against which we are judged.

Library decision makers must therefore determine how to meet new and evolving expectations for library services and materials. Clearly, libraries are operating from vastly different assumptions about the ways in which they might best carry out their responsibilities than they did a few, short years ago. While library practice is changing, it remains based in a commitment to service.

Collections of books and other information resources without accompanying access tools, instruction, or other library services are mere warehouses, not libraries. Librarians in all types of libraries work to ensure that their organizations provide high quality service in support of the goals of the library‘s parent institution. It would be rare indeed to discover an academic library, for example, that did not consider service quality an important aspect of carrying out its mission to support teaching, learning, and research in the college or university in which it operates. But how do library administrators know whether their libraries are meeting the new expectations of users or providing high quality service?

ROLE OF LIBRARIES

In the modern knowledge society libraries have a new role and there are various types of library models. In the modern society, where the use of electronic services and Web-based information sources constantly increases, libraries are managed in a more democratic way, have more flexible communication system and work organisation, and their service development is based on the quality and user-orientation of services. In the modern knowledge society libraries have a new role and there are various types of library models.

These are as follows:

- Traditional library as a memory institution
- Library as a learning and research centre
- Library as a cultural and communication centre
- Electronic library
- Digital library
- Virtual library as library without walls.

Libraries had been performed many important roles in the past agrarian and industrial societies. But those roles were limited in scope. In the 21st century, libraries have to perform pivotal roles in disseminating and sharing the culture of knowledge. In this age of knowledge libraries should be repositories of all of the knowledge and information accumulated by human kind.

They will have to store all kinds and forms of material and information and disseminate beyond the geographical boundaries. Today's advanced information technology is enabling libraries to accomplish this immense task. Exchange of knowledge has always been the most important objectives of libraries. Various systems have been developed to share and exchange the records of human knowledge. Universal Bibliographic Control and Universal Availability of Publications are two major Programmes of IFLA (International Federation of Library Associations and Institutions) to exchange knowledge world over. OCLC is the world leading library network in USA for sharing intellectual knowledge among academic community in all over the world. But libraries in the 21st century should fulfill more dynamic role. They should exchange knowledge and information with users inside and outside their country, thus going beyond their traditional reference and lending services. This would possible when libraries agreed to expand their roles beyond the geographical boundaries by using sate of art technologies.

The modern libraries certainly can not be passive repository for books and other printed materials. The opposite requirements of storing increasing collection in various forms and of maintaining easy access to most part of it can only be balanced by deploying information and communication technologies. Libraries should upgrade their services by digitising their resources for online use.

These services should be accessible to anyone, regardless of time or location, through digital communication devices. Libraries can play significant role in providing a good education and knowledge of high quality. Individuals around the world, no matter how poor they may be, can access whatever knowledge and information they need by visiting libraries via the internet, such as the library of congress.

PROBLEMS AND OPPORTUNITIES FACING LIBRARIES IN INDIA

Library and information services are fundamental to the goals of creating, disseminating, optimally utilising and preserving knowledge. They are instrumental in transforming an unequal society into an egalitarian, progressive knowledge-based society. It is well known that in India most of the libraries function in the government sector.

These are in academic and research institutions and under the public library system, which is again under the state and central governments. At present, education being a state subject and coming under the purview of different apex agencies, there is no common direction or coordination among them. It is imperative that all libraries (public, academic, research and special) change gear and develop at an accelerated pace. Developments in information communication technology (ICT) have enabled libraries to provide access to all, and also bridge the gap between the local, the national and the global. Yet the Library and Information Services (LIS) sector in India has not kept pace with the paradigmatic changes taking place in society.

There are a few libraries which are using state of art technologies to disseminate knowledge to their respective user community. There is lack of cooperation among the libraries of different organisations and which cause the lack of union catalogues at national level.

The national library failed even to do this immense task. One of the major problems faced by LIS sector in India is lack of bibliographic control at national level which causes duplication in research. A considerable number of libraries had not been developed bibliographic databases of their documents for putting them on network. To summarise, the major constraints faced by the libraries which militate against effective dissemination and use of information are:

- A considerable percentage of the population is illiterate or functionally literate making libraries of minimal use to them.
- Poor resource allocation for infrastructure improvement and collection development for public libraries.
- Lack of sufficient sanctioned posts, forcing most services to be operated by voluntary Non-professional staff, which damages

information organisation and services.

- Lack of national policies promoting ICT as a tool for development of library systems and services.
- Lack of adequate trained manpower in the use of IT.
- Lack of funds for acquiring necessary hardware and software facilities.
- Resistance on the part of library staff to change from their traditional practices to the use of IT.

Despite the problems, Library and Information Services (LIS) sector in India has got remarkable achievements. Efforts had been made to set up networks at local, regional and national level to deploy information and communication technologies and to build electronic information sources. Besides INFLIBNET at the national level to support university and college libraries, a number of other national networks and various library networks have also been developed including NICNET (National Informatics Centers Network), ERNET (Education and Research Network), CALIBNET (Calcutta Library Network), DELNET (Developing Library Network), etc.

A number of educational institutions are members of such networks. These networks, especially INFLIBNET and DELNET, are engaged in compiling union catalogs, creating various databases of experts, providing training to library staff, ILL, online facilities, reference service, assistance in retrospective conversion, etc. To overcome the problem of financial crunch and the rising costs of journals, librarians have formed consortia to subscribe all the required journals and databases. Some special libraries and research organisations have established consortia known as FORSA (Forum for Resource Sharing in Astronomy) to share electronic access to journal literature.

NISCAIR (National Institutes of Science Communication and Information Resources), one of CSIR labs, has formed a consortium for CSIR labs for accessing e-journals and databases. In order to solve the problem of universities and college libraries, UGC launched a major initiative called UGC-INFONET that provides high speed Internet connections so as to have electronic access to professional literature including research journals, abstracts, review publications, and databases from all areas in science and technology, as well as in social sciences and humanities.

The Ministry of Human Resource Development (MHRD) has set up the "Indian National Digital Library in Science and Technology (INDEST) Consortium" for the subscription to electronic resources for 38 academic institutions, including the Indian Institute of Sciences, Indian Institute of Technology, Regional Engineering Colleges, Indian Institute of Managements, and about 60 centrally-funded/aided government institutions through the consortium. For the improvement of quality of library and information services through the systematic acquisition, organisation and dissemination of knowledge, various library associations have been set up at national and state level.

They annually organised conferences, seminars and training Programmes to trained and update library professionals with latest development in LIS. Recently libraries and research organisations realise the importance of digital libraries and they started the work of digitisation of important documents. NISCAIR and the Department of Indian Systems of Medicine and Homoeopathy (ISMandH) have entered into an agreement for establishing a Traditional Knowledge Digital Library (TKDL) on Ayurveda. TKDL will be available in English, German, French, Spanish and Japanese Since, these languages account for more than 98 per cent of the international patent applications.

TKDL in the first phase targets Ayurveda. But as a whole it would encompass, in addition to Ayurveda, Siddha, Unani, Yoga, Naturopathy and Folklore medicine. The Indian Institute of Science (IISc), Carnegie Mellon University (CMU), the International Institute of Information Technology, Hyderabad (IIITH) and many other academic, religious and government organisations, totaling about 21 'Content Creation Centers', have become partners in the Digital Library of India (DLI) initiative for the digitisation and preservation of Indian heritage present in the form of books, manuscripts, art and music.

Each centre brings its own unique collection of literature into the digital library. DLI has a vision to build a universal digital library of world knowledge. One million books have already been available through this project. India perhaps has one of the oldest and largest collections of Manuscripts in the world. These manuscripts are in different languages and scripts; written on different materials such as birch bark, palm leaf, cloth, paper, etc. They are in the custody of libraries, museums, monasteries, mutts and individuals.

A significant proportion is not preserved scientifically. Experts estimate that almost all palm leaf manuscripts may perish due to wear and tear over next 50 to 100 years. In this regard the National Mission for Manuscripts has taken a step to save the most valuable, intellectual property of our cultural inheritance. The missions has started a pilot project for digitising the manuscripts in five states across India covering five caches of manuscripts and for the same four digitising agencies have been selected.

Importance of open access archives, institutional repositories and open access journals has been realised by the library and information professionals in India. This movement has been accelerated by the availability of open source software namely DSpace, EPrints, Greenstone, etc., Indian Institute of Science, Bangalore, INFLIBNET Centre, Ahmedabad and Documentation Research and Training Centre (DRTC), Bangalore are the leading institutions who made this movement a great success. Among the top 25 publishing countries, India ranks 12th for the overall number of journals, but drops to 18th for journals with online content. At present there are more than 150 open access journals in India. The open access journals in India are mainly initiated by six journal publishers, namely, Indian Academy of Sciences, Indian National Science Academy, Indian Medlars Centre of National Informatics Centre, Medknow Publications, indianjournals. com and Kamla-Raj Enterprises. The Indian Institute of Science was the first in the country to set up and interoperable institutional archive ePrints@IIScr.

The archive now has more than 7000 records, with over 90 per cent having full text. Presently there are 25 institutional archives in India which are registered in the Registry of Open Access Repositories (ROAR). An open access statement is likely to be ready by this year. The CSIR also has a plan to setup a national digital repository of research literature. NISCAIR has already started to work on the project known as National Science Digital Library. National knowledge Commission is also formulating similar open access policies and guidelines for the higher education and R and D sectors to improve access to research literature and disseminate research literature to the global communities. The National Knowledge Commission has submitted its report to the government on how to redefine the information services sector. The report of Knowledge Commission on library sector suggests that "Every state should establish a registry and archives of knowledge based digital resources which should be made accessible to all".

MEASURING LIBRARY QUALITY

The recent emphasis on assessment in higher education has affected every facet of post-secondary institutions. Administrators in college and university libraries are no exception; they need assessment tools that provide data for continuous improvement, documentation of assessment, and evidence of the thoughtful use of assessment data for accreditation organizations. The traditional measure of academic library quality has been collection size.

In fact, many institutions still organize special events to commemorate the acquisition of a library's millionth volume. Rather than providing a census of its collections, however, the Middle States Commission on Higher Education now requires the institution to demonstrate the "availability and accessibility of adequate learning resources, such as library and information technology support services, staffed by professionals who are qualified by education, training, and experience to support relevant academic activities. Colleges and universities are therefore required to determine adequacy without prescriptive measures such as volume counts or numbers of professional staff.

The other regional associations have similarly broad statements, leaving librarians and institutional effectiveness staff to figure out a new approach. This shift in the assessment of libraries has been described as a "move beyond the rearview mirror approach" of simply reporting what libraries acquired or how many users walked through the front gates in a given year. This emphasis on assessment for accountability has motivated librarians to seek out more meaningful measures of quality. Rather than focusing solely on inputs such as collection size or staffing level, the first new library measures were output measures that sought to describe what libraries produced with their inputs.

That is, in the 1990s librarians began to report outputs such as the number of items borrowed or the number of reference questions answered. Those measures alone, however, still fell short of addressing whether library services were sufficient. As colleges and universities created student learning outcomes beginning in the late 1990s, librarians also created measures that were based on outcomes, or the extent to which student and faculty contact with libraries affected them and contributed to the mission of the university. New instruments and protocols, however, were needed for libraries to meet demands for accountability, measure service quality, and generate data for effective library management.

LIBQUAL+™

Service-based industries in the private sector began using an instrument called SERVQUAL for assessing customer perceptions of service quality in the 1980s. SERVQUAL was developed by Parasuraman and grounded in their Gaps Model of Service Quality. In 1995, 1997, and 1999, the Texas A&M University Libraries, seeking a useful model for assessment, used a modified SERVQUAL instrument. Their experience revealed the need for an adapted tool that would use the Gaps Theory underlying SERVQUAL and better address the particular requirements of libraries. In 1999 the *Association of Research Libraries* (ARL) partnered with Texas A&M University to develop, test, and refine the adapted instrument.

As a result of their collaboration, LibQUAL+™ was "initiated in 2000 as an experimental project for benchmarking perceptions of library service quality across 13 libraries". During 2006 the LibQUAL+™ survey was administered in 298 institutions. This study analyzed data collected from the two administrations of LibQUAL+™ during 2006. A description of the instrument will facilitate an understanding of the investigation. With each administration, the LibQUAL+™ instrument was improved and it is currently composed of 22 questions and a comment box. The three dimensions measured by LibQUAL+™ are service affect, information control, and library as place. The perceptions of customers about library staff competency and helpfulness are derived from nine questions that compose the service affect dimension score.

The information control dimension is derived from eight questions and focuses on whether the library's collections are adequate to meet customer needs and whether the collections are organized in a manner that enables self-reliance for library users. Finally, the library as place dimension is derived from five questions that address user perceptions regarding the facility‘s functionality and adequacy for academic activities. All of the scores are scaled from 1 to 9 with 9 being the highest rating, so that scores can be compared.

RELIABILITY AND VALIDITY

A number of studies have examined the LibQUAL+ ™ instrument for score reliability and validity. In a key study by Heath, Cook, Kyrillidou, and Thompson, validity coefficients replicated closely across different types of post-secondary libraries, leading them to conclude that *"LibQUAL+ ™ scores may be valid in reasonably diverse library settings"*. This study explored that conclusion as it relates to institutional size, institutional type, and level of investment by the institution in its library. Since 2000 LibQUAL+ ™ has been administered in every state except Alaska and South Dakota, and. . . in various language variations in Canada, Australia, Egypt, England, France, Ireland, Scotland, Sweden, the Netherlands, and the United Arab Emirates. The 2005 cycle saw administration in several South African universities. And the summer of 2005 brought training in Greece. The instrument has consistently tested as psychometrically valid and the protocol has "a universality that crosses language and cultural boundaries at the settings where LibQUAL+ ™ has been implemented to date".

CUSTOMER SATISFACTION AND SERVICE QUALITY

In the for-profit sector, customer satisfaction measurement and management has long been a common practice, and contemporary service quality assessment has its roots in customer satisfaction measurement. During the past 40 years, the concept of customer satisfaction has changed a number of times. From the corporate image studies of the 1960s to the total quality approach in Western economies in the late 1980s, several approaches to customer satisfaction led to the contemporary conceptual model of service quality.

The first phase of customer satisfaction measurement took the form of corporate image studies in the 1960s. Customer satisfaction and perception of quality were often included indirectly in image surveys as questions about company characteristics such as progressiveness or involvement in the community. The second phase saw the birth of product quality studies beginning in the late 1960s. The primary measurement was the adequacy–importance model that created an index of satisfaction to explain customer attitudes.

The index was created by "summing measures of satisfaction with product performance multiplied by measures of feature importance". Beginning in the 1970s, a new phase was evidenced by some early customer satisfaction studies that were implemented in regulated industries, notably by AT&T. Without market-based performance indicators, monopolies sought to justify rate increases by garnering favourable customer satisfaction measures. The 1980s marked the next major evolution in thinking about customer satisfaction. The increased competition in the American automobile market from foreign companies gave rise to syndicated automotive studies, such as the J. D. Powers and Associates studies. The current focus of customer satisfaction measurement can be traced most directly to the 1980s, when the total quality movement captured the attention of businesses in Western economies and businesses recognized the need for a model that addressed the fundamental shift to a service-based, rather than product-based, economy. There was no longer a specific, tangible product to assess, and businesses turned to customer perceptions of whether their expectations were being met or exceeded.

THE GAPS MODEL OF SERVICE QUALITY

The marketing research group of Parasuraman, Zeithaml, and Berry developed an approach to customer satisfaction measurement in the 1980s called the Gaps Model of Service Quality. The Gaps Model assessed customer satisfaction by identifying the differences, or gaps, between customer expectations and customer perceptions of service. In this model, customer expectations are established by the customer, who defines the minimum acceptable and the desired levels of service. The customer then describes his or her perception of the level of service he or she received and the gap is thereby defined by the difference between perceived level of service and desired level of service. Hernon and Nitecki noted that service quality definitions vary across the literature and are based on four underlying perspectives.

1. Excellence, which is often externally defined.
2. Value, which incorporates multiple attributes and is focused on benefit to the recipient.
3. Conformance to specifications, which enables precise measurement, but customers may not know or care about internal specifications.
4. Meeting or exceeding expectations, which is all-encompassing and applies to all service industries.

Most marketing and library science researchers, however, have focused on the fourth perspective and the Gaps Model of Service Quality uses that perspective as a framework to identify the gaps created when performance either exceeds or falls short of meeting customer expectations. In fact, the Gaps Model expands the fourth perspective to five, with the addition of "gaps that may hinder an organization from providing high quality service". In the Gaps Model customer *expectations* are viewed as subjective and based on the extent to which customers believe a particular attribute is essential for an excellent service provider.

Customer *perceptions* are judgements about service performance. Furthermore, expectations are not viewed as static; they are expected to change and evolve over time. Hernon wrote that

- The confirmation/disconfirmation process, which influences the Gaps Model, suggests that expectations provide a frame of reference against which customers‘ experiences can be measured . . . customers form their expectations prior to purchasing or using a product or service. These expectations become a basis against which to compare actual performance.

The measurement of service quality using the Gaps Model, therefore, focuses on the interaction between customers and service providers and the difference, or gap, between expectations about service provision and perceptions about how the service was actually provided. The difference between the minimum acceptable and the perceived levels of service is the adequacy gap; larger adequacy gaps indicate better performance. The difference between the desired and perceived levels of service is the superiority gap; ideally, these scores would be identical so a perfect score is zero. As the superiority gap score gets further from zero, either positive or negative, it indicates poorer performance.

CUSTOMER SATISFACTION AND SERVICE QUALITY

Consumer satisfaction research "matured into a respectable research stream" in the mid-1960s. Several approaches to customer satisfaction have emerged since then that contributed to the conceptual model of service quality used in contemporary measurement efforts. From the corporate image studies and product quality studies beginning in the late 1960s, measurement approaches emerged based on customer expectations or values. The adequacy–importance model, for example, was one such measurement that moved from just measuring consumer satisfaction with product performance to enriching those product performance measures with consumer values.

It added ratings of the importance of each product feature. The level of satisfaction with performance was then multiplied by the product feature importance to create an index of consumer satisfaction.

Expectancy Disconfirmation Theory

One of the primary areas of exploration in the emerging field of consumer satisfaction research in the 1960s was from the perspective of expectancy disconfirmation theory. Expectancy disconfirmation is a process theory that creates a framework for examining the formation of customer expectations and the subsequent confirmation or disconfirmation of those expectations through comparisons with product performance.

Consumers are thought to compare post-purchase performance to their expectations prior to purchase "using a "better-than, worse-than heuristic" to arrive at a judgement of simple confirmation if the product performs as expected. If performance is better than anticipated, there is a positive disconfirmation of the consumer‘s expectations; if the performance is worse than anticipated, there is a negative disconfirmation.

THE SERVICE-BASED ECONOMY

In the 1980s, consumer satisfaction theorists and businesses alike began to realize that, in terms of the gross national product and employment statistics, the economy in the United States had become dominated by service industries. For the purposes of customer satisfaction measurement, there was no longer just a physical product to assess in terms of durability or number of defects. The commercial sector was beginning to recognize the need for a new customer satisfaction model that addressed the fundamental shift to a service-based economy and it turned to examining customer perceptions of whether their expectations were being met.

Total Quality Management

Crosby contends that the contemporary emphasis on quality is "largely attributable to the quality movement in business" that took hold in the United States in the mid-1980s. The success of foreign companies in the American market in the late 1970s and the 1980s was unprecedented. The success of Japanese companies in particular, such as Toyota and SONY, led many American companies to look at how the Japanese had become so successful. Since the end of World War II, Japanese companies had focused on quality and embraced *Total Quality Management* (TQM). American companies subsequently looked for ways to integrate TQM into their own organizations.

TQM requires every part of a company to be organized in terms of a single, integrated philosophy encompassing quality through teamwork, productivity, customer understanding, and customer satisfaction. A critical perspective in TQM is that only the customer may judge quality. In a paradigm where the customer judges quality, measuring customer satisfaction and customer perceptions of quality, not just product performance, becomes significant.

THE GAPS MODEL OF SERVICE QUALITY

As TQM became popular in the United States, the marketing researchers Parasuraman developed the Gaps Model of Service Quality. The Gaps Model is based on the expectancy disconfirmation perspective with a focus on service quality rather than product quality. In his review of quality assessment, Hernon wrote that:

- "the confirmation/disconfirmation process, which influences the Gaps Model, suggests that expectations provide a frame of reference against which customers' experiences can be measured. . . . customers form their expectations prior to purchasing or using a product or service. These expectations become a basis against which to compare actual performance".

The Gaps Model is described by Hernon as a way to measure customer perceptions of service quality by identifying gaps, or differences, between customer expectations and customer perceptions of service. In the Gaps Model, customer expectations are viewed as subjective judgements based on the extent to which customers believe a particular attribute is essential for an excellent service provider. Expectations are affected by experience and are not expected to remain the same over time.

In this model, customer perceptions are the judgements about how well service was performed. To deploy the Gaps Model, a survey instrument is used and customers are asked to define the minimum level of service they will accept and the level of service they desire. Customers are then asked to describe their perceptions of the service that was actually provided. The gaps between perceived performance level and customer-defined desires or expectations can be used to identify and target areas for improvement. Hernon's examination of the Gaps Model identifies five types of gaps created by discrepancies between:

- Customer expectations of service and management's perspective on these expectations;
- Service quality specifications and management's perspective of customer expectations;
- Service quality specifications and service delivery;
- Service delivery and external communication to customers about that delivery; and
- Customers' expectation of service and perceived service delivery.

The fifth type of gap, between customers' expectation of service and perceived service delivery, is the one used by Parasuraman in defining the framework for SERVQUAL, the instrument they created to assess service quality in the for-profit sector.

SERVQUAL

The SERVQUAL instrument is a multi-item scale that was developed to assess customer perceptions of service quality in retail businesses. It is based in the Gaps Model of Service Quality, which is grounded in expectancy disconfirmation theory.

Customers Define Quality

The SERVQUAL instrument was designed from data gathered in an exploratory customer study by Parasuraman. The exploratory customer study conducted focus-group interviews of customers in four distinct markets: retail banking, credit cards, securities brokerage, and product repair and maintenance. The focus-groups were designed to discover the elements that form the concept of service quality from the customers' perspective. Using a focus-group methodology reflects the TQM focus on quality as well as the precept that "only customers judge quality; all other judgements are essentially irrelevant". The definition of service quality that emerged from the customer focus groups was "the extent of discrepancy between customers' expectations or desires and their perceptions". The investigators also found that "the criteria used by consumers in assessing service quality fit into 10 potentially overlapping dimensions . . . tangibles, reliability, responsiveness, communication, credibility, security, competence, courtesy, understanding/knowing the consumer, and access".

Refining SERVQUAL

The first version of the SERVQUAL instrument was composed of 97 scale items designed by Parasuraman to gather data that would address those 10 dimensions. In the next phase of development, SERVQUAL was administered and data were collected for the 97 items. The investigators performed a factor analysis and applied reliability testing. Using Cronbach's alpha coefficient, with alpha values ranging from .72 to .83 across the 10 dimensions, the instrument was refined to 54 items.

Factor analysis of the resulting 54 items changed the factor loadings, suggesting reassignment of some items and deletion of others. Each time the factors were changed, the factor analysis was repeated and this iterative process ultimately resulted in 22 items loading on five dimensions. The final five dimensions in SERVQUAL included three of the initial dimensions: tangibles, reliability, and responsiveness, as well as two new, combined dimensions: assurance and empathy.

METHODOLOGY OF LIBRARY QUALITY SERVICES

The purpose of this study was to explore and expand on the current understanding of the meaning of LibQUAL+™ scores in college and university libraries. Specifically, this study addressed whether the scores were related to characteristics that express institutional mission, institutional size, or level of investment in libraries. The definition of service quality that underlies the LibQUAL+™ protocol is the definition that was used in the present study. Service quality was defined as "the result of the consumer's comparison of expected service with perceived service".

VARIABLES

The independent variables that were investigated for potential relationships with LibQUAL+™ scores were institutional type, institutional size, and investment in libraries. For this investigation, institutional type was defined as the classification assigned by the Carnegie basic classification, institutional size was defined as 12-month FTE enrollment, and institutional investment in libraries was defined as total annual library expenditures. The dependent variables in this investigation were the mean perceived scores for the three dimensions of LibQUAL+ ™ and the overall, weighted LibQUAL+ ™ score.

SAMPLE AND POPULATION

This study investigated potential relationships between institutional characteristics and LibQUAL+ ™ scores in American colleges and universities. According to the *National Center for Education Statistics* (NCES), the population of post-secondary, degree-granting institutions that confer at least four-year degrees is 2,217. The sample of institutions for this investigation was a non-random, convenience sample.

Selecting the Sample

The sample was limited to an existing group of American college and university libraries that opted to participate in the LibQUAL+ ™ survey during 2006. Furthermore, institutional score reports were included in the sample only if all of the following conditions were met.

- The institution agreed to share its results.
- The institution used the American English version of the survey.
- The institution placed itself in the "Colleges and Universities" category.

Finally, two more libraries were removed from the sample because complete data for this study could not be obtained. In both cases, the libraries participated in LibQUAL+TM as single institutions but did not report individual institutional statistics to the NCES Academic Library Survey; NCES data were subsumed in the reports of a parent institution.

Size and Representativeness

Of the 298 institutions that participated in the 2006 administration of LibQUAL+ ™, the sample was composed of 159 institutions that met all of the selection criteria. The resulting sample of 159 institutions is an adequate sample size since it is generally considered acceptable to have a minimum of 30 cases in each group for a correlational study. For an exploratory, goodness-of-fit analysis, a one-sample Kolmogorov-Smirnov test was computed for the independent variables: library expenditures, FTE enrollment, Carnegie basic classification, and library expenditures per FTE. The test results were significant for all of the independent variables, which indicated that the distribution was significantly different from a normal distribution. Since the distribution did not meet the assumption of normality, the data analysis required non-parametric procedures. The one-sample Kolmogorov-Smirnov test was also computed for the dependent variables, which had distributions that were not significantly different from a normal distribution.

LIMITATIONS AND DELIMITATIONS

Since the sample of score reports included in the study is a convenience rather than a random sample from a self-selected group of institutions, it may not be representative of all academic libraries. In addition, the findings of this investigation cannot be generalized to institutions that administered the survey in other languages, including British English. Finally, since the study analyzed data related to college and university libraries, findings cannot be generalized to other types of libraries.

DATA ACQUISITION

The data analyzed in this study were originally collected and published by the *Association of Research Libraries* (ARL), the Carnegie Foundation for the Advancement of Teaching, and the *National Center for Education Statistics* (NCES). A number of validity and reliability tests have confirmed the integrity of the LibQUAL+ ™ protocol. Data were retrieved from the publications of these organizations to enable an analysis designed to address whether, and to what extent, there were relationships between LibQUAL+ ™ scores and the following characteristics of colleges and universities: institutional type, institutional size, or level of investment in libraries. The following research questions were posed as a framework for the study.

- What were the 2006 LibQUAL+ ™ scores for American college and university libraries?
- What were the characteristics of the American college and university libraries that administered LibQUAL+ ™ 2006?
- To what extent, if any, were scores for the information control dimension related to institutional type as expressed by the Carnegie basic classification?
- To what extent, if any, were scores for the library as place dimension related to library expenditures per FTE student?
- To what extent, if any, were scores for service affect related to institutional size as expressed by FTE enrollment?
- To what extent, if any, was institutional investment in the library, as expressed by library expenditures, related to scores for each of the three dimensions, or to overall LibQUAL+ ™ scores?

The data for the dependent variables were LibQUAL+ ™ scores that were collected for this study from the LibQUAL+ ™ score reports of libraries in the sample.

The data for the independent variable, "institutional type" were collected from the Carnegie Foundation's published basic classification of each institution. The library expenditures and 12-month FTE enrollment data were obtained from the NCES publication, *Academic libraries: 2004*.

STATISTICAL ANALYSIS

The first two questions were addressed by conducting descriptive statistics procedures that summarized the distribution of LibQUAL+ ™ scores and institutional characteristics for the libraries in the sample. Frequencies for all values of each variable were determined; mean and median scores were calculated as measures of central tendency.

Variability was described by variance and standard deviation calculations, and outliers were identified. For the remaining four questions, correlations and regressions were performed to discover whether, and to what extent, the relationships existed. Simple linear correlation, non-parametric correlation and bivariate linear regression were used to assess the potential relationships of the independent variables with the dependent variables.

DATA ANALYSIS

PROBLEM AND APPROACH

The recent emphasis on assessment in higher education has prompted university administrators, including library administrators, to develop new ways of evaluating services and programs. Libraries are service-oriented organizations, yet the traditional measure of academic library quality has been collection size.

The emphasis on formal assessment in recent years has motivated librarians to seek out more meaningful measures of service quality. There is a need for assessment tools that produce data that can be used to inform improvement, as well as document assessment practices for accreditation organizations, funding agencies, and governing boards.

The LibQUAL+™ Instrument

In the 1990s, the Texas A&M University Libraries began using a survey instrument called SERVQUAL, which had been designed to measure customer perceptions of service quality in the private sector. After administering the instrument three times to assess library service quality, the Texas A&M University Libraries entered into a partnership with the *Association of Research Libraries* (ARL) to develop, test, and adapt the instrument for academic libraries. That collaboration created the LibQUAL+ ™ survey, which was first administered in 2000 by the ARL across 13 research libraries as an experimental project for benchmarking perceptions of service quality. Since that first administration, the LibQUAL+ ™ survey has become an increasingly popular tool. In 2006, there were 298 libraries that participated in LibQUAL+ ™. The instrument has been improved and refined and it is currently composed of 22 questions and a comment box. Each question is answered on a scale from 1 to 9, with 9 being the highest rating.

The *service affect dimension* is concerned with the perceptions of customers about library staff competency and helpfulness; the *information control dimension* is concerned with whether the library's collections are adequate to meet customer needs and organized in a manner that enables self-reliance for library users; and the *library as place dimension* is concerned with the library facility's functionality and adequacy for academic activities.

PURPOSE AND DESIGN OF THE STUDY

Considering the increasing level of participation in the LibQUAL+™ survey, and the relatively small body of research about the meaning of LibQUAL+™ results, this study was completed for the purpose of adding to the library profession's understanding of the meaning of LibQUAL+™ scores. Previous research found that validity coefficients for LibQUAL+™ replicated closely across different types of post-secondary libraries in one study, leading the authors to conclude that *"LibQUAL+™ scores may be valid in reasonably diverse library settings"*.

This study explored an aspect of that conclusion by seeking to determine whether institutional characteristics would impact LibQUAL+™ scores. The data analysis was designed to address whether, and to what extent, there were relationships between LibQUAL+™ scores and selected institutional characteristics of American colleges and universities. Specifically, this study examined the following institutional characteristics for potential relationships with the 2006 LibQUAL+™ scores.

- Institutional type as defined by the Carnegie basic classification,
- Institutional size as defined by 12-month FTE enrollment, and
- Institutional investment in libraries, as defined by annual library expenditures.

METHOD

The sample was composed of libraries in American colleges and universities that conferred at least 4-year degrees and participated in LibQUAL+™ during 2006. This was a sample of convenience that included a total of 298 participating libraries. Initially, 82 libraries were removed from the total sample of 298 libraries because they did not identify themselves as libraries in colleges or universities. From the remaining 216 institutions in the sample, 55 additional participating institutions were removed because they were from countries other than the United States. The remaining 161 libraries became the initial sample. During the data collection phase of the study, two additional institutions were removed from the sample because complete data required for this study could not be obtained. In both cases, the libraries had participated in the LibQUAL+TM survey as independent institutions. However, during data collection it was discovered that neither library reported statistics as an independent institution to the Academic Library Survey administered by the *National Center for Education Statistics* (NCES). NCES data for both of the libraries were subsumed in the reports provided to NCES by their parent institutions.

The remaining 159 libraries formed the final sample that was used in this study. The research questions that framed the study were addressed by using SPSS for Windows to analyze the data. The calculations produced descriptive statistics, calculations of bivariate correlations, and bivariate regression analyses. The independent or predictor variables were annual library expenditures, FTE enrollment, Carnegie basic classification, and library expenditures per FTE. The design of this study employed an approach that required multiple calculations using the same set of variables. For this reason, the Bonferroni adjustment was applied to the significance levels to reduce the chance of a Type I error. The conventional .05 significance level was divided by four to account for the four questions that were addressed. Subsequently, data were accepted and interpreted as statistically significant at the .013 level or lower.

LIBRARY QUALITY ASSESSMENT

Historically, academic library quality has been expressed in terms of collection size. The "ultimate goal of bringing together a perfectly customized collection of books for the purposes of fulfilling users‘ needs" drove collection sizes higher and led to assessing a library‘s quality by the "magnitude of its resources". In this environment, libraries relied upon collecting statistics and analyzing input measures.

Input measures, the financial, human, and material resources available to the library organization, have been measured in some form by research libraries since 1908. With the increasing emphasis on assessment and accountability, coupled with the changes in libraries and library collections made possible by information technology, librarians began to seek new measures of quality that would be more meaningful.

From Inputs to Outcomes

In the first phase of seeking out new measures, librarians shifted from focusing solely on what libraries had acquired, and developed measurement models beyond simple inputs. In the 1990s, library measurement expanded to include output measures: the activities that libraries produced from inputs, such as the number of items borrowed or questions answered. Library professional associations, including the *Association of Research Libraries* (ARL) and the *Association of College and Research Libraries* (ACRL), as well as the *National Center for Education Statistics* (NCES) continue to collect collection- and activity-based data from academic libraries. NCES maintains an academic library comparison tool on its website for the purpose of comparing such data among institutions in the United States. Input and output measures are useful yardsticks, but they do not capture the full extent of the impact a library has on its institution. In its 1998 report, the ACRL Task Force on Academic Library Outcomes Assessment captured the limitations of such measures, noting that "measurement of inputs, or the specification of quantities of them by standards, is viewed by some as a primitive, or at least insufficient way" of assessing libraries.

The Task Force argued for libraries to develop outcomes-based measures. In the late 1990s the movement to hold schools, colleges, and universities accountable for establishing and meeting outcomes was becoming formalized by accreditation requirements and pressure from State legislatures for accountability. Educators had been using learning outcome measures for about 15 years at that time, but until the 1990s, most of them had not been required to use formal outcome measures in accreditation reports or legislative budget requests. Libraries tapped into this activity on campus and began to develop outcomes and outcomes-based performance measures.

Library outcomes were intended to measure "the ways in which library users are changed as a result of their contact with the library's resources and programs" as well as document how libraries contribute to meeting institutional outcomes.

Service Quality from the User Perspective

It is only since the beginning of the 21st century that libraries have engaged in directly measuring service quality from a user perspective. As recently as 2001 the library assessment literature did not, for the most part, consider direct measurement of quality. For example, as late as 2001, Shim, McClure, and Bertot observed, in a report on measures and statistics for ARL, that "to accurately indicate the success or quality of an academic library, measurement should be implemented at three key levels: outcome level, use/capacity level, and resources level. In other words, prominent library science researchers were still relying on measures that assessed quality indirectly.

Of the measurement methods Shim, McClure, and Bertot identified, there was no instrument or protocol for directly measuring service quality in a library, and there was certainly no instrument to measure service quality across libraries for benchmarking purposes. Pritchard offers a cogent description of the measurement challenge that faced librarians.

- The difficulty lies in trying to find a single model or set of simple indicators that can be used by different institutions, and that will compare something across large groups that is by definition only locally applicable—*i.e.,* how well a library meets the needs of its institution. Librarians have either made do with oversimplified national data or have undertaken customized local evaluations of effectiveness, but there has not been devised an effective way to link the two.

As library practitioners and scholars worked to develop meaningful measures for libraries, the need for reliable and meaningful assessment instruments intensified. In their quest to discover better measures, the Texas A&M University Libraries turned to marketing research in the 1990s to identify instruments for measuring library service quality. At that time the SERVQUAL instrument had been widely used in the private sector for about 10 years; moreover, SERVQUAL's creators, Parasuraman, were members of the Texas A&M University faculty.

The Texas A&M University Libraries used SERVQUAL three times, in 1995, 1997, and 1999, to track perceptions of library service quality from samples of its library users. Through that experience, the assessment team recognized that the instrument could be improved for libraries by adapting it to address the concepts most critical to library service and removing "items not considered relevant by some library users.

The Texas A&M University group approached ARL about working jointly to adapt SERVQUAL for libraries and they collaborated to apply for a grant from the *Fund for the Improvement of Post-Secondary Education* (FIPSE). The FIPSE award funded the effort to develop a modified protocol, which they called LibQUAL+™.

VALIDITY AND RELIABILITY

The LibQUAL+™ survey is the first assessment instrument that is claimed to produce reliable and valid national benchmarks for library service quality. A number of studies have supported the instrument's score reliability. LibQUAL+™ has also consistently tested as psychometrically valid. Roszkowsli, Baky, and Jones criticized one aspect of validity by examining LibQUAL+™ scores from a slightly different perspective. In a 2005 investigation, they analyzed data from 709 respondents at one institution that participated in LibQUAL+™ during 2003. The study found that the perceived performance rating was a more valid indicator of user satisfaction than the superiority gap score.

This criticism of the LibQUAL+™ protocol focused on the validity of the superiority gap score, which is the difference between users' perceived and desired levels of performance. The investigators argued that user-defined desired levels of performance are irrelevant and only user perceptions of actual performance are valid measures of library service. In a study by Heath, Cook, Kyrillidou, and Thompson, validity coefficients replicated closely across different types of post-secondary libraries, from which they concluded that LibQUAL+™ scores may be valid in different types of library settings. The study described in this report investigates that conclusion by exploring whether and to what extent there are relations between LibQUAL+ ™ scores and the following key characteristics: institutional size, institutional type, and level of investment by the institution in its library. Only one study was identified in the literature review that specifically explored potential relationships between LibQUAL+ ™ scores and institutional characteristics. However, this previous study used an earlier version of the LibQUAL+ ™ instrument with four dimensions and used a different set of institutional characteristics for the independent variables than those in the present study. Kyrillidou and Heath found a "moderate negative relation of the ARL Membership Criteria Index with LibQUAL+ ™ scores". The ARL Membership Criteria Index is composed of volumes held, gross volumes added, current serials, total staff, and expenditures.

In other words, the Index is composed of traditional input and output measures of library quality. Kyrillidou and Heath concluded that students and faculty members in libraries at large research institutions have higher expectations for library collections, which results in lower LibQUAL+ ™ scores. The negative relationship found between the ARL Membership Criteria Index and LibQUAL+ ™ scores occurred, they asserted, because such library users "are highly skilled, have specialized and diverse information needs . . . are clearly more demanding and harder to please" than library users at other types of institutions.

CONCEPTUAL FRAMEWORK

This literature review served as the basis for the conceptual framework underlying this study. It is clear that demands for assessment are directed at post-secondary institutions and their libraries by internal and external constituencies including governing boards, state and federal agencies, accreditation organizations, and administrators who need data for decision making. In addition, library users bring expectations to the library about services and resources based on their understanding of the institution as well as their experience and skill in using libraries.

VALUE OF LIBRARY SERVICES IN DEVELOPMENT

We live in the 'end-of-everything' era: the end of time and space, the end of ideology, the end of geography, the end of history, the end of the nation state. In this same vein, the end of libraries has been proclaimed. Libraries are supposedly being swept away by the digital revolution.

Yet, library power is still very alive, and has become even more potent in this new age. This priceless power leverages accumulated human intellect efficiently into human progress. From this power issues the springs of literacy and knowledge, the seeds of democracy, and the fuel of productivity.

The library as a catalyst for human progress is irreplaceable. In spite of their enormous power to propel human progress, libraries are increasingly asked to justify the resources spent on them, to justify even their very existence. In this climate, libraries must be accountable, responsive, and effective in portraying the value of their services to funding authorities, be they public or private.

These imperatives have led to a new emphasis on quantitative assessments to provide hard evidence about the extent of their value to the society or their sponsors. Secondly as online information become more and more available, arguments against funding of libraries are increasing in number and loudness.

Therefore, assuring the proper functioning of libraries depends on demonstrating their value in the widest sense and to their widest audiences.

LIBRARIES ADD VALUE EVEN IN MONETARY TERMS

Research has produced hard facts that libraries pay fully for their existence, and even produce positive returns on the investments made on them.

For example, long-term studies of technical libraries using return on investment analysis (ROI) established that in monetary terms libraries produce 515 per cent annual return on investment, that is five times more than what is invested on them per annum. Cost-benefit analysis also showed that the benefits derived from library services outweigh the cost of providing them.

These results were mainly based on the following value dimensions:

- The cost of library users' time, weighed against the cost of providing professional library services.
- All costs associated with obtaining a piece of library service on an ad-hoc basis weighted against the costs of obtaining it from a professionally organised in-house library servic.
- The value of having the right information at the right time to increase the speed of an operation or prevent the undertaking of a potentially useless or wasteful process or project, modifying work, or stopping an unproductive line of work.
- The cost a person is willing to pay for library services to enable him or her to successfully complete a project.

Return on investment analysis of public library services also show evidence of high value-added. For example, which is from an annual report of a public library district of a developed country, shows how investment in library service yielded more than fivefold returns when compared to the monetarily valued outcomes.

From research reports reviewed, it may be deduced that depending on the type of library, and the cost of a professional's time in relation to the cost of reading materials, the savings achieved by an organisation or a community that has a well-functioning library, may range from 2 to 8.5 times if the cost of running the library is weighed against the cost of obtaining library services from outside sources, libraries of high technology firms, research centres and institutions working on mission-critical projects may achieve savings of up to 8.5 times.

Materials and Services	Estimated Value of Benefits
4,751,514 books and materials borrowed at an average retail price of $20 each.	$95,030,280
4,614,903 books, periodicals and newspapers were used in libraries, if purchased the average retail price of each would be $10.	46,149,030
5,435,095 reference questions were answered in person by library Staff, if each charge were $2 per enquiry.	10,870,190
625,292 Internet sessions (45 minutes per session) at a $2\per session access fee.	1,250,584
420,581 persons attended special programmes and exhibitions, if there were a $2 admission fee.	841,162
19,000 children and teenagers participated in the Mayor's Summer Reading Programme, if there were a $5 registration fee.	95,000
279 literacy tutors provided 10,015 hours of one-on-one tutoring to 239 project participants, if each charge were $25/hr.	250,375
Total Benefits	$154,486,621
Less Taxpayers' Investment on libraries -$24,645,113	-$24, 645, 113
Total Return on Investment from Libraries.	$129, 841, 508

The magnitude of the value-added reported by the studies is quite striking, as is the high degree of their consistency, both across different measures, and across different library types and cases. This gives a high degree of confidence that the findings reflect a genuine phenomenon. It can therefore be concluded that library services pay for themselves by orders of magnitude. When library services are non-existent, the costs in terms of lost long-term productivity are infinitely high.

WHAT DEVELOPMENT

Yes, libraries achieve high value-added at the level of the institution, but of what value are they in community and national development? The answer to this question depends on what we think the goals of development are. In classical terms, the purpose of development is to attain increased productivity for economic growth.

Economic growth has not however, provided solution to rural exodus, marginalisation of the weak, galloping urbanisation, proliferation of shanty-towns, mass unemployment, increased poverty and spread of deadly diseases. As Julius Nyerere stated, "the truth is that development means the development of people. Roads, buildings, the increases in crop output, or other things of that nature, are not development, they are only tools of development".

This and similar thread of thinking lead to the notion of human development: the increasing of people's chances to acquire knowledge and have access to resources that would enable them to lead healthy, gainful and dignified life. To be pragmatic, development efforts should be aligned with the current regional and global development strategies such as the *New Partnership for India's Development* (NEPAD) and the *Millennium Development Goals* (MDGs) which are multidimensional and lay emphasis on human development and sustainability. Libraries can play direct as well as catalytic roles in contemporary development initiatives.

LIBRARIES HARNESS INFORMATION AND KNOWLEDGE

Libraries increase the value of human intellectual outputs by increasing access to them through professional processing, storage and dissemination. Processing and organisation moves ideas, data and other primary intellectual outputs from raw bytes to information. The world's intellectual outputs would be useless, even constitute a nuisance, if libraries were not there to gather, analyse, classify, catalogue and provide access to them. The hundreds of bibliographic records of published and unpublished materials ensure their use and reuse to satisfy commercial, educational, cultural and recreational needs.

CRITICAL IN THE EDUCATIONAL PROCESS AND CONTINUING DEVELOPMENT OF INTELLECTUAL CAPITAL

The educational and research role of libraries cannot be over-emphasised. Research has found that libraries make significant contributions to the effectiveness of the education process. Learners from institutions where library use is part of the learning process are more likely to become equipped for the society and occupational effectiveness than those without proper library habits.

Libraries are also central for the development of literacy, a critical component of the development of intellectual capital of a community, an attribute which initiates a ripple effect on an individual's ability to become gainfully employed, increase his or her income and make effective contributions to society. Community members use library services and library programmes for everything from introducing their children to the habit and joy of reading, to tapping into their professional networks.

CATALYST FOR ECONOMIC DEVELOPMENT AT THE LOCAL AND NATIONAL LEVELS

Economic development effort is simply any activity that raises real incomes, thereby offering new hopes of expanded opportunities for people, communities, and enterprises. As both the global and national economies become more and more knowledge-driven, specialised knowledge has become the indispensable asset for further economic development.

Local businesses benefit greatly in specific ways from libraries, including access to new ideas, knowledge and information. In particular, relocating businesses, start-up businesses, and small businesses of all kinds are perceived as enjoying the greatest benefits from library products and services. Indeed, existence of libraries has been cited as a reason for a business' decision to relocate to a particular community. Studies also found that business information resources were significantly more valuable with expert help of library staff. In other words, not only are information sources themselves viewed as important resources for people seeking mission-oriented information, but professional services provided by librarians are believed by many to be critical factors in finding, accessing and utilising information resources to the fullest extent, especially with regard to electronic resources.

Studies further suggest that for any nation to be effective in the global economy, its institutions of higher learning must do more than just prepare an educated workforce and expand knowledge through research and scholarship. They must get involved in local economic development. Libraries in these institutions can play an important role in effecting extension of economic development knowledge to the community. The main physical manifestations of economic knowledge extension services by higher institutions are *Economic Development Information Centres* (EDICs).

The type of information provided in EDICs includes: general economic and industry-specific statistics, economic forecasts, trade statistics, market surveys, census data, tax and regulatory requirements, cost-of-living and cost-of-doing-business data, information on general business practices, financial planning, as well as employee benefits and compensation. 'How to' materials ranging from starting a business to entering foreign markets are also an important part of a typical core collection. Training in basic business planning and management could also be provided. A library may offer extension services as part of its service portfolio or develop an EDIC unit to focus on local economic development services.

DIRECT ECONOMIC BENEFITS TO MEMBERS OF THE COMMUNITY

Many direct benefits from library services accrue to individuals. These include cost savings from borrowing materials rather than having to buy them; borrowing of such items as audio books and videotapes, which save significant expenditures; and the use of periodicals and newspapers which result in financial benefit. There is a dual nature to this: first, users save the cost of purchasing these items themselves; and second, many users have been better able to manage their lives as a result of information obtained.

In fact, some quality of life indexes, for example best places to live, best places to raise children, and best places to retire, include 'library books per capita' statistic when profiling communities. Libraries enhance productivity of individuals and organisations.

Access to the right information is a very critical component in the productivity of information workers, and consequently the productivity and good decision-making of the organisations employing them. For the self-employed knowledge worker, use of libraries make them more productive on their jobs, especially as they can obtain job related training in the areas of computer and information literacy skills and good business practices.

SOCIAL INCLUSION AND COHESION, PARTICIPATION AND EMPOWERMENT

Libraries perform an important role of social inclusion when they serve the needs of disadvantaged populations such as the poor, the elderly, the physically disabled, the unemployed and those with learning disability, because these are exactly the groups least likely to have the means to acquire such assets as information sources, computers and Internet access. Libraries also serve as agents of social cohesion.

In one study, a participant said: "we are brought closer to other members of our community through the very act of sharing books with them". For this reason, social inclusion and life-long learning agenda of most developed countries include the founding of new public libraries and increased information and library provision for learners at all levels and of all ages.

CIVIC CENTRE AND COMMUNITY INFORMATION SERVICE

For many communities and organisations, libraries serve as civic centres, which assist them in meeting their civic duties by offering meeting space for civic organisations, assisting with voter registration, and making government forms available, including tax forms. Libraries also serve as a posting place for proposed changes in local ordinances, and other local government proposals.

As a community centre, the library introduces users to new systems of doing things during changeover programmes. A variety of other programmes are offered, such as story telling, technology education, and recreational activities. Valued in most places is the availability of meeting rooms for voluntary groups, which represent monetary savings to them. Libraries also serve the public by providing assistance in finding answers to many basic questions: from how to find jobs to where to find up-to-date health and legal information. The information the library provides to answer some of these important questions can lead to significant economic benefits and impacts.

ESSENTIAL ELEMENT OF PHYSICAL DEVELOPMENT

Research also found that communities value their libraries as physical assets and a source of community pride. Indeed, libraries, especially public and national libraries, are important landmarks in many cities and other communities. Participants in a survey stated many times that the presence of a new library, or the redevelopment of an existing one, favourably impacted on its immediate surroundings.

LIBRARIES AND CITIZEN EMPOWERMENT, DEMOCRACY AND E-GOVERNMENT

Effective citizen action is possible only when citizens know how to gain access to information of all kinds and have the skills to become responsible, informed participants in democracies. This is especially so as e-government evolves. Libraries offer real and virtual civic spaces where citizens can speak freely, share similar interests and concerns, and pursue what they believe are in their public's interest. Ultimately, free discourse among informed citizens assures civil society; and civil society provides the social capital necessary to achieve common goals.

Through this role libraries prevent the lack of information and idea exchanges which in a closed society stifles creativity, suppresses the imagination and creates a barrier to social, economic and technical progress. e-government is about using the power of information technology to provide better public services. The main dimensions of an e-government strategy include: building services around citizens' choices, making government and its services more accessible, ensuring social inclusion and ensuring two-way communication between the government and the governed.

Governments have always depended on libraries to collect and disseminate government information, but egovernment adds very new and valued dimensions: the citisen empowering potential reinforced by virtual access and the possibility to hold governments accountable without physical confrontation. For librarians, a special challenge by e-government is to obtain recognition as the professionals best suited to provide guidance on e-government's need for information analysis, indexing, organising of digital documents, and the design and development of versatile interfaces for information retrieval as well as for data harvesting and communication.

BRIDGE DIGITAL DIVIDE ALONG WITH THE ECONOMIC GAP

Studies show that, only people and businesses in the higher income brackets are able to afford the hardware, software and connectivity costs required to participate in the information revolution, including e-commerce. The need for access to the Internet is however not limited to people and businesses with discretionary income, and it is here that libraries are well positioned to help bridge the economic gap along with the digital divide. From individuals who might not be able to afford computer technology at home to many small and home-based businesses, the library can provide the necessary connections to help prevent the division of our society into information 'haves and have-nots.' The western-style universal access is not a practical reality in

Indian countries where much of the population cannot afford individual access.

Instead, focus should be on providing access through community facilities like libraries and schools. In this role, libraries can help in poverty alleviation since, information poverty often is the basis of economic poverty. In the information age, access to information has a place alongside adequate food, health care, education, and other basic needs. This phenomenon has broadened the definition of poverty to include information poverty.

More so, when it has become clear those people and nations who cannot or will not participate fully in the new information economy will find it all the more difficult to climb out of poverty. Just as today, books are a chance for ordinary people to better themselves, in the information society, access to cyberspace will be a route to better prospects. But just as books are freely available from libraries, the door of libraries should lead everyone to cyberspace toll-free. In the information society this real chance for equality of opportunity through libraries should remain.

LIBRARIES AND THE INFORMATION SOCIETY

Despite the popular misconception, libraries have never confined themselves to books. Indeed, libraries pre-dated the invention of the book, collecting papyrus scrolls and manuscripts. For libraries therefore, content is much more important than the medium.

In fact, the information revolution is aiding the library movement by reinforcing the material-virtual duality of knowledge and information and helping in transforming our society into an information society based on a strong foundation of knowledge which is universal, objective, timely and drawing from a variety of sources.

In developed countries, libraries are taking the lead in Internetisation, digitalisation and virtualisation of access to knowledge. Special online services are being developed to support lifelong learning, provide health advice and information, and give citisens access to official documents free of copyright restrictions.

Thus libraries are becoming not only Internet access points, but also places where people may receive help in using the Internet and other information sources. Governments implementing digital opportunity programmes do them in cooperation with libraries. For example, in implementing its policy to ensure universal access to the Internet, the UK Government located two thirds of the 6,000 ICT learning centres billed to open in 2002 in public libraries.

Libraries are helping to build viable global communities based on local-global networks that enable individuals and groups to explore their respective and common futures, and create synergy through sharing of knowledge and experience. Local-global networking will become a means of making globalisation to suit local conditions, as knowledge and information sharing will make globalisation desirable through universalism, a new form of understanding that results from shared values engendered by constant exchange of experience.

WITH THE INTERNET, DO WE STILL NEED LIBRARIES

Yes, because, although a great deal of information is available from the desktop of anyone with a computer linked to the Internet, much of it is spurious and disorganised. Some of it is of course misleading. Much of the information that is authoritative is available only to paying subscribers. Such information can be accessed usually through libraries with site licences.

Thus users seeking value-added information need to access information sources through libraries, resources selected and organised by professionals. Besides, libraries enable users to learn to search the Internet efficiently, as well as help to identify free authentic sites.

ARE TODAY'S INDIAN LIBRARIES CAPABLE OF PLAYING THEIR RIGHTFUL ROLES IN DEVELOPMENT

To this question we can answer both yes and no, depending on the locality, but the fact is that the majority of Indian libraries are in real crisis. They were not always in this situation though. Between 1960 and 1980, libraries in India were built and resourced with determination in the hope that they would support the rapid development of their communities. Rightly, then national governments, organisa-tions and donors funded libraries as basic needs. However, since, the early 1980's, libraries across India have experienced a very deep decline in resources and services.

The so-called 'great Indian library decline' can be characterised as follows:

- Funds provided are grossly inadequate. In fact, most libraries do not get up to half of their minimum requirements. In most of the places, available fund just cover staff salaries.
- Libraries lag behind global trends due to inadequate resources, reliance of process inefficient processes, and weak professional networking.
- Lack of current books, journals and other information sources.
- Total lack of, or inadequate application of library information technology.
- Unavailability of, or unreliable access to the Internet;
- Empty reading rooms due to lack of library habit resulting from years of poor customer service.
- Rusty professional skills and outlook affected by lack of resources for training and development.
- Demoralised management and poor co-ordination within their parent organisations.

- Poor or absence of library support of the learning process across all types and levels of educational institutions across much of India, with student to book ratio as low as 30 students to 1 book in certain places.
- Library shelves in public libraries with old and irrelevant books that gather dust.
- Little or no physical development to match current needs.
- Little or no professional library activism and advocacy.
- Where in existence, library boards that overshadow the libraries they govern.

In this situation, libraries in India are in a very weak position to effectively play their roles in economic and human development. This is an unfortunate situation since, libraries do not yet have viable substitutes and may not have any in the near future. Do policy makers and leaders perceive this crisis? May be, yes! May be, no! But not much is being done about it.

Foundations and development organisations interested in libraries and educational development in India, such as the Carnegie Corporation of New York, have called attention to this crisis and invited in all stakeholders to join hands in dealing with it. Some of those organisations are actively funding or implementing projects aimed at alleviating this decline, but the situation may not improve significantly without the attention of all levels of government in India. This is because of the enormity of the need and the fact that eventually, government whether by design or by chance, determine the course of human progress wherever they operate.

THE PLACE OF LIBRARIES IN NATIONAL INFORMATION POLICIES AND INFRASTRUCTURE PLANS

National information policies can be viewed as the embracing framework to put into practice the basic notion that social and economic systems will function more efficiently if the right information resources are available to individuals, households, civil society, businesses and government agencies whenever they are in need of them. Placing libraries and other repositories of knowledge prominently in this framework is the pragmatic starting point, but studies show that in India, national information policies usually do not put libraries within the mainstream of issues addressed, instead technology is overemphasised. National policies and frameworks for information in most countries are fragmented, leading to limited coordination and ineffectual strategies.

For example, in most of the countries where library laws have been enacted, national library boards with overly political dispositions were created, resulting in a situation where the boards draw attention to themselves rather than to the libraries they were set up to promote. In these situations, vision and strategic directions are not well articulated or neglected.

POLICY IMPLICATIONS

The foregoing analysis has policy implications both for developing national and local strategies by governments and their agents; and for managing resources, services and operational relationships by institutions, library boards and librarians.

Identified implications are outlined:

- It should not be taken for granted that the value of libraries is widely recognised. This value should be demonstrated to all stakeholders, as often as possible. Return on investment analysis is particularly powerful in demonstrating the monetary value of libraries to their parent organisations and communities. This calls for efforts from library managers and boards to develop detailed frameworks to ensure data collection and communication of impact.
- Funding of libraries should be viewed as profitable investments in development, and as provision of public goods which help in efficient use of scarce financial resources.
- Library administrators and boards should recognise their economic and human development mission by developing programmes that directly impact on their local economies. In this respect, they should participate in projects that further local and national development, such as export promotions and youth skills development projects. Specialised outfits such as Economic Development Information Centres (EDICs) provide focussed means of delivering such services.
- To be effective e-government programmes must rest on viable libraries and information networks. Therefore, governments at all levels, should strengthen libraries, including university, school and public libraries to enable them to play their central role in strengthening the interactive exchange of information that is the essence of e-government.
- It is good policy to use libraries as agents for bridging the digital divide because libraries ensure wider access to information technology, the Internet and specialised information networks. In fact modern library services concretise the benefits of the information society to the grassroots of communities.
- Library governance in much of India needs a reappraisal. Library boards in a number of Indian states are preventing libraries from developing as strong brands. Successful libraries around the world are recognisable brands. Such libraries attract funds from a variety of sources and have the confidence of information seekers. A board should occupy the background so as to project the library it governs, to such a not overshadow it. This call may also go to any department to which a library is attached.

- National information policies in India should have substantial library services component. An information policy without the provision for libraries as the main purveyors of information resources and services is bound to lack substance in the long run. Libraries may not appear glamorous, but any information policy not based on this foundation of knowledge will normally not succeed to serve the aims of development.
- It is implied that any legislative agenda for the development of a national strategic information framework must include elements for library development in the areas of infrastructure, funding, human resources, technology, information sources, services and governance. Effective legislative and strategic framework for library-friendly policy environment should include the following elements:
  - A ministerial level organisation with respon-sibility for policy, resource allocation, introduction and administration of relevant laws, as well as representation of the interests of libraries at the highest level of government. This ministry may cover other related sectors such as science and technology, research and culture.
  - A national commission on libraries that provides strategic leadership and crossministerial advocacy on libraries, ensures policy and technical focus on how to maximize resources by coordination and networking across types of libraries as well as governmental departments and the private sector.
  - A national library established by legislation as the repository of all publications issued in a given country. A national library may have a wide range of responsibilities depending on the complexity of its operating environment.
  - A system of public libraries, supporting communities of all sizes and recognised as a vital component of the national strategic information management framework. Legislation may be used to define their roles.
  - A public records access legislation that establishes the structures for selecting, conserving, processing and giving access to records and documents of all levels and branches of government.
  - Intellectual property laws, which cover the ownership and use of copyright, patents and other forms of tradable intellectual assets. Provisions on lending rights for published materials may be included in this set of laws.
  - Professional body or bodies chartered or recognised by law and authorised to promote professionalism and standards.
  - Professional education and accreditation system that ensures dynamic human resources development in this area.

— National conference on library services that discusses policy issues related to libraries. A good example of this format is the White House Conference on Libraries and Information Services convened by the President of the United States.
— Prominent provisions should be made for the place and roles of libraries in national and regional information policies and infrastructure plans in India.

2

Managing Quality of Academic and Research Library

The application of computing to library work in India has a history of at least three decades because since, the time the computer entered premier academic institutions and selected R & D facilities, it has been explored for improving information processing and management routines. Information technology (IT) enriched library services arrived initially for science and technology (S&T) information handling and for the special libraries attached to research and development (R&D) centres and academic libraries in higher education institutions. In comparison to other libraries, academic and research libraries have better infrastructure and skilled manpower in greater numbers, making them able to offer information services comparable to advanced countries. Like qualified teaching and research personnel and well-equipped laboratories, the right information service is another vital element in the trinity which completes a fruitful academic or research environment.

MARKET-DRIVEN COLLABORATION

Academic and research libraries, especially in developing countries, are passing through a very challenging phase in their existence due to unfriendly trends in the emerging information market. On the one hand, these libraries are still left with many of the old problems such as poor budgetary support and weak infrastructure, as well as staff in fewer numbers and often with less expertise. But the new information marketing techniques, like the possibilities of delivering and accessing electronic information in diverse channels, force these libraries to be very vigilant and cautious in their approach towards information acquisition and services. Libraries and professionals in India were quick to understand the emerging information environment was forcing their users to depend largely on those resources, which are becoming more expensive day by day due to the rise in production costs, fall in subscriptions and inflationary trends of Indian currency.

When individual libraries found that alone they are not in a position to satisfy the information requirements of their clients, they formulated various collaborative arrangements with other libraries such as, interlibrary loan (ILL) services, document delivery services (DDS), resource-sharing, and consortia-based subscriptions.

PRESENT PRACTICES AND EMERGING GOALS

The special libraries attached to research and higher education were lucky enough to garner resources to automate their in-house routine operations and for hosting online public access catalogues (OPACs); some of them also set up facilities to search electronic databases. A few of them evolved the desired infrastructure for Internet surfing, for hosting of full-text database access, and for setting up digital libraries. The major advantage of the progress in computerisation is a considerable increase in the amount of information available online.

We have experienced that at the start of computer applications only the surrogates existed online, but some full-text content has been made accessible online in recent years. These libraries are experiencing the virtues of electronic information in different forms such as e-journals, e-books, bibliographic/full-text electronic databases on CD-ROMs and through Web access. Due to publishers' 'electronic plus' policies, libraries are able to access electronic versions of printed sources such as journals either for free or by paying an additional fee.

However the goal these libraries in specialised research and academic centres should have set for themselves is to enhance their information facilities to fully functional digital libraries, comparable with similar facilities in the developed countries.

CULTURES AND CONFLICTS FACED BY LIBRARIES

The fixed roles suggested by Levy for researchers, publishers and libraries are either overlapping or changing in the electronic scene. There are cases where an author or a library is acting as electronic publisher, and there are publishers providing a wide variety of information packages beyond the contents of printed journals. The real question is: has the library really lost ground in the emerging information scene? Even the critics will not say so.

The concerns expressed are only to revitalise the professional skills of librarians, rejuvenate the style of working and reorient the library towards its rightful place in effective dissemination of information. Maybe the common feeling that the library is a central place in the institution visited everyday by large numbers of users, like any public utility, has lost some ground in the electronic scene. Non-etheless, apart the continuing provision of information services for print sources, the electronic revolution has reaffirmed the library more as an information service and access centre than as an information storehouse.

ACADEMIC LIBRARIES IN INDIA: A HISTORICAL STUDY

Research in library history in India has remained largely neglected area which has resulted into availability of very limited and scanty literature. Commenting on the status of library history in India, Donald G. Davis, Jr. of the University of Texas at Austin, writes that "although a core literature on Indian library history exists, it has many imbalances and gaps. The scholars are very dispersed in their interests and their geographical location. With one person rarely contributing more than one work. There is little pattern to existing research efforts."

In this context, the role of historian happens to be much more crucial and significant to make an assessment of the growth and development of libraries in India, the factors responsible for their development and the impact of those factors on the library progress. Rajgopalan, in his 1987 presidential address to the Indian Library Association rightly said, "it is generally acknowledged that our libraries are underutilized in relation to investments being made in them.

Non-use and low-use of libraries amount to wastage of facilities being made available. Maybe the literacy rate, lack of reading habits, etc., are the causes for low use from the side of patrons... User education programmes must be organized by libraries in a way that libraries are fully utilized." He further remarked that, "if library historians would address the roots and trends of library issues, they would provide a valuable service to the profession and society."

The Father of Library and Information Science in India,Padmashri Dr. S.R. Ranganathan while giving a radio talk in April 1956 said: "an account of the libraries in the first four periods must necessarily depend upon the historical research. This has not yet been done. The library profession is too small in India to spare a person to fill up this antiquarian gap. Those trained in the scientific method of tracing history are too preoccupied with dynastic and political history to spare sufficient time for cultural history in general and library history in particular."

Thus, an historical study of the growth and development of academic libraries in India, is a desideratum, the fulfilment of which should go a long way in removing the imbalances and gaps. Such a study becomes significant not only in view of the tremendous activity concerning the growth and development of libraries in India, but also because their growth has been shaped in the first phase by the phenomena that have shaped the historical course of this period and, secondly, the rise of library as an important instrument in the advancement of knowledge and socio-economic transformation.

Source Material for Writing History of Libraries

For the purpose of scientific writing of history of libraries, an understanding of the nature of existing source material and knowing the art of using it is essential. The sources for writing the history are available in Pali, Sanskrit,

Chinese, Arabic, Persian and European Languages and most of them have been translated into English. These exist in various formats, such as Manuscripts, inscriptions, copper plates etc.

They are either indigenous or foreign. The contribution of foreign travelogues such as Tibetan, Chinese, Muslim, Portuguese, English and other Europeans is highly useful. Some noteworthy foreign travelogues are Itsing, Fahien, Hieun Tsang, Alberuni, Ibn Batuta, Minhaj, Firishta, Badauni, Afif, bernier, mandelso, Manrique de Lara, Martin, Count Noer.

In addition to the contribution of the travelogues, the contribution of historians like Henry M. Eliot, John Dawson, Stanley Lane-Pool, Ishwari Prasad, R.C. Majumdar, Jadunath Sarkar, V.D. Mahajan, Mohammed Muhammed Zubair, J.S. Sarma and N.N. Law etc. is also significant.

Though scanty, yet there are articles written by the library professionals on history of libraries. A few efforts have also been made for conduct of research in the area of history of libraries and such like works have been consulted for the purpose of writing this paper.

University Libraries in Ancient India

In the Vedic age instructions were imparted "orally, without the medium of books." Taxila from 700 B.C. to AD 300 was considered to be the most respected seat of higher learning and education in India but still there is no evidence found so far in the archaeological excavations at Taxila that there had been a good library system in the Taxila University.

Fa-Hien noticed such libraries at Jetavana monastery at Sravasti. In A.D. 400, there came into being one of the biggest known universities, the Nalanda University, which by A.D 450. became a renowned seat of learning, its fame spreading beyond the boundaries of India. Nalanda near Patna grew to be the foremost Buddhist monastery and an educational centre. Most of what we know of the Nalanda University during the 6th and the 7th centuries A.D. is due to the accounts left by Hiuen-tsang, who lived in the institution for three years in the first half of the 7th century, and I-tsing who also stayed there for ten years towards the latter part of the same century.

Information on the Nalanda University Library is also found in the Tibetan accounts, from which we understand that the library was situated in a special area known by the poetical name the Dharmaganja, which comprised three huge buildings, called the Ratnasagara, the Ratnodadhi and the Ratnaranjaka of which the Ratnasagara was a ninestoried building and housed the collection of manuscripts and rare sacred works like Prajnaparamita Sutra etc.

The library at Nalanda had a rich stock of manuscripts on philosophy and religion and contained texts relating to grammar, logic, literature, the Vedas, the Vedanta, and the Samkhya philosophy, the Dharmasastras, the Puranas, Astronomy, Astrology and Medicine. The University of Nalanda and its library flourished down to the 12th century A.D. until Bakhtiyar Khalji sacked it in A.D. 1197-1203. and set fire to the establish-ment of Nalanda.

The world famous universities, such as, the Vikramasila, the Vallabhi and the Kanchi were coming up in other parts of the country during the period from the 5th century A.D. to the 8th century A.D. All these universities possessed rich libraries and in the hall containing such books there used to be an image of the goddess Saraswati with a book in her hand.

The Nalanda and the Vikramshila universities were under the control of the king Dharmapala. He founded the Vikramshila monastery in the 8th century A.D. It had a rich collection of texts in the Sanskrit, the Prakrit and the Tibetan languages.

Regarding the library of the university, the *Tabaqat-i-Nasiri* informs us that there were great number of books on the religion of Hindus there; and when all these books came under the observation of the Mussalamans, they summoned, a number of Hindus that they might give them information regarding the import of these books; but the whole of the Hindu community was killed in the war.

Muslim vandalism caused the disappearance of the excellent collection at Vikramashila. The Jaggadal Vihara in Varendra-bhumi was also an important centre of learning with considerable collection of the reading material. It was established by the king Kampala, who ruled from A.D. 1084 to 1130.

The provision of facilities for reading, writing, editing and translating manuscripts shows that this library was in no way less than its contemporary libraries in importance. Though not as large as the library of Nalanda, it abounded in private collection of texts.

Likewise Mithila had been famous for its scholars since the days of Rajrishi Janaka and had a rich collection of various commentaries on the different branches of the Hindu *Shastras.* The library of its university played an important role in teaching and learning. A needle *(Shalaka)* was pierced through the manuscript on the subject of the student's specialization and he was expected to explain the last page pierced.

In this way the student's all-round mastery of the subject was tested. Mithila continued to enjoy its all India importance in the field of learning till the end of the 15th century AD. The university at Sompuri, like that of Vikramshila, occupied a significant position since the days of Dharampala.

Like Nalanda, this university also had its own library. Atisa Dipankar, a noted scholar, lived there. He with the help of other scholars, translated into the Tibetan the *Madhyamkaratnapradipa* of Bhavaviveka. This university was destroyed by fire in the middle of the 11th century A.D. Efforts were made by the monk Vipulsrimitra to renovate the university but it could not regain its past glory.

At a time when Nalanda was famous for its *Mahayana* courses of study, the Maitrakakings provided their patronage to the Mahavihara of Vallabhi. This university was famous for its *Hinayana* studies. The fact that this university had a good library is supported by a reference in a grant of Guhasena, dated A.D. 559, wherein a provision was made out of the royal grant for the purchase of books for the library.

This important seat of learning at Kanheri, on the West Coast, flourished during the reign of Amoghavarsha in the 9th century A.D. The library occupied a significant position within the establishment, and the donors provided money to buy books for the library.

The last of the famous seats of learning in Eastern India was Navadwipa in Bengal. It reached its height of glory from 1083 to A.D. 1106 as a centre of intellectual excellence as well as its rich library facilities, when Lakshman Sen, a king of Gauda, made it his capital. However, this library was also destroyed along with the centre by Bakhtiyar Khalji.

Situated in South India at Amaravati, on the banks of the Krishna, the Nagarjuna Vidyapeeth flourished in about 7th century A.D. Its library housed in the top floor of the five storyed building of the university had an enormous collection on the Buddhist philosophy, particularly of the *Mahayana* school that Nagarjuna had founded, science and medicine.

There is enough archaeological evidence that supports the existence of this 7th century university and its library. The enormity of the collection in this library is borne out by the fact that it not only had works on the Buddhist literature and the *Tripitakas,* but also works on several branches of scientific knowledge, such as, Botany, Geography, Mineralogy and Medicine. It was a great attraction for scholars from the different parts of India and from countries, like, China, Burma and Ceylon.

University Libraries in Medieval India

The existence of academic libraries during the medieval period of Indian history is not known, though the Muslim rulers did patronize libraries in their own palaces. A lone exception, however, was a library attached to a college at Bidar, having a collection of 3000 books on different subjects. Aurangzeb got this Library transferred to Delhi to merge it with his palace library. During the medieval period, due to Muslim invasions and political troubles, the powerful empires and kingdoms of Indian rulers fell one by one. This affected higher education and the development of academic libraries as well.

Libraries in Modern India

During the British rule in India, number of academic institutions were established by the East India Company, and by the Christan missionaries. Some of the worth mentioning events which led to the growth and development of higher education in India during this period were the establishment of the Calcutta College in 1781, Jonathan Duncan, then a British agent, founded the

Benaras Sanskrit College in 1792. The Calcutta Fort William College was founded in 1800. All these colleges were having their own libraries.

The Charter Act of 1813, the foundation of Fort William and Serampore Colleges, Calcutta, Madras and Bombay universities and their libraries, Hunter, Raleigh and Calcutta University Commissions, library training programmes, the establishment of Inter University Board, Sargent Report and appointment of the University Grants Committee, the establishment of Madras University, University of Bombay, University of Calcutta and their libraries, the constitution of Inter-University Board, the appointment of Hartog Committee, the Montague-Chelmsford reforms of 1919, the Government of India Act of 1935, and the Sargent Committee Report etc. laid foundation for establishment of libraries in various parts of the country.

The Fort William College was founded in Calcutta on 18th August 1800 by the Marquis of Welleselay, the Governor-General of India during 1798-1805. Reverend David Brown, Provost of the college was instrumental in setting up the library which had a well rounded collection of Eastern manuscripts.

In the absence of adequate financial support, the library could not survive for long and in 1835 it was decided to close the library and its valuable collection was transferred to the Asiatic Society Library in Calcutta between 1835-39. The Charter Act of 1813 passed by the British Parliament gave the East India Company complete responsibility for educating Indians.

The establishment of C.M.S. College in Kottayam, Hindu College in Calcutta in 1816 and Raven Shaw College in Cuttack in 1816 was the immediate result of the Charter Act 1813. These and other colleges came into existence thereafter had their own libraries the day they were established. Serampore College during this period was founded by the Danes in 1818 and the King of Denmark in 1927 agreed to give this college an academic status by providing equivalence to the Danish Universities with power to confer degrees.

The library of this college too was established along with its foundation and at a later stage the college was given affiliation to the University of Burdwan for the purpose of conferring degrees. The 7th March 1835 decision of the British Indian Government to promote English literature and sciences in India was resulted into the spread of number of colleges in India and by 1839 there were over forty colleges with attached libraries in the British territory in India.

For their establishment, lots of money was made available by the Indians in the form of donations. In 1840 Presidency College was founded in Madras, followed by a medical college in Bombay in 1845. This progress in education was instrumental in establishing universities in India.

The Charles Wood dispatch of 1854 popularly known as the 'Magna Carta of English Education' in India also paved the way for the establishment of the universities in the presidency towns. Sir John Colville introduced the Bill to establish universities in India and it was passed by the Governor General of India

Lord Dalhousie on 24th January 1857, paved the way for the foundation of three universities based on the London Universities Model in the Presidency towns of Calcutta, Madras and Bombay.

Indian Education Commission, popularly known as Hunter Commission was appointed by the British Indian Government in 1882 to study the progress of education under the new policy adopted in 1854 by the East India Company and transferred to the Crown and accepted by the Secretary of State in 1859. Sir William W. Hunter in his report had clearly stated that the conditions of the libraries was in a very poor state and declared them "hardly creditable." The Commission paid special attention to the colleges and their libraries and other facilities.

The direct result of the Commission was the establishment of Panjab University, Lahore and Allahabad University in 1882 and 1887 respectively but still the condition of the education and libraries remained in a poor state.

The Raleigh Commission 1902 appointed by Lord Curzon to investigate the conditions and prospects of the Indian universities and to recommend measures to improve their constitution and working and standards of teaching also paid special attention to the academic libraries and found that, "the library is little used by graduates and hardly at all by other students." Further, the Commission commented, "In a college where library is inadequate or ill arranged, the students have no opportunity of forming the habit of independent and intelligent reading."

Thus, the Commission specifically recommended that reference services must be made an integral part of all libraries in colleges and universities, and that one of the prerequisite conditions for the grant of university affiliation to a college be the accessibility of students to the library of the institution.

The recommendations of the Raleigh Commission were included in the Universities Act of 1904 and provided the power to all universities to require that all colleges applying for affiliation maintain proper libraries, equipment, library building, and lend books to all students but the situation and the status of libraries could not be improved much simply because the recommendations made by the Commission and the provisions made in the act could not be implemented properly. The Calcutta University Commission popularly known as Sadler Commission was appointed by the government in 1917 to study the situation and the status of education in the country and to make recommendations to solve the existing problems.

The Commission noticed that "one of the greatest weak-nesses of the existing system is the extraordinarily unimportant part which is played by the library" and found that "in some colleges the library is regarded not as an essential part of teaching equipment but merely as a more or less useless conventional accessory." The Commission made the recommendations regarding the libraries that college libraries be strengthened and that training should be given to the students and occasionally to the teachers about use of the library.

One of the immediate result of the Calcutta University Commission was the establishment of a few new teaching-cum-residential universities at Patna in 1917, Osmania in Hyderabad in 1918, Dacca, Aligarh, and Lucknow in 1921, Delhi in 1922 and Nagpur in 1923 and all of them were established along with the establishment of libraries as an integral part of the university system.

As stated earlier, the impact of the Commission could very well be seen in the establishment of several universities along with their libraries. This was the period when in the libraries scenario, a person appeared who at a later stage turned the entire scene and become the father of library science in India.

The man was none other than Dr. S.R. Ranganathan. The University of Madras appointed Dr. S.R. Ranganathan as its Librarian in 1924. He was trained at the University of London Library School before joining his duties at Madras. Things did change rapidly after his joining. For example, he introduced the lending and reference services at the Madras University Library and extended the library hours for the benefit of the readers.

Whereas the hours had previously been 7 a.m. to 4 p.m., they were changed to 7 a.m. to 6 p.m. He delivered a series of lectures to about two thousand teachers at the conference of the South Indian Teachers' Union in 1929 regarding the use and importance of the library services.

The Madras Library Association started a summer course in librarianship and the lectures for this course were mainly delivered by Dr. Ranganathan. The main objective of the course in its beginning was to spread the ideas of the value of good library services and modern library methods among potential users of the library. The budget of the university library of Madras had been very poor from the beginning and it was really a difficult task to manage, run and administer the library effectively within it.

Ranganathan brought this poor financial position to the notice of the then Chief Minister, Dr. P. Subbaroyan, when he delivered a speech during an educational conference held at Madras in 1926. In his speech, Ranganathan "gave a graphic account of the library network in Europe and the United States of America and compared it with the poor, appalling facilities existing in India.... added that paucity of funds prevented him developing his library."

The Chief Minister was highly impressed by Ranganathan's speech and promised to give more State help to the University Library. Its immediate result was a grant of rupees 6,000 which was added to the annual grant from the State, and, in addition, rupees 100,000 in lump sum were sanctioned by the Madras State Government in the same year to buy books and periodicals in pure sciences, humanities, and social sciences.

Provision was also made for additional grants to the library, as and when new departments of study and research were established. In the words of Ranganathan, "This was the first time when such a forward financial step in the history of the university libraries in India was taken in the second quarter of the 20th century."

The University of Madras library made a good start under Ranganathan's effective leadership and administration. In 1930, the library had five well-trained reference librarians to help the readers, and they "carried the work to a high pitch of efficiency."

This was the first time in the history of Indian libraries that a special reference service was introduced in a university library. The library collection increased to 93,000 volumes in 1935 and on September 3, 1936, the library was shifted to its first new and permanent functional building. By 1944, when Ranganathan resigned from the position of the Librarian, to become the University Librarian at the *Banaras Hindu University* (BHU), the collection of the Madras University Library had augmented to 1,20,000 volumes.

The contribution of Dr. Ranganathan to the growth and development of libraries in general and the Madras University Library in particular is undoubtedly tremendous and unforgettable. It will not be wrong to say that the Library School of Madras and the Madras University Library were the laboratories of Ranganathan to propound his ideas in library science and to test them practically.

Some of the important and major ideas of Ranganathan were the Five Laws of Library Science which were enunciated by him in 1924, and their formulation and publication in 1929 and 1931 respectively. These laws are still considered a unifying theory for all library practices and services, and set of guidelines for the dynamic development and study of library science as a whole.

The University of Bombay Library received a special grant of rupees 50,000 from the Central Government in 1939 to strengthen its collection for graduate studies. During the period from 1931 to 1939, a few more special grants were given to the library for its collection development. A very special grant of rupees 10,000 was given by Kikabhai and Maniklal, sons of the late Premchand Roychand, in 1931 to replace the electric clock of the library tower. The collection, which stood at 4,504 volumes in 1900, rose to 70,000 in 1939 and 73,582 in 1947. Though higher education and academic libraries made some progress during the first quarter of the present century, yet their growth and development was not very well organized.

Academic institutions and their growth after 1916 created a few problems also and the general feeling was that the "quality of Education was being sacrificed for quantity." While such a situation prevailed, the Indian Statutory Commission, popularly known as the Simon Commission, was appointed by the Government in 1927 to study the conditions prevailing in India.

The Simon Commission appointed an Auxiliary Committee to look into the growth of education in India. Sir Philip Hartog, a former member of the Calcutta University Commission, and a former Vice-Chancellor of the University of Dacca, was appointed its Chairman. In its report, submitted in 1929, the Committee stated that "the dispersal of resources for university teaching among a number of colleges had made it difficult to build up university libraries of the type required for advanced work both at the Honours and the research stage majority of the university libraries were inadequate and all needed great additions."

In addition to want of books, libraries also lacked good current periodicals in their collections. The Committee also made a special note of the low academic standards in many colleges and universities and the "unhealthy competition for candidates between neighbouring universities". This report, however, did not offer any comprehensive, detailed, and realistic solutions to the problems. In 1935, Ministry of Education was formed in each province, as per the provisions of the dyarchy in the Montague-Chelmsford Reforms of 1919, supplemented by those of the new Government of India Act of 1935.

The Ministry of Education in India requested the Central Advisory Board of Education in 1944 to survey the educational conditions in the country. The Board's report, known as the Sargeant Report, after its Chairman, Sir Sargeant, the Educational Advisor to the Government of India, came up with a master-plan for the development of education in the post-World War II India. Its terms of reference covered education at all levels-primary, secondary, and higher.

The Indian universities, as they existed then, despite many admirable features, did not fully satisfy the requirements of a national system of education. During the British rule, several committees and commissions set up periodically, paved way for the foundation of several colleges and the establishment of many universities and in many cases the libraries were also established along with them.

It is also true that as compared to the first two decades the development of university libraries after 1924 did make better progress but the college libraries were still neglected and were struggling to get their recognition.

There were only 12 universities in India in 1924 and their number swelled to 18 by the time India got freedom in 1947. In fact, the academic libraries during the British rule had no significance in the academic life of the institutions of higher education and the pivotal role that can be played by the academic libraries in the life of the institutions could very well be seen in the policy statement of higher education of the free India and the fact was also proven when at the time of national reconstruction, the importance of libraries in teaching and research was recognized, and libraries received the early attention of the Government of India.

Academic Libraries in India after Independence

The actual process for the development of university libraries in India can be said to have been set in motion with the appointment of the University Education Commission presided over by Dr. S. Radhakrishnan and its recommendations, such as, annual grants, open access system, working hours, organization of the library, staff, steps to make students book conscious and the need to give grants to teachers to buy books.

The section on libraries of the report opens with a powerful statement on the importance of libraries in university education and states, "teaching is a cooperative enterprise. Teachers must have the necessary tools for teaching purposes in the shape of libraries and laboratories as also the right type of students."

The Commission in the course of its study of the academic libraries, found that "libraries were hopelessly inadequate to serve the curricular needs of a modern university. They were ill-housed, illstocked, and ill-staffed and were totally lacking in standard literary and scientific journals. Service was in the hands of personnel that had hardly any notion of the objectives of university education. The annual appropriation for book purchase seldom exceeded the ten thousand mark."

In addition, the annual grant for these libraries were not sufficient. Therefore, the Commission recommended that at least six per cent of the total budget of each academic institution should be set aside for the library. It added that if institutions were not willing to allocate six per cent of their budget to libraries, they should spend ₹ 40 per student enrolled. The Commission also suggested that greater attention should be paid to improve the reference services in the university libraries. Documentation and biblio-graphical services must be developed in order to promote research among the faculty and students, make libraries proper centres for research activities, and to raise the standards of services.

As far as the library staff is concerned, the Commission was of the view that it is very important to have well-qualified staff, including the Director, in order to provide excellent service in any library. The Director's qualifications must include Ph.D. in Library Science and he must have the rank and salary of a professor, capabilities of organization and management, and should have full powers of an administrator to run the library effectively.

University Education Commission. There is no doubt that the recommendations of the Commission "were based on the needs of the modern library services in universities for the promotion of research and creative learning." It was for the first time that such detailed attention was paid to the library matters by a commission on university education in India.

Ranganathan Committee (1957)

The most comprehensive and significant document on the university and college libraries is the Report of the UGC library committee, chaired by Ranganathan. The Report was published by the University Grants Commission in 1959 entitled 'University and College Libraries.' It was perhaps the first attempt by any Library Committee in India to systematically survey the academic libraries on a national basis, and it was also the first time that the government of India had decided to seek advice from a professional librarian regarding academic libraries. The committee was to advice the UGC on the standards of libraries, building, pay scales, and library training.

After the survey the library committee invited all academic librarians to a seminar on "Work flow in university and college libraries," at Delhi from March 4 to 7, 1959 to keep them informed about the progress the committee had made surveying the academic libraries. It wanted to discuss its recommendations with them. Some of the recommendations of the Committee included the provision that the UGC and the State Government should help the college and the university libraries in the collection development of both books and periodicals.

The formula suggested by the committee was that funds be given "at the rate of ₹ 15 per enrolled student and ₹ 200 per teacher and research fellow. There should also be special initial library grants in the case of a new university and of a new department in an existing university, a similar scale should be followed for the college libraries. In order to promote co-operation among libraries, a Union Catalogue of books and a Union List of periodicals to be prepared.

The Committee strongly recommended that an open access system be introduced in every academic library. Committee also stressed "that reference service is the essential human process of establishing contact between the right reader and the right book by personal service. Reference service is vital in promotion of reading habit in student each library should provide an adequate number of reference librarians to function as library hosts and human converters."

Other recommendations included building up a microfilm collection, copying facilities for microfilms and book material, appointment of a committee to look into the standards of teaching, examination and research in the library schools, and appointment of full-time teaching faculty members rather than asking librarians to teach part time in the library schools.

The Committee added that "the status and the salary of the library staff should be the same as that of the teaching and research staff', *i.e.*, Professor, Reader, and Lecturer etc." The recommendations of the committee had a farreaching effect on the development of the university libraries later.

They had not only provided a framework to the UGC to implement its grants-in-aid programmes but also given to the university authorities important guidelines. Particular mention, in this connection, may be made of the recommendations concerning the library finances which had helped libraries to secure enough finances by way of annual grants from the universities themselves and of development grants from the UGC.

The recommendations on the library personnel and staff strength have given to the library staff status and salaries equivalent to the academic staff and ensure provision for adequate staff for various library operations. The Committee submitted its report to the UGC with the hope that it will provide a blueprint for the systematic development of university libraries in the country.

Hence, inspite of many hurdles like education being a state subject in the Indian Constitution, considerable development in the university libraries has taken place and as such the condition of these libraries in 1953 was much better than in the 1940's and even the early 1950's.

Kothari Commission

The Education Commission under the chairmanship of Dr. D. S. Kothari marked another important stage in the history of university libraries in India.

The Commission devoted considerable attention to the development of the university libraries and made suitable recommendations on the following points:

- Norms for financial support;
- Long range planning for library development;
- The need for the establishment of a well equipped library before the starting of a university, college, or department;
- Suitable phasing over of the library grants;
- Encouraging the students in the use of books;
- Interdisciplinary communication; and
- Documentation service in libraries etc.

The Education Commission had also addressed itself to the role of libraries in adult education and recommended establish-ment of a network of public libraries. It wanted the school libraries to be integrated with public libraries for purposes of the adult education programmes. The Report, submitted by Dr. D. S. Kothari, on June 29, 1966, emphatically pointed out that "nothing can be more damaging than to ignore its library and to give it a low priority. No new college, university or department should be opened unless adequate number of books in the library are provided."

The Commission was shocked to note that the recommen-dations of the Radhakrishnan Commission had not been fully implemented, for only four universities in India has spent five per cent or more of their budget on books and periodicals acquisitions, though the 1948's Commission has suggested that six per cent of the total budget be spent on libraries. Other universities had spent less than five per cent of their budget on libraries, "Surprisingly enough there are five universities which spent even less than one per cent of the total budget on the libraries."

It was clear proof that the university libraries in India were not functioning properly to fulfil the needs of higher education. The Kothari Commission recommended that a long range plan for library development should be drawn up for each academic institution taking into consideration anticipated increase in enrollment, introduction of new subjects and research needs etc., and documentation service be encouraged in libraries, and documentation experts be appointed to help researchers and do indexing and abstracting. It was further recommended that "the book selection should be oriented towards supporting instruction and research." The library should "provide resources necessary for research in fields of special interest to the university; provide library facilities and services necessary for the success of all formal programmes of instruction."

Monetary guidelines were also suggested by the Commission. "As a norm, a university should spend each year about ₹ 25 per student registered and ₹ 300 per teacher depending on the stage of development of each university library." It was also suggested that "the foreign exchange needed for university and college libraries should be allowed separately to the UGC."

The Wheat Loan Programme

During the 1950's and early 1960's the Indian academic libraries received huge grants from the UGC amounting up to ₹ 100,000 for books, buildings, equipment and even for additional staff. At the same time many libraries got additional grants from a special US fund called the 'Wheat Loan Programme.' The American Congress passed a special Act, in 1951 known as the 'Public Law 480' to loan India $ 19,000,000 to buy much needed wheat from the US. Under the agreement of the loan, India had to buy American books, periodicals and scientific equipment worth $ 50,000 to be used for research purposes in the Indian libraries.

This, money India had to pay as interest on the loan. Part of the money was to be spent on the exchange of scholars, including librarians, between the two countries. The United States authorities bought some educational material and equipment from India for research purposes and higher education in the American Universities.

During 1951-1961 Indian libraries spent US $ 1,400,000 of the purchase of American books, US dollar 160,000 on libraries, US $ 40,000 on the travel and study grants for thirty three Indian librarians to visit the United States and US $ 75,000 on the travel and study grants of the five Americans.

College Libraries

The College libraries in India have a significant role to play in higher education. Majority of the undergraduate students, *i.e.*, 88.5 per cent and graduate students, *i.e.*, 53 per cent, attend these colleges. When India attained Independence many among the 533 affiliated colleges did not have their own libraries, but at present, every college in the country has a library.

Majority of the college libraries do not have proper facilities to meet the needs of their users. Their collections are not up-to-date, budgets are their very inadequate and limited, and a large number of them are single libraries. In many colleges, there is neither a library hall nor a sufficient big room, not to think of a separate building for the library.

Any unused room, quite often somewhere out of sight, would be considered adequate to house a few shelves of books. And in most college libraries there is complete darkness even during the day time, as the windows are closed out of a fear that the books may be stolen.. Different studies, conducted by scholars and Srivastva have explicitly established that the condition of the college libraries in India are far from satisfactory.

The college libraries are open only six to eight hours a day. Many do not have any qualified librarian on their staff and have closed stacks only. The several commissions and committees, like the Radhakrishnan Commission of 1948, did not stress the importance of the college libraries in their reports. However, the University Grants Commission gives more importance to the college libraries.

As the quality of higher education and research, especially at the graduate level, depends upon, among other things, the standard of the college libraries and their services. Therefore, the UGC has played a significant role in the growth and development of college libraries since 1953 by giving grants for books, equipment, staff and library buildings and has done a remarkable job in salary improvement of the college librarians. The UGC's contribution to the college libraries is at the rate of ₹ 15 per student with a maximum of ₹ 10,000 with some additional and special grants for text books, when a new subject is introduced in the Curriculum.

On the other hand, the colleges and the state governments have failed to provide their equal share. The total Expenditure on the college libraries according to the recommendation of the Education Commission should be 6.25 per cent of the total budgets of the colleges, but in most cases it has remained between 1.5 per cent and 2.3 per cent.

Sardana Collection development of the college libraries are done without taking into consideration the actual needs of the faculty and the students of the colleges as sixty per cent of them consist of text books and 20 per cent cover fiction.

Even this small inadequate collection, in depth and content, is not used effectively due to the closed stacks system and lack of staff and facilities for instruction concerning their use. The net result is that the utility factor of the college libraries comes practically to nothing.

In most college libraries, books are neither properly classified nor catalogued. In several libraries no systematic classification is followed for collection arrangements. The only service the college library renders to its clientele is book-lending. There are colleges where students are not even allowed inside the library.

The UGC is aware of the slow progress of the college libraries. In addition to providing financial help for development, it has also from time to time organized seminars to keep the college librarians aware of the new developments in the field. But these seminars have made only a limited effect on the progress of the college libraries. The condition of the college libraries in the country should be a cause for alarm among the academic community.

In the interests of the development of higher education in the country along proper lines, it is important to make a detailed study of the style of functioning of the college libraries and of the utilization of the library resources and facilities by the students and teachers. This will help in the preparation of more realistic and operational policies and programmes for ensuring the proper functioning, utilization and development of the college libraries. The college library has to be made the intellectual hub of the institution, serving equally, both the students and teachers.

This is all the more necessary because about 90 per cent of the students in higher education in India pursue their studies in colleges and they have only very small and substandard college library resources to fall back upon. Although, owing to various efforts of the UGC as well as other forces, the traditional concept that the college library is a custodian of books has changed, yet there is evidence enough to show that the condition of the college libraries is generally poor, their development is rather slow and that the position of the college libraries and their librarians in India, with a few exceptions, is pitiable.

University Libraries

University libraries all over the world have their own place of importance in the scheme of higher learning. Libraries are not only repositories of knowledge but also dispensers of such knowledge. There is no doubt that where libraries of universities and institutions of higher learning are ignored or not given due recognition, the country as a whole suffers because the standards of study, teaching and research very heavily depend upon the qualitative and quantitative service rendered by the university libraries.

The Radhakrishnan Commission expressed that "the library is the heart of all the university's work, directly so, as regards its research work and indirectly as regards its educational work, which derives its life from research. Scientific research needs the library as well as its laboratories while for humanistic research the library is both library and the laboratory in one. Both for humanistic and scientific studies, a first class library is essential in a university."

The growth of university libraries since Independence can be seen in respect of the initiatives taken by the Central Government considering the vital importance of higher education and role of libraries in the educational development, commitment to fulfill the demand of higher education, and the foundation of the UGC in 1953 by an Act of Parliament. The Radhakrishnan Commission recognized the value and importance of a well equipped and organized library system and its role in higher education.

It had found many drawbacks and pitfalls in the university libraries and had made many recommendations for the improvement of library facilities. The Ranganathan Committee, appointed by the UGC in 1957, made some outstanding recommendations, which included standards for library building, collection development, staff and services and furniture etc. These recommendations were accepted by the UGC and forwarded for implementation.

The Kothari Commission also made valuable recommen-dations for this purpose, but the role of the University Grants Commission deserves special mention, because it has played a vital role by "regularly providing appropriate grants and funds to all universities for development of libraries, to purchase books and journals. . . ., construction of new library buildings and for library equipment and furniture."

Dr. D. S. Kothari, the Chairman of University Grants Commission, said, "Libraries play a vital role in the development of institutions of higher learning. The University Grants Commission attaches great importance to the strengthening of library facilities in the universities and colleges and their efficient administration. The commission has also been giving grants to institutions for books and journals construction of library building and appointment of library staff."

One of the most remarkable and identifiable development in the history of higher education and libraries was the foundation of the INFLIBNET in 1991. Information and Library Network Centre is an autonomous Inter-University Centre of the UGC of India. It is a major National Programme initiated by the UGC in 1991 with its Head Quarters at Gujarat University Campus, Ahmedabad. Initially started as a project under the IUCAA, it became an independent Inter-University Centre in 1966.

Its objectives are:

- To promote and establish communication facilities to improve capability in information transfer and access, that provides support to scholarship, learning, research and academic pursuit through cooperation and involvement of agencies concerned.
- *To establish Inflibnet*: Information and Library Network a computer communication network for linking libraries and information centres in universities, deemed to be universities, colleges, UGC information centres, institutions of national importance and R&D institutions, etc. avoiding duplication of efforts.

Inflibnet performs following major activities:

- Provides grants to universities to automate the libraries, establishing the network facilities and create an information technology environment.

- Developed and distributed Software for University Libraries (Soul) which is an integrated userfriendly library management software. The latest version of the software is 2.0 which is competent to operate with the latest technologies and international standards such as MARC21, Unicode based and NCIP 2.0 based protocols for electronic surveillance and control.
- Indian Catalogue of University Libraries in India (IndCat) is Online Library Catalogue of books, theses and journals available in major university libraries in India which provides bibliographic description, location of the material in all subjects available in more than 112 university libraries. Thus, IndCat has over 10 million bibliographical records of books from more than 113 universities. In addition, the database of theses, expert databases, project databases and Sewakoffline database access facilities are also extended to the libraries of higher learning institutions.
- To enhance the skills of university library staff for implementation of Inflibnet programme, it conducts training programme for library staff, onsite training for member library staff, training on SOUL software, holding Calibre convention every year and workshops for senior level staff of the university libraries are conducted.
- It has brought out a document entitled 'Inflibnet Standards and Guideline for Data Capturing' prepared by a task force of experts based on Common Communication Format (CCF).

Another very important and significant landmark in the history of higher education and development of libraries in India is the establishment of "Ugcinfonet Digial Library Consortium" by the UGC on the concluding day of its Golden jubilee celebrations by his Excellency the then President of India, Dr. A.P.J Abdul Kalam at Vigyan Bhawan on 28th December 2003. UGC-Infonet is an innovative project launched by UGC to facilitate scholarly e-resources to Indian academies through joint partnership of UGC, Inflibnet and Ernet.

This includes interlinking of universities and colleges in the country electronically with a view to achieve maximum efficiency through Internet enabled teaching, learning and governance. The UGC-Infonet is overlaid on Ernet infrastructure in a manner so as to provide assured quality of service and optimum utilization of bandwidth resources. The network will be run and managed by Ernet India.

The project is funded by UGC with 100 per cent capital investment and up to 90 per cent of recurring costs. UGC and Ernet India have signed the necessary MoU for this purpose. A joint technical and tariff committee, has been setup to guide and monitor the design, implementation and operations of Ugcinfonet. Information for Library Network (Inflibnet) an autonomous Inter-University Centre of UGC, is the nodal agency for coordination and facilitation of the linkage between Ernet and the Universities.

Under this programme, information and communication technologies (ICT) and internet will be used to transform learning environment from a monodimensional one to a multidimensional one. This was created to help and benefit more than 310 universities and about 14,000 colleges affiliated with these universities and approximately 10 million students with the e-journals, thus, is a boon to higher education system in many ways.

The UGC-Infonet digital Library consortium has the following objectives: Bhatt,

- To subscribe electronic resources for the members of the consortium at highly discounted rates of subscription and with the best terms and conditions.
- Promote the rational use of funds.
- Guarantee local storage of the information acquired for continuous use by present and future users.
- To impart training to the users, librarians, research scholars and faculty members of the institutions on the electronic resources with an aim to optimize the usage of the electronic resources.
- To have more interaction amongst the member libraries.
- To increase the research productivity of the institutions in terms of quality and quantity of publications
- Strategic alliance with institutions that have common interests resulting reduced information cost and improved resource sharing.

National Knowledge Commission

The National Knowledge Commission was set up by the Government of India on 13th June 2005 with a time-frame of three years, from 2nd October 2005 to 2nd October 2008. As a high-level advisory body to the Prime Minister of India, the National Knowledge Commission was given a mandate to guide policy and direct reforms, focusing on certain key areas such as education, science and technology, agriculture, industry, e-governance etc.

Easy access to knowledge, creation and preservation of knowledge systems, dissemination of knowledge and better knowledge services are core concerns of the Commission.

The Commission envisaged the future road map for the growth and development of academic libraries by imbibing core issues such as, set up a national commission on libraries, prepare a national census of all libraries, revamp LIS education, training and research facilities, re-assess staffing of libraries, set up a central library fund, modernize library management, encourage greater community participation in library management, promote information communication technology applications in all libraries, facilitate donation and maintenance of private collections, and encourage public private partnerships in LIS development, etc.

ACADEMIC LIBRARY STRUCTURES

Organisational structure can be defined as "one of the interrelated components that define any organisation referring to the definition of individual jobs and their relationship to each other as depicted in organisational charts and job descriptions." It clarifies how information is distributed, and jobs are organised. For decades the hierarchical structure of management was regarded as the most efficient way of managing an organisation. This system worked well in and environment where the future was predictable and librarians were in the driving seat. Hierarchies were not designed to foster creativity and lead workers to self-fulfilment.

It is therefore very difficult to introduce fundamental change within hierarchical structures which are naturally resistant to change. In an effort to bring about reorganisation within organisations institutions try to either modify the existing hierarchical structure or replace it with something else. Deming as cited by Mullins states that management systems still prevalent today have had a destructive impact on people. According to Deming "people are born with intrinsic motivation, self-esteem, dignity, curiosity to learn... " Qualities such as these are undermined by a management style that reward top achievers and punish those that do worse. Managers that exhibit such management styles use disapproval as a negative control measure. This approach leads to a climate where staff performance is primarily directed at pleasing their superiors and that inevitably lead to average performance.

According to researcher managers have a natural tendency to maintain the status quo. They would instinctively fall back on models and practices that worked in the past. The volatile nature and unpredictability of information services is forcing managers to adopt new management styles. It is beginning to dawn on people that the bureaucratic way of management is becoming outdated and that change will be more effectively achieved through education, sharing, motivation, teamwork and coaching.

Moran states that unprecedented change has forced managers to re-evaluate structures. Customary practices designed to maintain organisational stability are being questioned. To cope with change, organisations have started flattening structures to induce more flexibility within those organisations. These new structures being adopted have decreased levels of hierarchy, increased flexibility and resulted in diminishing boundaries between departments.

Issues to Consider when Introducing New Structures

Management theorists are very reluctant to prescribe to a particular structural model but advise that structure should rather be designed to meet organisational needs and goals. Organisations should try and learn as much as possible from others who have implemented organisational change. They should never introduce a structure simply because it is being used elsewhere but always to meet specific organisational needs. Of cardinal importance is to determine how people within the organisation will adopt the new structure. Researcher shares the following points learnt from a process of restructuring:

Before implementing a process of restructuring it is important to have clear vision, goals and objectives with the focus on service delivery. It is useful to establish a core team to lead the restructuring process. It is vitally important that senior management support the process, *e.g.,* a deputy vice-chancellor. It is important to involve the entire staff component, listen to their inputs and concerns since ownership by the staff is vital for successful change implementation. Staff development programmes should be part of the process to prepare staff for new functions or roles they may be involved in.

After implementation it is important to critically analise the performance of the academic library within the new structure. Managers often do not adapt easily to the flatter less bureaucratic structures that are generally being adopted. Even staff members at lower levels experience this problem. Generally it is very difficult to introduce change that goes against prevailing organisational culture. Proper planning is needed to take the organisation from the existing structure to the new one.

Employee input in developing such a strategy is crucial. Research indicates that organisational transformation had been most successful in scenarios where employees had maximum input. Finally evaluation is necessary after change implementa-tion to determine its success. In reorganised libraries structures are always flatter resulting in manager's roles reverting from directing to coordinating. The prime purpose of reorganisation is to create a more effective organisation. Reorganisation results in academic libraries becoming learning organisations.

The learning organisation is characterised by staff empowerment, is team based, decentralised, practices participative management and information sharing. In the learning organisation the person closest to a problem has the responsibility and authority to deal with it. Tom Wilson as cited by Moran states that the academic library is in bad need of reconstruction. To Wilson academic libraries were essentially designed to manage physical artifacts. The rise of the Internet has completely transformed the way information is created, distributed and accessed.

The e-journal is a typical example. Johansen and Swigart as cited by Moran states "we had outlived the usefulness of models from the Industrial era but don't yet have robust organisational models for the information era". It is therefore of paramount importance that academic librarians continuously re-evaluate current structures and through an experimental process adopt new models. Moran states that for people who advocate restructuring there is good and bad news. The good news is that people understand that technological change will compel fundamental organisational change. The bad news is that there is a lack of urgency. Generally organisational change appears to be incremental rather than radical.

IMPACT OF ICT CHANGE ON ACADEMIC IBRARIES

The Internet has made information access and retrieval both simplistic and complex. Information retrieval systems are being designed to suit the needs of end users and therefore try to simplify the process. Simultaneously however the user is overwhelmed with so much information resources and choices that the process becomes complex. This creates a situation where the users need skills and knowledge in terms of search strategies and conceptualisation. Herrington is of the opinion that information literacy instruction at the point of need can be very effective. Wood and Walther is of the opinion that unlike popular believe the Internet will not completely replace the skills of professional librarians but rather make them indispensable.

Changes in the Job Description of Academic Librarians

An overview of the core competencies required by academic library and information workers gives one an idea of how dramatically information and communications technology has changed the library profession.

Cheng identifies the following core competencies needed by the future librarian:

- Good communication skills.
- Should be more than just computer literate and should have a good understanding of ICT and its relation to information resources.
- Should have an in-depth understanding of organisational and user needs that is research based and should organise library resources to satisfy those needs.
- Competent in Web publishing techniques.
- Skilled in manipulating metadata to organise digital information.
- Skilled in training users in the use of e-resources.
- Skilled in filtering, evaluating and appraising Internet information.

Researchers identifies another quality required, an in-depth understanding of what information resources are available on the Internet, as well as insight in terms of its reliability and scope.

The Changing Nature of the Academic Library

ICT is busy transforming the nature of academic libraries. A variety of terms such as hybrid, digital and virtual library are used to refer to the academic library. A digital library can be defined as "a managed collection of information, with associated services, where the information is stored in digital formats and accessible over a network".

The virtual library has been defined as "remote access to the contents and services of libraries and other information resources, combining an on-site collection of current and heavily used materials in both print and electronic form, with an electronic network which provides access to, and delivery from, external worldwide library and commercial information and knowledge sources". Hybrid libraries are libraries that provide access to both electronic resources and paper-based resources.

From the definitions it is clear that most of today's academic libraries fall in either the hybrid or virtual category. The library of the future is unlikely to be a physical entity as we know it but would probably be a Web portal providing access to information.

The emphasis will be on access to information rather than physical ownership. Akeroyd supports this view and states that as a physical space entity the library, as we know it is unlikely to prevail in a digital environment. One reason for this is that because of Web access the digital library is accessible from anywhere.

Changes in the Information Seeking Behaviour of Users

Academic librarians have a good understanding of the tremendous value of printed and electronic resources available to students at academic libraries. Academic library users do not necessarily share this insight. New generation academic library users have a preference for Web resources rather than visiting the library.

Research done on undergraduate engineering students in 2004 revealed that they would turn to the Internet as the primary resource for information for their projects. Moyo refers to a scenario where users were asked what they expect from an academic library service.

They responded as follows:

- All resources should be available in full text and be printable.
- The library service should be fast and easily accessible.
- 24/7 availability of a virtual reference service.
- Wish to do all library transactions online.
- Web resources that is easy to use and Web search engines that meet information needs.

What is clear is that new generation academic library users prefer the convenience of digital access above reliance on assistance from librarians. This preference for the Internet poses a serious challenge to the academic library which has to move from a paradigm of the library as a physical cntity to a library where the users do not have to come to physically to make use of it's services.

Electronic access to information resources does have many advantages, *e.g.*,:

- Multiple access which implies more that one user can access a resource simultaneously.
- Lots of resources are available in full text.

- 24/7 access which means users can access resources remotely, *e.g.*, from off campus or from dormitories.

One of the disadvantages of remote access from an academic library point of view is that users are not always aware of the fact that they are using library resources. One user stated: “No, I don’t need to use the library, I use Internet resources”.

Despite the apparent preference for digital content the need for access to high quality digital content remains constant. Greater cooperation between library and faculty is necessary to develop ways to connect users and high quality digital materials.

IMPACT OF ICT ON COLLECTION MANAGEMENT

Collection development can be defined as the selection and acquisition of library materials based on current and potential user needs. Collection management goes beyond this. It is concerned with managing the utilisation, storage and accessibility of a collection. Collection development can thus be seen as a subdivision of collection management. Academic librarians find themselves in an era of unparalleled access to information.

The latest edition of Uhlrich’s has indicated the availability of more than 1,72,000 journal titles. Although this appears to be a most ideal situation it is not because the financial resources available in acquisitions departments have not necessarily increased. The sheer volume of information available also makes selection of the most suitable information a complex task. The impact of electronic resources has made collection management a very complex and challenging task. There are budgetary constraints, numerous formats, ever changing user needs. Collection management implies involvement in tasks such as analysis of needs, negotiation of contracts and evaluation of resources. There was a time when the size of an academic library collection determined its stature. At that time the library’s resources were generally adequate to meet most of its users needs. Since then the academic library has exchanged the ownership model for an access model where physical location becomes completely irrelevant.

Access versus Ownership

Information and communications technology has had a fundamental impact on library collection development policies. Academic libraries had traditionally applied an ownership or just-in-case approach to collection development. The premise was that users would need the material and make use of it. Having the material available in the library would also provide immediate access to it than having to borrow it from a third party. The cost of maintaining collections and increased demands for more information had forced academic libraries to reconsider the ownership model and adopt another model. Unparalleled price increases and shrinking budgets had ushered in a new model called access or just in time where the focus is to give the user the information that they need when they want it.

Cost

Technically it is more cost effective to produce an e-resource, for example an electronic journal, because the first copy costs are reduced. There is also savings in terms of packaging, delivery and storage. In practice these savings have not lead to reductions in the cost of e-journals. It has been suggested that the academic library adopts a pay-as-you-use approach. This make sense according to research done in 1997 that indicated that 22 per cent of science articles published in 1984 were never cited for the next 10 years. In the social sciences this figure goes up to 48 per cent.

Storage Space

With the access model there is no need for storage space, *e.g.*, back copies. Moahi cites Cooper who states that the storage cost per single copy is between $25 and $40. Calculations to determine JStor pricing lead to the conclusion that the cost per single volume was between $24 and $41. When costs for re-shelving and maintenance were included, the estimated cost rose to $45 per title per year for a core journal and $180 per title per year for a large research library.

Enhanced Access to Information

One of the benefits of ICT is enhanced access to library services and resources. The academic library can expose its users to a much larger collection than it can house physically because users can access information remotely. With online access it is possible to accurately measure utilisation of e-resources and that is invaluable in determining which resources to purchase. It is easier to search e-resources and access speed is greatly enhanced. Other advantages are that users can simultaneously access the same resource, and there are no incidences of lost copies or mutilated issues. Singh is of the opinion that a paradigm shift is taking place within the academic library as more academic librarians are doing collection management rather that collection development. The focus is rather on interpretation of information rather than selection. Librarians are becoming knowledge managers rather than collection managers.

Digital Preservation of Data

One of the major costs facing the academic library is the cost related to the conversion and preservation of information in digital format. The cost of this process amounts to $1 per page. This does not include the cost relating to the annotation for indexing purposes and the cost of conversion of audio-visual material. One of the problems with converting records into digital image is the fact that the technology used to store these pages as a digital photograph results in large files which have storage implications and place demands on band-with. Funding allocated to preservation of digital material is generally inadequate. This has to do with expectations that the costs of digital preservation over length of time might be very high. It is also difficult to forecast cost in terms of how long to retain digital material in an archive and computer architectures needed to access material. Preservation of digital materials poses many challenges. It is further complicated by the fact that computer technology changes at an unprecedented rate.

There are concerns that changing interfaces, standards, formats and operating systems will render it impossible to read today's computer discs at some point in future. The implication of this is that one needs migration strategies to move data to new operating systems and structures or have scenarios where computers can simulate data structures and operating systems of previous eras. This scenario will make digital preservation prohibitively expensive. A great deal of current research into digital preservation is based on overcoming the technical issues to ensure long-term preservation of digital content. The issue of digital preservation initially came to the fore as an impending crisis. Fears were expressed that large portions of our cultural heritage were in danger of disappearing forever. Examples were cited of Web sites available today that might be gone to-morrow.

Although digital materials are more fragile by nature than analog materials the risk varies within different categories of digital materials. Although it is true that a Web site currently available may disappear overnight, the same does not apply to electronic journals. This realisation has transferred the focus from the immediate rescue notion to an approach that sees digital preservation as part of a carefully planned digital access management process. One way academic libraries can deal with digital preservation is through cooperation. Through cooperation various institutions can share costs. Another advantage would be that it would reduce redundancy. Because of the fragile nature of digital materials libraries cannot put off decisions to preserve digital information *ad infinitum*. Time is of the essence.

Unlike a book that can be repaired or rebound, once a digital file becomes corrupt it may be impossible or prohibitively expensive to restore the data. Another problem facing the academic library is the long-term preservation of digital information. There are questions concerning the long-term stability of digital information stored on disks and tapes. There is the potential of these media deteriorating over a period of time. Another way digital preservation is approached is by letting the vendors do the preservation. These days there are also escrow repositories, *e.g.,* Elsevier has agreed to provide the National Library of Netherlands with a copy of Science Direct which the National Library will maintain and make available should Elsevier be unable to do so.

ELECTRONIC RESOURCES

ICT has fundamentally changed academic library collections. Forever gone is the era when an academic library's physical collection determined its stature. In the modern networked technological era the emphasis has shifted from ownership of physical resources to access to electronic resources that are globally accessible.

Internet Information

There are huge amounts of unedited information on the Internet. There are countless Web sites and no single listing of them all. There is also the phenomenon of Web sites disappearing overnight that create problems in terms of access.

The Invisible Web

Academic library users make use of search engines such as Google and Altavista to find information on the Web. As a result they are only exposed to a small portion of the Web called the 'Publicly Indexable Web' These students are only exposed to Web pages accessible via hyperlinks. Search engines do not index Web pages that requires authentication or Web pages behind search forms. The Web consists of two components namely the 'Publicly Indexable Web' also referred to as the visible Web and the invisible Web. The invisible Web refers to all those information resources available yet not indexed by conventional search engines yet accessible via the Web.

Masses of information available via the invisible Web are found in subject databases. Most of the databases that academic libraries make available to their users resort under the invisible Web, *e.g.,* EbscoHost and Eric. Conventional search engines can find databases such as EbscoHost but cannot access them. Search engines can only find content that was indexed by their software called spiders or crawlers. The problem is that they only index Web content available in formats such as HTML and PDF. Michael K. Bergman in year 2000 in a paper on the invisible Web for an Internet Search Company called Bright Planet suggests that the invisible Web is 500 times larger that the visible Web with approximately 550 billion documents.

The Issue of Quality of Resources Available on the Visible Web

The Internet had become a very important research tool for academic endeauvour. Slaouti as cited by Stapleton notes that the relevance and importance of the Web as a research tool should not be underestimated. There is a stark contrast in the way resources are published on the Web versus traditional publishing. In the traditional print environment publishing generally was done by a publisher hence a controlled environment that impacted on quality as well as the scope of the audience being reached. The open nature of the

Web, the development of sophisticated search engines, browsers, Web creation and publishing software and easy access to networks via low cost connectivity has developed the Web into a tool that can be easily utilised by the masses for publishing purposes, people who were formally shut out of the publishing process.

This has lead to a flood of Web publications of variable quality. During the 1990's library scholars recognised this dilemma and suggested criteria to evaluate Internet resources, *e.g.*, authority, purpose, coverage and objectivity and accessibility. These days a single search can yield hundreds of thousands of items. The unfiltered nature of Web resources has made evaluation of these resources essential. One often finds that unlike in traditional printed media, e-resources found on the Web often lack important criteria such as author or date. Web pages because of its non-linear textual nature has added new effects to the search process such as sound, videos and access to thousands of items by clicking a mouse. These new elements imply that new sets of skills are required on the part of the researcher.

Reference Works

According to Moyo reference statistics in academic libraries are plunging. At the same time electronic access of these resources are increasing. This tendency can be ascribed to the fact that users can access these resources remotely via the Internet. Internet connectivity and e-resources had become absolutely essential for the new reference service paradigm. One of the key elements of e-reference service success is that the service is available at the point of need. The tremendous growth in the use of online reference works has created a need within the academic library to develop services to support this type of service.

Academic libraries are turning to on-line real time reference tools also referred to as ORR to support students remotely. The Pen State University library has more than 300 databases that students may access. On-line real time reference support is used to assist students at the point of need. E-reference works share all the benefits of e-resources, *e.g.,* 24/7 remote accessibility, concurrent access for multiple users and the potential for online updating to keep content up to date. Electronic communication had become the primary mode of communication in e-reference services. Online chat had become the method of choice. Some e-reference application providers have added *Voice over IP* (VOIP) to their products which enable voice dialogue with the library user.

E-reference services have many advantages, *e.g.,*:

- Availability via the Internet.
- Service at the point of need.
- Easy for people who are unable to come to the academic library, *e.g.,* the physically disabled.

- 24/7 availability.

Moyo cites Stormont who states that online real time reference support is very labour intensive. In order to cope academic libraries have adopted a distributed staffing model where the load of the service is shared among various libraries.

E-Journals

The e-journal can be defined as "a version of the traditional print or paper-based journal which is disseminated electronically in some form or other directly to the end user." Although e-journals had been in existence since 1976 it became prominent during the 1990's. Since it's inception in 1665 the printed journal remained the primary vehicle for communication among academics and researchers. The advent of the Internet transformed publishing radically as it made it possible to publish cheaply. Internet also made access universally available. Because of the Internet academics and researchers became more creative and productive.

Cost Factors

There had been major increases in the cost of journal subscriptions during the last two decades. According to researcher between 1986 and 1996 the average increase per journal subscription had been a whopping 147 per cent. This state of affairs had been laid at the door of the commercial publishers. Moahi states that simultaneously there had been a significant increase in the number of science and engineering journals published. Because of ever decreasing budgets academic libraries are unable to purchase the titles they deem necessary. Falk cites McCabe of Georgia Institute of Technology stating that publishers offer libraries bundled packages of e-journals under the pretense that it is cheaper but these deals actually inflate prices.

Moahi is of the opinion that a consequence of these bundled deals is that academic libraries end up with titles they do not want or need. Despite the fact that publishers have substantial cost savings on first copy production of e-journals and also save on distribution costs, these savings are not passed onto their customers. Cost of e-journals tend to be similar or higher that their printed counterparts. What further complicate matters are the fact that provision has to be made for connectivity and desktops, which means additional costs. Aggregate publishers also tend to drop titles without prior consultation with academic librarians.

Academic Library's Response to Publishers

Despite general expectations that e-journals should be cheaper than printed versions publishers maintain the status quo by maximizing profits. Publisher's attitudes have forced academic institutions to take a tougher stance against them. Recently the Senate of the University of California instructed the library to sever all ties with Elsevier, *e.g.*, cancel subscriptions and cease submission of research papers if negotiations with them fail to obtain a reduction in the price of subscriptions. Harvard University has cancelled their Elsevier subscriptions of bundled journals. The Senate of North Carolina State University urged that excessive prices from publishers be resisted.

Four North Carolina universities had signed a deal for a bundle of 1300 journals in 2003 with the proviso that no titles are dropped. When these institutions wanted to renew subscription for 2004 the price was so exorbitant that they all cancelled the deal. Cornell University and the University of Missouri also cancelled subscription with Elsevier for the same reasons. Three North Carolina universities have drafted policies to only forward research to publishers whose journals are reasonably priced and widely accessible.

In the event of this not being possible they will include an "authorisation to publish' clause in contracts that empower the author to retain copyright to reproduce research for academic and research purposes. Kansas University includes a clause in their contracts that give them permission to use their research for teaching and research purposes and retain the right to make it available on public accessible Web sites.

Open Access Journals

The open access initiative is aimed at making scholarly research freely available via the Internet. Open access journals are journals available on the Internet for academics, researchers and the general public. The open access journal philosophy received a tremendous stimulus with the birth of the *Public Library of Science* (PLoS). At its conception 30,000 scientists promised their support in terms of submitting research. The first open access journal to emerge was PLoS Biology in the year 2003 which was received with great enthusiasm. In the publishing arena the Biomed Central publishing house embarked on free access to peer-reviewed journals. Recently the *Directory of Open Access Journals* (DOAJ) made open access journals available covering different languages and subjects.

Open Access Archives

Many leading universities are setting up electronic archives as depositories for their research output and are granting access to it. There are plans in progress to use theses archives as a platform to provide open access journals. The *Massachusetts Institute of Technology* (MIT) has made software freely available for managing electronic archives. Currently there are approximately 140 universities that have established open access archives. The number of journals held in these archives have increased from 20,000 in 2001 to 1.3 million in 2003. Although this is still fairly insignificant compared to the 2 million peer reviewed journals printed annually it nevertheless sends out a clear warning signal to commercial publishers of what is to come. In Europe the Open Archives Forum was established. The goal of this forum is to establish electronic archives and make it globally available.

e-Books

There are various definitions for e-books but e-books are essentially published books and reference materials that were digitised and are distributed electronically. In the year 2000 e-books were heralded as the new publishing revolution. One market research company predicted that by 2005 there would be 1.9 million users. Forrester Research predicted that income generated from e-book sales would increase from $9 million in 2000 to $414 million in 2004.

Unfortunately e-book popularity never rose to expected heights. Despite the negativity surrounding e-books it had not demised completely. There are still some companies dealing with e-books that are profitable and experiencing growth. One of the first commercial e-book services, NetLibrary, was established by OCLC in 1998. The NetLibrary collection has since grown to over 400 000 titles. The shortcoming in the NetLibrary system is the fact that an e-book can only be used by one user at a time. Questia, another commercial e-book service went live in 2001. Their target market was students and they employed librarians to manage collection development. By 2003 Questia had more than 400 000 titles from more than 200 publishers.

Advantages of e-Books

E-books have numerous advantages. There are no printing, storage, warehousing and shipping costs. Consequently e-books can be published at costs much lower than conventional books. Additional advantages are online availability, keyword-searching capability, cross-referencing, adjustable fonts, electronic bookmarks and imbedded audio. Updating e-books will be easier than re-editing conventional books. From an academic library point of view benefits would include cost savings in terms of shelving, binding, circulation, overdue notices and management of fines. All needed would be a person to maintain the collection and a person to manage user accounts. Print collections in academic libraries are very expensive to acquire and maintain. E-books are also environmentally friendly in the sense that no tree pulping is necessary to for its production. The flaws in current e-book technology will be overcome. When that day dawns e-books being much cheaper to produce and publish than printed books as well as economies of scale will tip the balance in favour of e-books.

Disadvantages

The devices needed to read e-books are relatively expensive, *e.g.*, hand held devices, PC's and laptops. In order to minimize piracy publishers use proprietary hardware devices and software platforms. This lack of universal standards is a problem. The question many ask is whether e-books pose a threat to libraries. Can it eventually put libraries out of business. Although e-books did not take off as well as expected within the public domain, the use of e-books at schools, colleges and universities are rapidly increasing.

Use of e-Books

Falk refers to research done by Forrester that indicated that 4 million e-books were sold at campus stores in year 2000. Forrester forecasted that by year 2005 e-book sales should have increased to 140 million. Research indicates that students are developing a preference for e-books above printed books. At the University of Rochester Rush Rhees Library course reserve section students were exposed to printed books and their e-book equivalents. Statistics compiled on a weekly base indicated a three to one preference in favour of the e-books.

SOME OF THE PROBLEMS RELATING TO ELECTRONIC RESOURCES

Online full text implies availability of articles rather that the entire content of a particular journal. The complete contents of a publication are seldom put into a full text database. This implies that an author one might have seen in a physical publication may not be traceable in electronic format. This predicament also applies to archiving where there is uncertainty about the percentage of a journals content that is archived in digital format.

Another concern is that the academic library in a sense has lost control over the resources it make available to its users. When academic libraries subscribe to aggregator databases, *e.g.* EbscoHost or ProQuest they subscribe to a service, a list of titles bundled together of which many are useful and many not so useful. One of the problems is that aggregators sometimes drop titles. Typically this would happen when publishers withdraw all their titles.

The Chronicle of Higher Education has reported in 2003 that Elsevier has been removing articles from aggregator files because of various reasons, *e.g.*, scientific misconduct, plagiarism and errors. On the Web there are masses of information available. With search engines, *e.g.* Google or Yahoo one may find useful information and record the URL or title. There is however no guarantee when one wants to revisit the site that it may still be available. Sites on the Web sometimes disappear overnight. An organisation may have merged with another one or the host server might have become dysfunctional.

The quality of information available on the Web is also sometimes questionable. Any individual with access to the Web and basic hardware and software can publish on the Web regardless of whether the person's views are factually correct. On the Web are more than an estimated billion Web pages and this create problems for users of the academic library to distinguish between what is useful or not. Another problem is that search engines cover only a small portion of what is what is available on the Web. There are lots of information behind firewalls and thus inaccessible. Many crawlers of search engines only focus on html and ignore graphics. Generally ASCII files will not be found. To assist users academic library services should try and inform users when sites have relocated or are no longer available.

CHANGES IN THE EDUCATIONAL ENVIRONMENT

ICT have changed every fibre of society including education. Lifelong learning has become essential. A very competitive working environment has influenced this. Even educational methodologies have changed. Greater interaction between learner, educator and material is becoming the norm. Learners have greater choices in terms of curricula. The 24 hour networked classroom became reality leading to the birth of the virtual library.

Network technologies and new educational methodologies have empowered learners, given them a greater measure of control and participation in the learning process and enabled network interaction with both fellow students and lecturers. Change in institutions of higher education will compel academic libraries to change accordingly. The most dramatic change according to visionaries will take place in distance education. This was a direct influence of the Internet. When the day dawns when distance education becomes the norm, universities the way we know them may vanish and virtual libraries may become a reality. Recently an author warned that the railroad managers overlooked the fact that they were in the transport business. He noted that universities must remember they are in the education business and not the campus business. If campuses disappear libraries will disappear.

There are already examples of cyberspace universities, *e.g.,* Phoenix. If academics should fail to restructure their institutions' external forces will do it. Of cardinal importance is to focus on what education wants to achieve and how one can fulfill it. Survival of the academic library will depend on its ability to continuously reshape and reorganise.

Distance Education

New technologies driven by ICT innovation have enhanced the virtual delivery of academic programmes and stimulated unparalleled growth of distance education at institutions of higher learning. The phenomenal growth in distance education technologies has lead to an escalation in the availability of online academic programmes and a tremendous increase in remote users. In order to support these programmes academic librarians have developed excellent portfolios and programmes for remote students. One aspect that is neglected is evaluation of these programmes.

What is of critical importance is to establish how these programmes are used, which ones are used more frequently than others and why. Monash University library in Australia provides online curriculum content to their students all over the world. The university library provides online access to more than 440 online databases, 140,000 e-books and 20,000 e-journal subscriptions. Apart from full text databases and e-books the university library also provides digital audio recordings of lectures that become available minutes after conclusion of lectures.

According to Ho Monash University library has made a paradigm shift to a complete new service module that utilises e-commerce technologies. Moyo is of the opinion that the transformation in distance education has created a need for distance librarianship.

Changes in Scholarly Communication

The rising of the Internet and subsequent Web during the 1990's has resulted in the decline of the printed journal as the principal medium of scholarly publication. The costs of journals have increased dramatically driven by commercial publishers trying to control research content. This resulted in depriving many researchers of access to needed resources. The Web has also made fast and easy electronic publication possible and has increased direct communication between researchers.

Publishers immediately started making electronic versions of printed journals available on the Web. This was however seen as perpetuating the status quo in a new medium. Scholars started seeing in the new technology the potential to develop a new model for publishing research and an opportunity to return ownership of scholarly output to the rightful owners of the research.

These sentiments were driven by shortcomings in existing scholarly journal publishing which were:

- The time to publish an article was to too long.
- The existing model demanded transfer of copyright to the publishers.
- A too rigid peer review system that tends to favour publication of authors from the more prestigious institutions.
- Journal prices had become unaffordable.

One of the outcomes of this dissatisfaction was the birth of the e-print which is essentially an electronic version of a research paper. E-prints lead to the development of e-print repositories that are an archive of e-prints accessible to the public. Some of the advantages of e-print repositories are the reduction of publishing barriers, increased visibility of research and rapid dissemination of research results to a wide audience.

Consortia Collaboration

Initially libraries got involved in consortia in order to reduce costs particularly with regard to the acquisition of e-resources. Consortia development is thus an attempt to maximize limited resources through co-operation and resource sharing. In the consortia scenario the emphasis is on access to information rather than ownership. Consortia collaboration provides more power when it comes to negotiating contracts. It also provides a platform for libraries to co-operate in terms of services. Nowadays libraries also turn to consortia to provide advice and guidance in complex decision-making. The input of consortia is also valuable in terms of evaluating e-resources in terms of quality, different options, *e.g.,* whether to subscribe to journals or pay article-by-article.

The South African Scenario

In terms of network infrastructure South Africa is not on par with first world countries where consortia cooperation is very effective. For the establishment of an information society in South Africa proper connectivity infrastructure is an absolute prerequisite. There is an uneven distribution of telecommuni-cations infrastructure across South Africa stemming from the political ideologies of the apartheid government. This inequity is also prevalent in South African academic libraries. Institutions for the privileged white people were well financed and resourced under the apartheid regime. Institutions for blacks were under funded and thus under resourced; hence the distinction between advantaged and historically disadvantaged institutions. Because of this there are great differences in wealth and the collections of academic libraries.

In South Africa there are five academic library consortia.:

1. CALICO (Cape Library Cooperative) based in Cape Town.
2. ESAL (Eastern Seaboard Association of Libraries based in Kwazulu-Natal.
3. FRELICO (Free State Libraries and Information Consortium) based in Free State.
4. Gaelic (Gauteng and Environs Library Consortium) based in Gauteng.
5. SEALS (South Eastern Academic Libraries System in the Eastern Cape.

Essential for the development of successful consortia is low cost tariffs coupled with high bandwith connectivity. Academic institutions constantly engaged with government agencies to achieve this ideal. Library consortia can also be invaluable in assisting member libraries with change management because "An organisation needs external coaches to catalyse, guide and facilitate a change process", the reason being that people within the academic library are sometimes to closely involved with daily activities to see things objectively. An outside view often helps to see things in the right perspective.

ICT MANAGEMENT ISSUES

Libraries are caught midstream between print versus a digital setup. To navigate the transition from print to digital remains enormously challenging.

Rapid ICT development had resulted in lots of incompatible systems being used within libraries. To manage ICT is a complex and daunting task. To select the right ICT technologies is a major management issue. It is very difficult in a world where hardware and software changes at a phenomenal rate.

The shift in the academic library from printed resources to electronic resources that are accessible via campus networks or remotely and the fact that users can even request services via the network has lead to a decline in users visiting the library. The growing electronic nature of the academic library is resulting in it becoming less visible as a physical entity to its users.

What is also disturbing is the fact that users are often oblivious to the fact that they are using library resources because of the seamlessness of access. Users are not aware of the fact that to make those resources available are costly in terms of subscriptions, infrastructure and staff. Academic libraries need to find a way to reverse this scenario of the library loosing its visibility. Hooper suggests that the academic library should use ICT to stimulate interaction between user and the library. It should be done in such a way that the user could identify with the academic library providing the service and experience a sense of ownership.

As a starting point the academic library can interact with the user relating to loans, database searches and other services available. It is also important to create an environment where the user can provide feedback relating to service shortcomings and suggestions that could lead to improvement. Stakeholder relationships are also very important. It is of vital importance for the academic library to ensure that their operations dovetail with the strategic goals of the university it supports. In these days where accountability is becoming the norm it is essential to run operations in such a way that the academic library at any point is in a position to provide proof of the value of its services as a return on investment made by the university authority.

TECHNOLOGY-ENHANCED LIBRARY SERVICES

TECHNOLOGY ADVANCES

The major technology breakthroughs in the context of libraries include:

- Advent of printing press and mass production of printed documents enabled democratisation of information. Libraries had a major role in the print era, as no one can own a large number of books on a particular subject whereas libraries by their very purpose concentrated on doing so.
- Microforms helped to preserve less used information in a compact space and as a smoother delivery option for voluminous sources. Libraries had their unchallenged role even in the microform era as the special purpose readers for microfilms and microfiche were costly and exclusively housed in the library.

- The economical and affordable copying technology revolutionised the concept of information use as it spearheaded the trend of owning copies of relevant portions of library resources. The copying technology freed the user from sitting in the library for long duration for reading, since, one can simply get a copy quickly and leave.
- Computing is the biggest technology revolution so far, as it is a major enabler in the information dissemination chain; also it is not a stand-alone technology unlike earlier technologies and can be networked and integrated with a whole lot of other devices and technologies. It not only revolutionised the production of books and microforms but also brought the arrival of online and CD-ROM databases, electronic information resources, Internet and the digital revolution.

PRODUCTS AND SERVICES

Adapting IT for library applications is an ongoing process, right from procuring or developing IT enabled information products through computer aided processing and management to delivering IT-enriched services. Library professionals in India are already exposed to the different offshoots of IT for library organisation and information services.

LIBRARY AUTOMATION PACKAGES

The availability of a wide variety of library automation software to suit the varied needs of libraries themselves is a reflection of the progress libraries have made in automating the operations of procuring, processing and providing information sources. Procurement is the end of the story for many other software/databases used in a library, whereas library automation systems will open a floodgate of issues. What the vendor provides is a structure to build information concerning the collection and users, to conduct various aspects of organising the collection and offering information services.

Thus software needs to be evaluated for its suitability for the target library before purchase. This may include case studies from other libraries using the software, evaluation of hardware and operating system required, computer awareness among staff and users, network as well as computer infrastructure in the institution, and all estimation of cost and charges for after-sales support. Using suitable software for library automation will significantly reduce manual operations and enable professionals to dedicate more time for professional jobs.

CD-ROM AND ELECTRONIC DATABASES

Due to the poor communication infrastructure prevalent in India and to the immense costs involved, online database services were used only by few institutions. The distribution of the same content of online data repositories subsequently in CD-ROMs made it affordable to a larger number of institutions.

While the library automation package gave search-and access facility to information sources present in the local collection, CD-ROM databases attempted consolidated access irrespective of holdings to the bibliographic data of publications in a discipline. CD-ROM databases have also freed library professionals from conducting searches and allowed the end user to conduct the searches. CD-ROM is so common nowadays that a library holds a good number of them not only for bibliographic, numeric and full-text databases, but also those received along with printed books and other reference sources. Managing and serving these high capacity discs was a problem earlier due to the stand-alone software required, whereas the onset of networking and hard-disk cached solutions provides an effective and functional way to enable access to them through the intranet.

WEB

Since, the 1990s, the Internet has changed the dissemination of information, such as electronic copies of traditional paper-based journals and conference proceedings, free electronic-only refereed journals, haphazard copies of all kinds of material on home pages and a handful of electronic preprints archives. Most libraries in India now have a web site and they use the site to present the basic strengths of the library and to host services such as the OPAC and Web access to electronic information.

The 'size of the catalogue card' and the field lengths of primitive database technology are surpassed in the Web era. Types of information resources on the Web also vary from authentic primary information about the latest research results to ephemeral product catalogues. Issues worth consideration are often the content of the sites that are deleted, modified or changed to new machines without proper redirection and the extraction mechanism through search engines, when a flood of sources is retrieved against a query, of which few are relevant.

The Internet and Web demonstrate that a large amount of electronic information can be hosted in a decentralised fashion in a cost-effective manner. The Web has also freed the user's dependence on library resources for finding information related to address and contact details of a person/institution, contents pages of books, journals, etc. As far as possible, especially for reference and information services, looking at the Web has become an innovative trend in the reference service to complement dated print sources.

Many publishers visibly feel the benefits and reach of the Web, and have considered it as an alternate medium for delivering information sources; some publishers even permit unrestricted access of tables of contents and abstracts of their primary journals.

As a result of these initiatives, the 'print and distribute' paradigm is challenged by 'distribute and print' paradigm.

CONSORTIAL LICENCES

The term 'consortial licences' designates library groupings to negotiate access rights to (print and) electronic information with publishers and vendors aiming at enhanced access to more resources at better pricing. "Consortia can be a means to introduce products to a previously untapped market" for vendors and "consortia provide shared expertise, access to new electronic and print resources, professional development, new sources of funds, and safety in numbers" for libraries. In contrast to earlier library collaborative arrangements such as ILL and resource sharing, the publisher and trade community are parties in the consortial agreements. In resource-sharing, libraries concentrate on collaborative subscriptions by avoiding duplication, where as in consortial licences, the emphasis is to strike the 'best deals' even if the library suffers some duplication.

The publisher community experience is that increased subscription costs lead to a reduction in the total number of subscriptions, further raising the subscription cost every year. Publishers also found it difficult to enforce ownership rights with electronic sources, even after adopting the latest technology tools and forcing libraries to sign the toughest of the legal clauses. The good marketing wisdom of the publisher and trade community prevailed to open up information access rights through consortial licences for a large part of the product spectrum to at least those libraries or groups of libraries which procure products beyond a certain threshold value.

The Indian National Digital Library in Engineering Science and Technology (INDEST) is the first and the major consortium in India. It is under the aegis of the Ministry of Human Resource Development (MHRD).

Before the creation of the consortium, access to electronic journals in these institutions remained at 60 per cent of subscribed titles, but the number of online journals has increased 10 times after the establishment of the consortium.

The rates for access offered to the consortium are lower by 50 per cent to 90 per cent depending upon the category of institution and the consortium paid only 11 per cent of the list price to access these resources. Info net, another consortium, floated by the University Grants Commission (UGC) for Universities, is also gaining strength. Similar consortia are also operational for research institutions under the Council of Scientific and Industrial Research (CSIR) and the Department of Atomic Energy (DAE).

DIGITAL LIBRARIES

Libraries in India are engaged in the development of prototypes of digital information resources, as influenced by developments in other countries. There are certain types of content which lie inaccessible or less used in their present physical forms that can be put to more visible and enhanced use through digitisation. Also heavily used content presently available in limited numbers of copies can be identified for conversion to electronic format.

The linear text in many of the print sources presents difficulties for providing a hypertext approach or a multimedia feeling, for simulating learning by doing; sustaining attention and interest for long duration calls for using electronic technologies to enable content to be more functional. The static content in printed sources fails to attract users who are increasingly exposed to the widely appealing features of broadcasting and IT-intensive presentation tools. Multimedia-enabled digital information will be useful to a large percentage of illitreate and older population also. There are cases such as papers in journals and conferences in print form that never get their deserved visibility and often end up with out reaching the target population.

The digital dissemination of this content may lead to very effective teaching and more focused research in most areas. To demonstrate the efficacy of digital libraries and collections, libraries must be able to identify materials in the public domain, sources generated in-house, and similar materials to overcome the constraints of copyright. Digital library (DL) development needs a two pronged strategy to digitise local content as well as to devise options for providing access to external resources obtained as free or as part of existing subscriptions or access licences.

The typical academic or research library in-house digital library on an Intranet must include the following components:

- Consortial access to electronic journals and electronic databases.
- Free/paid Web access to journals subscribed in print format.
- Subject gateways and virtual libraries.
- Free/paid e-books from publishers and portals.
- Intranet access to bibliographic and full-text databases, and CD-ROM publications.
- Local archiving of free and paid e-books.
- LAN serving of e-supplements of purchased books.
- In-house digitisation of copyright-owned and copyright-free printed books in the collection.
- Born-digital in-house publications such as research reports, annual reports, convocation reports, teaching materials, theses and dissertations, in-house journals, proceedings of conferences, seminars, workshops, etc., conducted by the institution.
- Preprints and post-prints of research papers sent for publication to journals, conferences, and books, especially with respect to the Open Archives Initiative gaining ground to provide further access to research published in toll journals and to make the results of publicly funded research available to those who need them.
- Publications in the public domain, such as government publications, publications from non-profit institutions, etc.

But many libraries are unable to provide these components due to lack of awareness or due to the hurdles invariably faced by libraries in India. The lack of interest on the part of parent institutions and the absence of action plans or priorities is the major hindrance. Though computer and communication infrastructure is improving, their availability for information work is not appreciated in many organisations. Paschoud commented how several of the speakers and many of the delegates at the International Conference on Digital Libraries (ICDL) 2004 conference in New Delhi focussed on addressing what most European libraries would consider very basic issues such as network/ Internet connectivity and management.

Even in places where infrastructure is available, there is an acute shortage of competent labour to take up the task of digitising local content and evolving digital information repositories. The students, faculty, curriculum and training methodology at the disposal of library schools have to be improved visibly to meet this challenge. Coupled with this is the need for continuing education for retraining the working professionals. Institutions, individuals, or private publishers have rights over content, and motivating them to ease these rights when they are not inclined towards digitisation is not a simple task. Levying charges for access is a distant proposition; instead sponsorships from institutions, government bodies and library suppliers can be explored.

Even when hosted as a free facility, enough security mechanisms must be evolved to prevent any trespassing by hackers. Selecting useful content requires careful review and evaluation by subject experts, as digitisation will only help to preserve the record, and not its enhanced and continued access. Internet bandwidth in India has to be sufficiently augmented to allow faster access to Web content as more content is being hosted on the Web. The different funding agencies, research councils and institutions are not currently offering monetary support to the desired extent for digital library development.

THE IMPACT OF INFORMATION TECHNOLOGY ON ACADEMIC LIBRARIES

In the 1990s, academic libraries are undergoing unprecedented change deriving from a combination of accelerating prices of library materials and space, an enormous increase in the amount and types of materials available, and rapid development in electronic technologies. Whatever the local differences in academic librarianship in the countries today, there is no question that information technology is transforming research, scholarship, teaching and learning, and with it, the role of libraries and librarians. Day strongly believes we are already seeing a shift from measuring library services in terms of size and comprehensiveness of collections to one of measuring the quality of service delivery: delivery of documents irrespective of origin, increasingly in electronic form, with access to the electronic library from the users' desktop.

THE EMERGENCE OF DIGITAL LIBRARIES

Definition of Digital Library

A working definition of digital libraries provided by Waters are: "Organisations that provide the resources, including specialised staff, to select, structure, offer intellectual access to, distribute, preserve the integrity of, and ensure the persistence over time of collections of digital works so that they are readily and economically available for use by a defined community or set of communities."

Digital Libraries Concepts

The digital library concepts requires librarians to be information architects in order to build effective, scalable Web sites to serve the digital demands of patrons. 'Just in time", a method introduced in the early '80s to manage inventory, is now an expectation of consumers for any business providing online. 'Just in time' applied to libraries is information delivered "where you need it, when you need it, and in a format that is useful. This strategy requires libraries increasingly to adopt 24/365 service to keep up with the demands of their patrons for core services, and to offer services through what is often called the digital, electronic, or virtual library or reference desk.

Technical Requirements of a Digital Library

The United States National Information Infrastructure programme has identified a number of critical technical challenges that need to be resolved if usage of electronic networking is to be both simple and efficient.

The listing of them below illustrates that all are important for the proper running of a digital library:

- Network components that can handle voice, and text simultaneously, and can operate seamlessly
- Information appliances and services that can provide access and services in a scalable, efficient and inter-operable way
- Information access techniques that can enable efficient searches of large distributed information repositories, making the myriad of information resources understandable
- Multimedia information technologies that can, for example, synchronise and integrate real-time delivery of voice, and can support search and retrieval based on image content
- Infrastructure for application development that can provide common solutions
- Technologies that are dependable and manageable
- Technologies that are easy to use and services that are accessible by users with widely varying skills, experiences, abilities and backgrounds

- Inter-operability among heterogeneous systems will be required on an unprecedented scale
- Security and privacy technologies that are easy to use and provide appropriate levels of security to suit the requirements, cost constraints and convenience of the end user
- Technologies and services that provide portability, mobility and ubiquity.

The Roles of Digital Libraries in the Academic Environment

Researcher provide a comprehensive remarks of the roles of digital libraries in teaching and learning. A library is fundamentally an organised set of resources, which include human services as well as the entire spectrum of media. Libraries have physical components such as space, equipment, and storage media; intellectual components such as collection policies that determine what materials will be included and organisational schemes that determine how the collection is accessed; and people who manage the physical and intellectual components and interact with users to solve information problems.

Libraries serve at least four roles in learning:

1. *First, they serve a practical role in sharing expensive resources:* Physical resources such as books and periodicals, films and videos, software and electronic databases, and specialised tools such as projectors, graphics equipment and cameras are shared by a community of users. Human resources—librarians support instructional programmes by responding to the requests of academicians and students and by initiating activities for teachers and students. Responsive services include maintaining reserve materials, answering reference questions, providing bibliographic instruction, developing media packages, recommending books or films, and teaching users how to use materials. Proactive services include selective dissemination of information to faculty and students, initiating thematic events, collaborating with instructors to plan instruction, and introducing new instructional methods and tools. In these ways, libraries serve to allow instructors and students to share expensive materials and expertise.
2. *Second, libraries serve a cultural role in preserving and organising artifacts and ideas:* Great works of literature, art, and science must be preserved and made accessible to future learners. Libraries preserve objects through careful storage procedures, policies of borrowing and use, and repair and maintenance as needed. In addition to preservation, libraries ensure access to materials through indexes, catalogs, and other finding aids that allow learners to locate items appropriate to their needs.
3. Third, libraries serve social and intellectual roles in bringing together people and ideas: This is distinct from the practical role of sharing

resources in that libraries provide a physical place for academicians and learners to meet outside the structure of the classroom, thus allowing people with different perspectives to interact in a knowledge space that is both larger and more general than that shared by any single discipline or affinity group. Browsing a catalog in a library provides a global view for people engaged in specialised study and offers opportunities for serendipitous insights or alternative views. In many respects, libraries serve as centers of inter-disciplinarily—places shared by learners from all disciplines. Digital libraries extend such inter-disciplinarity by making diverse information resources available beyond the physical space shared by groups of learners. One of the greatest benefits of digital libraries is bringing together people with formal, informal, and professional learning missions.

- Formal learning is systematic and guided by instruction. Formal learning takes place in courses offered at schools of various kinds and in training courses or programmes on the job. The important roles that libraries serve in formal learning are illustrated by their physical prominence on university campuses and the number of courses that make direct use of library services and materials. By making the broad range of information resources, digital libraries open new learning opportunities for global rather than strictly local communities.

Much learning in life is informal—opportunistic and strictly under the control of the learner. Learners take advantage of other people, mass media, and the immediate environment during informal learning. The public library system that developed in the U.S., in the late nineteenth century has been called the 'free university', since public libraries were created to provide free access to the world's knowledge.

Public libraries provide classic non-fiction books, a wide range of periodicals, reference sources, and audio and video tapes so that patrons can learn about topics of their own choosing at their own pace and style. Just as computing technology and world-wide telecommunications networks are beginning to change what is possible in formal classrooms, they are changing how individuals pursue personal learning missions. Professional learning refers to the on going learning adults engage in to do their work and to improve their work-related knowledge and skills. In fact, for many professionals, learning is the central aspect of their work. Like informal learning, it is mainly self-directed, but unlike formal or informal learning, it is focused on a specific field closely linked to job performance, aims to be comprehensive, and is acquired and applied longitudinally. Since professional learning affects job performance, corporations and government agencies support libraries with information resources specific to the goals of the organisation.

The main information resources for professional learning, however, are personal collections of books, reports, and files; subscriptions to journals; and the human networks of colleagues nurtured through professional meetings and various communications. Many of the data sets and computational tools of digital libraries were originally developed to enhance professional learning. The information resources—both physical and human—that support these types of learning are customised for specific missions and have traditionally been physically separated, although common technologies such as printing, photography, and computing are found across all settings. This situation, is depicted in fig. 1.1.

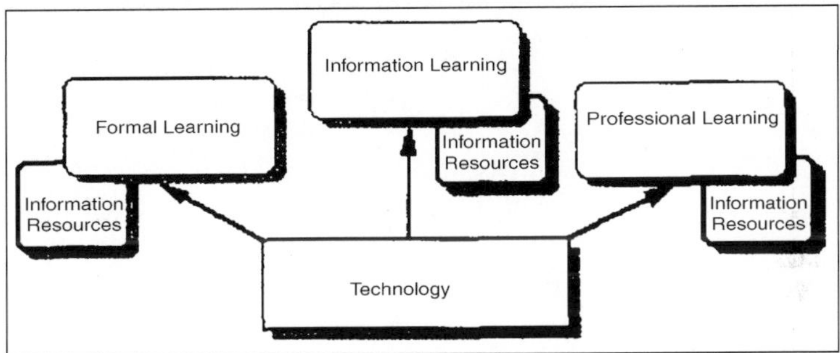

Fig. Current Models of Technological Support for Types of Learning

Digital libraries combine technology and information resources to allow remote access, breaking down the physical barriers between resources. Although these resources will remain specialised to meet the needs of specific communities of learners, digital libraries will allow teachers and students to take advantage of wider ranges of materials and communicate with people outside the formal learning environment. This will allow more integration of the different types of learning, as depicted in fig. 1.2.

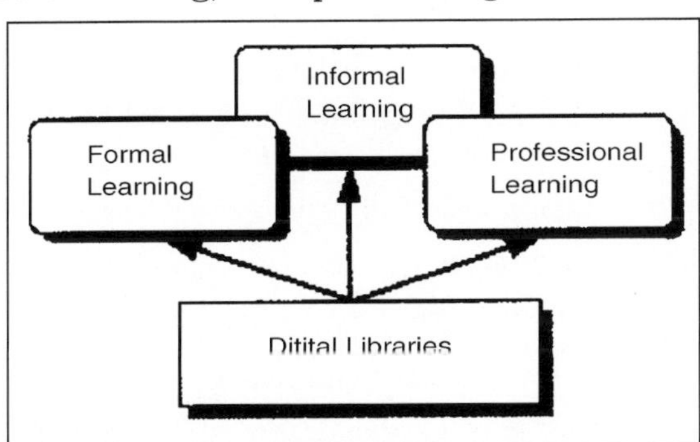

Fig. Digital Libraries Lead to Integrated Resources and Type of Learning

Although not all students or academicians in formal learning settings will use information resources beyond their circumscribed curriculum and not all professionals will want to interact even occasionally with novices, digital libraries will allow learners of all types to share resources, time and energy, and expertise to their mutual benefits.

Characteristics of Digital Libraries

A few of the now familiar characteristics that should distinguish digital libraries from traditional libraries.

The Evolving DL Faces Many Unknowns

For all of its problems and challenges, the print-on-paper environment is well known to us and largely understood. We know how to manage it; we are painfully aware of its costs; and we are familiar with its benefits and its limitations. Our digital library future, by contrast, is full of unknowns and unsolved problems. The list of these is too long and too well rehearsed to need reciting. In addition, the underlying digital technology continues to change. So, even if we could discover the unknowns and solve the problems today, we could not freeze our solutions. Consequently, we are faced with the prospect of creating organisations that are flexible and that accommodate changes, including large changes, easily and regularly.

The DL will Offer Ubiquitous Access

Digital libraries will be designed to support a great range of users at a distance rather than being limited to those on the premises. In other words, unless we create restraints, any and everyone with the necessary hardware can use our digital libraries. This characteristic means both that we should expect a larger variation in the types of users and that as suggested, be responsible to determine whether and what sort of limits will we place on access.

The DL will Host Remote Users

Since digital library users will ordinarily be off the premises, anew, entirely different set of challenges will arise with regard to what we have known as reference and other help services. Our experience with help services has largely been face to face and interpersonal, and efforts to create sophisticated, remote help services are still rudimentary today.

The DL will be more Fully Technology Based

From the creation of metadata to the provision of information services and training, digital libraries will be predominantly technology based. This stands in stark contrast to the essential character of traditional, residential libraries. This is problematical not only because librarians are reluctant to design systems that are technology as opposed to people based but also because often librarians do not possess the necessary expertise to do so. Yet we are not eager to let the process out of our hands. On the positive side, much of the cost of traditional libraries has resided in the manual processes and procedures. While no one supposes that digital libraries will be inexpensive, we should design them in so far as possible to avoid many of these costly manual procedures.

The DL will be open and Customisable and a Part of a Much Larger Information Smorgasbord

Though the qualifications of a digital library can be conveniently limited by definition, they cannot be so conveniently limited by practice. There is a debate over whether or not the Internet is a library. An approach to this question is rather more pragmatic: if growing millions of individuals use the Internet regularly as the source for information on all subjects, it is a library. For all its limitations, it may be a very poor library but it is one nevertheless. For this reason, it is unlikely that our digital libraries will monopolise the library activities of our constituencies in the same way that our traditional libraries have. Digital users today have already sampled the smorgasbord information world of the Internet and have correspondingly broadened their appetites. In addition, it is increasingly common for information users to desire to customise information retrieval, a desire that reduces patience with our more inflexible information systems.

The DL will Offer Distinctive Functions

As surely as digital libraries will discard functions common in traditional libraries, they will necessarily concern themselves with new functions. Commonly named among these are such activities as intellectual property management and database creation and management, the latter being normally associated with administrative computing and data processing. In terms of functionality, therefore, digital libraries will differ markedly from traditional libraries.

Radically Altered Job Descriptions for Information Professionals Will Evolve

To the degree that digital libraries are the business of librarians, this means the incorporation of radically changed or new functions in the librarians portfolios. Digital libraries ignore old boundaries and fall across lines currently marking divisions between libraries, computing organisations, and telephony/networking departments.

Therefore, that digital libraries are not solely the province of librarians and that the new constellation of functions inherent in digital libraries will require the evolution of new information professionals with job descriptions that are as yet unspecified.

Such new job descriptions will reflect new combinations of skills represented in these currently distinct agencies along with those from other areas, such as intellectual property law and business.

As Suggested, See New Focuson Original Materials

In the rapidly passing era of traditional libraries, most of our resources and energies were expended on acquiring, organising, managing, and explaining commercially published materials. Because of the slow but steady movement of commercial publishing into the Internet environment, it is likely in the future that access to commercially published digital resources will increasingly be provided directly by publishers.

The role of libraries as gateways to commercial academic materials, therefore, will diminish. At the same time, however, because of the capabilities of technology, digital libraries will increasingly focus on providing access to original materials, both those born digitally and those converted from analog formats. The effect of this will be to enrich vastly the research potential of our resources and to provide new opportunities for our institutions to benefit from the potential commercial value of such holdings. The new content paradigm for digital libraries will be raw, source materials.

The DL will have Commercial Characteristics

As a result of the shift in digital libraries to original materials, as suggested, find the means to exploit the commercial value of such materials to a degree never before possible. Digital libraries, therefore, must from the outset be designed to support commercial activities. Correspondingly, support for digital libraries will likely include business plans, replete with market assessments, commercial partnerships, and new concerns for cost-effectiveness and year-end financial performance. In other words, because of the value of their data, digital libraries will have an imperative to function in a more business-like, for-profit manner.

As Suggested, Experience New Competition

We must be increasingly aware that, as representatives of primarily traditional, not-for-profit institutions, we do not enjoy sole ownership of the future of digital libraries. Even as we gather here, a host of new competitors for the business of education and the distribution of knowledge and information resources is assembling.

For this reason, we must not presume that the digital library world will evolve to our specifications, especially if we work on digital libraries as a closed community of librarians. Just as the world-wide-web swept over us and, with unbelievable swiftness, changed the nature of our communication environment, so too may we be over-washed by some new inescapable digital library model from unanticipated sources.

Custom, User-Built Digital Libraries

Apart from large commercial interests, some user-built, highly focused information storage and retrieval services, such as the NASA Astrophysics Data

System or the on-line journal of high energy physics, suggest that elements of the digital library may best be developed by the users. Creating these technically customised data and information retrieval systems requires intimate familiarity with the subject matter, jargon, and academic habits of the user communities and likely could not be accomplished by librarians. Clearly we must ponder the implications of these examples for our assumptions and methodologies.

WORKPLACE ENVIRONMENT IN THE DIGITAL ERA

What might we expect of the workplace environment in the new millennium academic library?

Libraries will take Over Campus Computer Centers

Academic libraries will pursue bolder organisational experimentation. This will include focusing on the information and services needs of users. There will be wider distribution of administrative responsibility and authority, as hierarchical structures are broken down and key activities and operations are integrated.

We can expect more fluid and flexible structures, enhancement of team and small group processes, and more collegial and collaborative working relationships. Continuing a trend that is already taking root, the academic library will assume administrative control of campus academic computing services. With the expanding mandate for accountability, there will be a greater focus on data collection and analysis. This will entail a rethinking of standards and benchmarks for assessment and more creative approaches to defining output measures and quality impact.

Academic Library Funding will Remain Stable

Responsibility-center budget models will expand across higher education, embracing the library. This relatively new system of distributed financial authority places libraries into a more rigourous fiscal relationship with academic programmes. Units will be taxed to support library operations, requiting intensified communication and accountability. Library funding will remain stable. The greatest growth will continue to be in collection and information access programmes.

The library budget as a percentage of total campus budget will not change substantially. Library development and fundraising activities will accelerate, as more colleges and universities pursue external funding from private, corporate, and foundation sources.

This will involve a greater focus on endowments rather than on raisin funds for specified capital projects. Library budgets will increasingly fund research and development, infrastructure upgrade and replacement capabilities, and risk capital for innovation and advancement. The trend towards outsourcing of library operations and services will accelerate. We have already seen substantial success with serials jobbers, approval plans, binding, photocopy services, building maintenance, and security. This will lead to further experi-mentation in cataloging, collection maintenance, document delivery, and preservation.

Digital Acquisitions Budgets will Quadruple, and more, Eating up 40-50 Per cent of Acquisition Budgets

Print-based collections will remain dominant over the next decade. However, substantial resources will be allocated to the acquisition of electronic information, as reference sources and scholarly journals become computer-based and the economic feasibility of the scholarly monograph is increasingly questioned.

The percentage of investment in digital information will grow from the current 5-10 percent of acquisitions budgets to 40-50 percent. There will be an ongoing need for investment in local collection building, however, because what has not been acquired and preserved cannot be made available to users and other libraries. Even as collections continue to expand, the gap between what is being published and what we can afford to acquire will continue to grow. As a result, there will be a dramatic decline in ownership: new information accessible through libraries will plunge dramatically.

Nevertheless, the role of the academic library as a depository and gateway for government information will expand, as traditional print-based distribution models are eliminated.

The academic library will expand its role in scholarly publishing and communication. Project Muse at Johns Hopkins and High wire at Stanford, and the Journal Storage Project spawned by Mellon are examples of the library's central involvement in the management of current and retrospective electronic publications. More than 50 percent of reference transactions will take place over campus networks

Patron-initiated and Controlled Services will Expand Rapidly

Libraries are already beginning to employ self-circulation, computer renewals and recalls, direct interlibrary loan, and document delivery. Full-text databases are becoming commonplace. The role of library staff as interpreters and mediators of user information transactions outside of local collections and services will decrease. Inside the university, the librarians' role as instructor will be formalised in a separate college department focusing on information and network literacy.

The technology of the World Wide Web that is evolving rapidly and unpredictable with the World Wide Web Consortium co-ordinates many activities in the areas of user interface, technology and society. The World Wide Web which was first announced by CERN in 1991, 2-3 years ago most people had not heard of it but by the end of 1996, there were 300,000 Web sites.

Libraries are creating Web sites to help students to distinguish between relevant and irrelevant information. The Web is likely to have a profound impact on education, communication and research activities of the universities.

Examples:

- *The Web empowers individuals:* They can easily reach a worldwide audience. Anyone can publish material that would never have been published in the past, and it is instantly available to millions of people.
- *The Web offers us the best of both worlds. Anyone can publish:* Their views cannot easily be suppressed, for good or ill. And anyone can comment, validate and offer judgement or advice.

The E-mail for example is extremely valuable for communication between the library and its users. Users Borrowers are expected to return their books within about two weeks. Very many do without reminders, but for those who need reminding, for some reason e-mail is a more effective spur than other methods. Online catalogs will increasingly define accessibility and not just local ownership. Thus the links between the local collection, the bibliography of a discipline, and the text of the publications/sources will become blurred. Remote use of online catalogs and databases is increasing rapidly at most colleges and universities.

An example, at Carnegie Mellon, already 75 per cent of catalog use is remote. Remote access to information necessitates new instructional efforts. Levels of all traditional collection circulation activity - general and reserve borrowing and interlibrary loan - will decline significantly. They will fall prey to the rapid growth in options for electronic document delivery and the implementation of electronic reserve systems. The new electronic journals already offer facilities unavailable to users of paper.

These include:

- The ability to search for particular content within a paper or a complete journal;
- The ability to move easily between the table of contents of a journal and the abstract.
- Facilities to annotate articles to create a personal virtual filing cabinet and
- The ability to move quickly from the article you are reading to one which it cites in its references, and that includes forward citing, example the ability to go to articles that cited the one you have just been reading but which were published later.

An example, the American Astronomical Society has digitised into electronic form all the articles in the last 20 years of its journal which can now be accessed. Academic libraries will house and manage campus usability laboratories focusing on the needs of the user and will involve users as part of the design team.

Reference assistance to users will be electronic-based, with more than 50 per cent of transactions taking place over campus networks in batched or real-time communication, up from the current neglible levels. User profiles linked to SDI-type services will ensure delivery of relevant, cur-rent information to faculty and students on a scheduled basis. Academic librarians will increasingly pursue service goals as part of multiple consortia-based relationships. There will be joint investment in commercial services and acquisition of materials, in the purchase and use of technology, and in the hiring and development of staff.

Librarians will be Key Players in Developing Technological Innovations

Technology is currently poised to transform the fundamental nature of operations and services. From the early days of automation in the 1970s, academic libraries have moved to the cur-rent distribution and individualisation of technology and digital conversion and production. The challenge of the next decade will be the application of intelligence to the searching and retrieval capabilities of library systems.

The library will play a central role in the future development of the campus information environment. Rather than reacting to campus technology decisions, library staff will be integrally involved in determining what the next innovations will be. In the new world of the desktop workstation, academic libraries have a mandate to integrate high-speed access both to scholarly and institutional information. They need to provide tools for filtering, analysing, and manipulating information.

The predominant mainframe-based library management systems will be completely replaced by client-server technologies and applications that include robust full-text content and intelligent links to network-based sources. Automatic language translation software will be introduced, contributing to the development of a renewed global acquisitions programme for both based and digital sources. Campus network infrastructures will extend to all student, faculty, and staff work and living areas.

This will provide dependable connectivity for a growing array of applications, including distance learning. Wireless technology will be introduced and will receive its initial testing in library services. The retrospective digitising of library collections, particularly unique materials, will evolve as a central activity in academic libraries. Newly formed digital knowledge centers will manage the operations and partner with academic departments, publishers, and other libraries.

The Number of Librarians Working in Academic Libraries will Decrease

Libraries will increasingly view staff development as an integral and essential component of organisational success. With retooling of skills emerging as a three-to-five year cycle, participation in training courses will be mandated for all employee groups. As technology programmes advance and dominate library collection and service activities, technical staff as a percentage of total staff will increase significantly. This will produce a net reduction in the number of librarians employed in academic libraries.

It will also promote more effective working relationships between librarians and technologists, improving current conditions marred by distrust, inadequate communication, and lack of shared investment in planning. Academic libraries have not responded effectively to demographic cultural, racial, and ethnic shifts. They will collectively enter the next century still recognising the important trends producing a more pluralistic society but without well-developed and well-coordinated strategic directions for the role and contributions of the library. Telecommuting, which is increasingly commonplace in commercial settings, will become a viable and acceptable option for *academic* library employees.

An expanding array of library operations and services will be performed from home, enabling improved competitiveness for the recruitment and retention of talented staff. Academic libraries and library education programmes will collaborate on the development of internship and certification programmes for new professionals. This will be necessitated by the anticipated rapid increase in retirements in the next 15 years, as well as by the need to develop new approaches to the preparation and orientation of the next generation of academic librarians. An example of a university library, De Montfort University in the UK that has been developing a digital library environment for some years past.

The lessons they claim to have learnt might be summarised under the following headings:

- The digital library will develop more quickly than people think;
- The digital library is still a complex, unstable entity for which little theoretical structure exists.
- Because of this inherent instability, investment and implementation are still high risk.
- Digital libraries operate in a global environment: new products and services can become *de facto* standards very quickly.
- Co-operation is therefore a key factor for maintaining competitiveness.
- The content of the digital library will become the dominant factor.
- Copyright issues will be resolved or side-stepped because the market will demand it.
- The economics of the digital library are not yet well understood.
- Library jobs and roles will change very rapidly.

3

Multimedia Trends in Library and Information Services

INTRODUCTION

After the introduction of e-mail and internet in libraries, use of information in digital form has increased many folds. There is a considerable change in-libraries in their acquisition of library collection, organisation and providing services to users. The prospects for the development of a multimedia market have been transformed in the past two years by the explosive emergence of the internet and the digital revolution in the converging, IT, telecoms and entertainment sectors. There will be major changes in distribution networks and the implications of multimedia on the economy will be profound. The Internet has shown that there is a huge market for multimedia applications. The most exciting developments will come. from what is known as networked multimedia-the distribution of information using both telecommunication and broadcast technologies.

It is currently multimedia packages/products such as CD-ROMs and hand-held videogames-which are the favoured methods of distributing multimedia, mainly because communications networks cannot deliver the same level of functionality. However networks are rapidly being upgraded to distribute graphics, sound and video and should soon take over from packaged multimedia. Products which can be transmitted digitally such as CDs and books are already facing major challenges. Paper publishing may never be completely replaced by electronic distribution but the cost savings for content producers may be too large to ignore. Value in the multimedia market will move away from infrastructure provision, where the network operators are strong, towards service provision and packaging which require innovation and new skills for libraries and information services. Consequently, new types of companies are poised to wrench control of the multimedia market from the network operators who will have to act quickly to gain the skills necessary to compete in the higher value areas of the market. Their alternative is to be left with high volume, but low profitability infrastructure provision.

APPLICATIONS OF MULTIMEDIA

Multimedia systems are being used for many purposes by different people in different organisations/offkes/environment. The main functions include media integration, storing, organisation and dissemination at different places in different ways. This chapter attempted in reviewing the use of multimedia for library and information services in various countries from the published literature.

Some of the general applications of multimedia are given below:

- Instruction/training and technical presentations
- Multimedia communications such as multimedia e-mail, personal conferencing, video phones, video conferencing, etc.
- Public information points/kiosks for libraries, museums, hospitals, tourists sites, monuments, etc.
- Medical information systems
- Multimedia databases, multimedia information banks
- Multimedia newsletters, multimedia books, other information resources
- Reference tools, *e.g.,* Encyclopaedias, directories, etc.
- Archival systems
- Geographical information systems
- Electronic publishing and bookselling
- Point-of-sale displays,
- Product information catalogues
- Technical documentation, including engineering drawings, specifications, etc.
- Architectural information displays for example walk-through programmes for the new buildings or constructions/already constructed buildings/ monuments,
- Entertainment, leisure, home
- Exhibitions such as conferences, trade shows, new product, facilities, museums, libraries, etc.
- Interactive displays in museums, hospitals, libraries, etc.

Tourism is one of the industries that has exploited the full strength of multimedia for developing tourist information systems for public and libraries.

Glasgow Online is one of the best tourist information systems designed by the University of Strathclyde during 1989 using Hypercard software. Afterwards several commercial multimedia information products were introduced in the market.

MULTIMEDIA APPLICATIONS IN LIBRARIES

Hypermedia, not only helps the users in providing information from different media on one platform but also saves on space, money, maintenance, operational inconveniences, etc.

The other advantages of multimedia in libraries are:

- It can help satisfying different information needs such as reference, enrichment, entertainment, leisure, etc.
- It can help meeting various types of information preferences of the users, such as scholarly, scientific, vocational, ' artistic, recreational, etc.
- Being in digital format, information can also be accessed by remote users on a network. It also helps in over coming the barriers of boundaries, proximity and physical rapacity of a library to accommodate users.
- It is interesting and easy to use over the existing form such as print, microforms, online, etc.
- Its control and interactivity helps the users and provides the benefits of books and human beings.

Electronic information, and multimedia in general, is about to become a vital part of our cultural heritage. Libraries have throughout the history ensured a democratic, independent and free access to the knowledge and intellectual value represented by conventional books. It is evident that this principle is also valid for electronic information and multimedia. The availability of multimedia information through,data networks may also open completely new ways for the libraries to obtain information for the common users.

AMERICAN AND EUROPEAN LIBRARIES

Many big libraries including the *Library of Congress* (LC), British Library, OCLC, etc. are building their collections in multimedia form. Apart from multimedia collection development in 1990, LC began the American Memory Project, aided by Annenberg Fund; the David and Lucile Packard Foundation; and others, for preparing multimedia CDs. This covered several kinds of information including country's historical books, pamphlets, photographs, folk songs, movies, genealogical works, etc. LC brought out the first part of this project America at the start of a New Century 1880-1920, as a CD. Similarly, Elmer E Rasmussen Library and 'University of Alaska started a Project Jukebox-a Hypercard-based Multimedia Archival System. Project jukebox is used for archiving as well as providing access to recordings of oral history archives. For the past five years, many libraries in the developed countries started various projects such as archiving different forms of information, multimedia databases, multimedia catalogues, walk-through programmes, Instructional packages, electronic books, and digital libraries. There are a few surveys in the literature that are focused on the usage of multimedia technology in public libraries, academic libraries and special libraries. These studies primarily cover the use of multimedia CD-ROMs in libraries and also the use of world wide web and Internet.

INDIAN SCENARIO

Nowadays many librarians feels that the multimedia should be integrated into the regular services by the libraries. Even in advanced countries, libraries do not have a separate department or personnel responsible for multimedia products or services. For the past 2-3 years, use of electronic resources, particularly multimedia, in libraries has improved considerably. However, budget for multimedia products still seems to be less, but it is growing for bigger libraries situated in metropolitan cities.

Generally, for selecting multimedia products, libraries depend on retail stores displays, publisher's catalogues, reviews, advertisements, trade shows, demos, computer magazines and catalogues. The main type of multimedia products being sought in libraries are reference and educational. Other related categories include databases, electronic books, software and their training packages, entertainment, leisure, etc. Most of th'e libraries are using multimedia resources for reference service and instructional purpose. In this connection, a survey was undertaken by the author on the use of multimedia in Delhi libraries to have a clear picture of usage in Indian libraries particularly in Delhi. So far published results are not available in the literature. Overall, inspite of cost reduction in the multimedia hardware and software, use of the multimedia resources is limited to some of the national level institutions or organisations. However, the majority of the libraries are now setting up such facilities for their users. After the availability of internet in a very large scale in the offices, libraries, and houses, multimedia has become more popular, with the result most of the decision makers/financial authorities are realising the importance of multimedia in the daily life and particularly in libraries. American Centre Library, British Council Libraries and a few other libraries in Delhi are having good number of *multimedia PCs* (MPCs) for using Internet and multimedia resources to their users.

MULTIMEDIA LIBRARY INFORMATION KIOSKS/WALK-THROUGH PROGRAMMES

Improving accessibility to both collections and services has always been a concern of libraries. Several libraries made attempts to create plans and guides to help users. In this connection, multimedia is one of the best tools for creating electronic library guides or web library guides or electronic tours for their users. Many libraries in the US and Europe have started using hypermedia for designing library walk-through programmes for their users.

Reference service is one of the most visible services that can be provided by these systems. 1.1 one study, it was found that 44 per cent of reference questions were directional, 18 per cent were instructional, 32 per cent actual reference and 6 per cent were extended reference. In another study, it was found that 34 per cent of the queries are actual reference and 66 per cent are directional. So, Librarians designed Hypermedia Library information Kiosks for their users to provide quick reference and redeployed the reference staff in other library activities. Andruss Library Hypercard tour is one such hypermedia walk-through programme designed for library users to provide ready made reference. This programme does not tell the users where to find books on a specific topic, one has to still use the online or card catalogues which are briefly explained in this system, and also it is not an index to periodical or newspaper articles. However, these are described and their locations are given in this tour programme.

The Andruss Library has two catalogues for library material: a card catalogue for books, phone records, tapes, maps, and music scores; and a computerised catalogue called PALS. This tour programme helps the users by giving all the basic information that the library users require to use PALS. Sweet Briar College Library's Hvpermedra walk-through programme is another of this kind designed for the staff and students to provide information about the collection, catalogue, archives, services, and locations of various collections and responsible persons of various library services showing on the floor layout.

Some other important examples of multimedia library guide web library guides/electronic tours are:

- Electronic Library Guide in the University of Birmingham's main library, created 'using ToolBook
- Guide to South Bank University's Centenary Library, developed with HyperCard
- Guide to the Dickens House Museum Library, designed using Guide
- Multimedia Database of Tourist information developed using HyperCard by the Public Library of Gateshead Libraries and Arts Service
- Guide to the Edinburgh University Computer Services, designed using Guide
- Multimedia Library Tour of the Wayne State University Library, designed using HyperCard
- Multimedia Library Tour of the Sweet Briar College Library, designed using HyperCard
- Drexel Disk is a hypermedia walk-through programme to the Drexel University students, designed using Hypercard
- Multimedia Library Kiosk of the Defence Science Library, DESIDOC, designed using Hypercard.

INSTRUCTION/TRAINING

The role of multimedia in instruction has been well documented in several research experiments done in various discipline. So, librarians have started using multimedia as a tool to train their staff in the new library technologies/ applications and also to the users to provide training about using library resources. The main advantage of using multimedia for training is its interactivity Hence, it is being used by several schools, colleges, and universities for designing individualised library instructional packages for providing training to their users and also to provide in-depth subject training to their staff. The Paul Leonard Library at San Francisco State University desrgned a multimedia-based instructional programme on library skills to teach their users. This package is intended to serve as a prototype For subject tutorials using computing technology. This was integrated in the library skills modules being developed by the HyperCard Library Instructional Project. University of Tennessee, Knoxville libraries have made another hypermedia-based *computer-based training* (CBT) package for their new staff. To make this training more interesting, they have used pictures, animation, sound and graphics and iniplemented on Mac platform. The training programme covers library services, online catalogue, orientation to the libraries, circulation policy, access to journals literature, preservation of library materials, introduction to reference work, using e-mail, technical services, integrated online systems for libraries, and acquisition and processing library material's.

A few multimedia-based CAI packages designed using HyperCard used for library staff training/instruction are:

- *Illuminate* - a Multimedia-based CAI project about the University of Minnesota Library's OPACs.
- *Tour of the Internet* - a quick tour about the Internet
- *Information Access* - a library research skills tutorial for the university students
- *Hypercard-basedAACR2* - a self teaching CAI package for preparing catalogue cards
- *Hypercard-based University of Hawaii OPAC tutorial*
- *CatSkills* - an interactive Multimedia package to teach AACR2. It is a good professional training tool for students, beginners in cataloguing and working librarians. This multimedia CD is available in both Mac and Windows platforms. The Library Association, London is marketing this tool for $495
- *UGE 100 Library Skills* - designed by the Wayne State University Library
- *Teaching Mini Medline* - a training tool for Library users
- *STAR (Student Tutorial Access and Resources)* - CAI package designed for OSU Libraries
- *Hypermedia-based CBT package* for training the new staff of University of Tennessee, Knoxville libraries

SELF-LEARNING TOOLS

For people who need practical education in areas such as home ownership, vehicles repairing, etc, the multimedia CD-ROMs are a good medium for presenting the nuts-and-bolts tasks required to keep the house/machine functioning. For example, the House Repair Encyclopaedia provides a thorough compendium of well-illustrated repair guidelines, covering essential tasks such as stopping water leak, performing electrical wiring, pouring concrete, fixing a roof and patching the damaged walls and ceilings. Individual tasks are' depicted in animation, sound, video and providing far better information than the static pages of a book. The lnternet Resource Guide is an online book about lnternet that describes the various services available on it. Similarly many more commercial multimedia self learning tools are available in the market. Some of the important training applications available in libraries are National Geographic's Animal Samplings, ABC Golf, Music Data City, Cartoon Jukebox and Magic Flute, etc.

These are self learning tools that any library can purchase and provide free education/instruction to their library users. The linking capabilities of hypertext with multimedia provides an ideal learning environment for foreign languages. Addition of graphics, photographs, music, speech and video play a lot of impact on the learner's interest, speed of learning and retaining of information in their brain. Several popular multimedia packages were' designed for learning most of the European languages by foreigners, such as Think and Talk French/Spanish/German and Introduction to Russian and Chinese, etc.

DIGITAF/ELECTRONIC LIBRARIES

Digital libraries are basically decentralised and easily extensible, able to support interoperability between different tools, applications and systems; support heterogeneity both in terms/forms of data and systems/tools supported; able to support a rich information seeking environment; and scaleable in terms of the size of the system. Digital information may include digital books, scanned images, graphics, data, digitised A-V clips, etc.

The first *Digital Libraries* (DL) project initiative was started, in 1995 in the following Universities in USA:

- University of Illinois Urbana-Champaign,
- Carnegie-Mellon University,
- Stanford University,
- University of California at Berkeley,
- University of California at Santa Barbara and
- University of Michigan.

Later on several organisations/universities/libraries in different countries started such projects. In the UK, an important DL projects were started by British Library is ELINOR-Electronic Library Project of De Montfort University, University of East Anglia, University of Bath, University College

London, University of Wales, University of Ulster and University of Surrey. Some Digital Library related projects are listed below:

- IBM Digital Library provides a hardware/software solution for the libraries to develop their own multimedia digital libraries or multimedia archival systems. It is an integrated system for capturing, indexing, storage and retrieval of tabular, textual, audio, still images, and video data at compressed and full resolutions. A search engine that can combine parametric queries, free text searches, and Query by Image Content. Workflow processing to manage approvals and routing of data is also provided. !t has an integrated rights management including electronic watermarking, encryption, licensing, accounting, metering, and authentication. It is scaleable storage and network management system that allows libraries to grow without sacrificing the convenience of anytime, anywhere access. It also provides a hierarchical storage system to protect the assets from loss and ensure fast access to most frequently used media. A world-wide web client that facilitates the multi-search capability and delivers ranked results. This system has an integrated frame-accurate VTR control of continuous media. IBM Digital Library provides a way for libraries and users of content to store and retrieve multimedia information along with textual information that describes it. Regardless of who the end user is, IBM Digital Library allows the users to capture information and images quickly, find them when needed, and build them into new products quickly, whether it is today's broadcast, a new multimedia CD-ROM, magazine, or Internet product.

Some other important Digital Library:
Initiative projects and their site information.

- The Networked Computer Science Technical Reports Library - a collection of computer science technical reports from CS departments and industrial and government research laboratories.
- The Networked Digital Library of Theses and Dissertations - a project which aims to increase the availability of theses and dissertations by placing them online with the content in an accessible form. The works may be accessed through the Electronic Thesis and Dissertation Library.
- Library Without Walls - a broad based digital library project to make information available to researchers on their desktops on a network environment.
- Thesaurus Linguarum Hiberni - an interactive on-line searchable database archive of literary and historical materials in the various languages of early, mediaeval and modern Ireland.

- The Perseus Project - a collection on ancient Greek and Roman world. Perseus contains texts in Greek and its translation.
- The RYHINER - consists of more than 15,000 maps, charts, plans and views from the 16th to the 18th century, covering the whole globe.
- Project Bartleby - a public library on the Internet.
- Digital Libraries - a collection papers discussing digital libraries and their research efforts.
- The Visible Human Project - a complete, anatomically detailed, three dimensional representations of the male and female human body.
- National Digital Library the American 'Memory project, Special American Collections at the LC and Country Studies.
- Digital Library Programme at Tilburg University is to provide staff and students with excellent support facilities for teaching, learning and research.

MULTIMEDIA DATABASES

Now-a-days a large number of photographs, artifacts, audio recordings and textual $material in various collections are available in libraries. Multimedia is helping the librarians in integrating all the information from various forms/sources subject-wise and making meaningful multimedia databases both for day-to-day use and archiving. Mendocino County Library, Ukiah has developed a multimedia database of historical and cultural information that is relevant to the Californian Indians in that area. In addition to the historical photographs, this database is also having parts of oral histories from the state and local archives. Ultimately this library is trying to bring out a CD-ROM on 'Gathering together a Native American History'. Ancient Biblical Manuscript Centre in Claremont; California has ancient texts, photographs, negatives, related to the Bible. This centre has undertaken an ambitious programme 'Dead Sea Scroll Imaging Project', which involves digitising and reformatting photographic negatives for the past four years. The Centre has converted this collection into a comprehensive digital library and it has sophisticated search/sort enquiries on Dead Sea Scrolls.

MULTIMEDIA INFORMATION RETRIEVAL SYSTEM

Hypermedia Information Retrieval System (HIRS) is a hypertext version of a large and comprehensive annotated bibliography of hypertext/hypermedia information. Compiled from a variety of sources including periodicals, academic journals and online informational databases, it is intended for educational and training purposes only and no warranty is made as to the suitability of anything included in this stack for any specific purpose. HIRS was created in association with Project Rivendell, at the University of Toledo. Rivendell focuses on the application of hypertext/hypermedia research to address training and educational needs. It is an interdisciplinary centre for applied hypermedia research serving as the focal point for the collection, synthesis, evaluation, and dissemination of the most current research available for using hypermedia to solve instructional problems in a variety of learning settings. HyperKRS is another commercial package being used for developing hypermedia-based information retrieval systems.

MULTIMEDIA CATALOGUES

Interactive multimedia Catalogues are electronic forms of catalogues distributed in the mail-order catalogue market. Printed catalogues are one of the important information sources particularly in technical libraries. These catalogues consume large percentage of postal carrier bags. Today, the interactive multimedia catalogues offer a high volume of information on a small disk. Several international publishing companies are also bringing out their catalogues in interactive multimedia CD-ROMs. For example, CD-ROM Catalogue Shopping, SW. Catalogues, Macromedia Showcase, Silverplatter Directory of Electronic Resources, etc. Under the *Colorado Alliance of Research Libraries* (CARL) System, Denver Public Library has designed a Kid's Catalogue is for children. The Kid's Catalogue designed to capture the imagination and the natural curiosity of children and connect them with intellectual and emotional delights of information. This catalogue was designed in *graphical user interface* (GUI) using Hypercard software. It was found that this catalogue made a considerable impact on the children's usage of the library collection. The Hans Helgesen Elementary School Library, British Columbia, Canada have also developed a Hypercard-based school card catalogue for the school children. Hypercataloguer is a Hypercard-based cataloguing tool. It can take text, graphics, animation, audio and video information for preparing multimedia-based digital catalogues. Several libraries are using multimedia Catalogues and OPACS' in their libraries for various purposes.

MULTIMEDIA INFORMATION RESOURCES

The kinds of multimedia systems/information resources available in libraries and information centers include:

- CD-ROMs.
- Video discs.
- Laser discs.
- Audio 8 video cassettes.
- Web.
- Databases on servers.
- Digital video.

Many big publishers have now converted their reference books including, Encyclopaedias, dictionaries, handbooks, etc. from the traditional print form to multimedia format. Thus libraries have a choice of selecting either print or multimedia publications.

Some of the multimedia publications are listed below:

- *Encyclopaedias*:Crompton's lnteractive Encyclopaedia, 1998; Britannica CD 98 and Britannica Video CD; Encyclopaedia Americana 98; Grolier Multimedia Encyclopaedia, 1998; World Book Multimedia Encyclopaedia; Microsoft Encarta 98, etc.
- *Dictionaries and Directories*: Oxford English Dictionary; Webster English Dictionary; The Dictionary of Living World; National Geograpic's Mammals; British Birds; Microsoft Dinosatlrs, etc.
- *Reference Manuals*: MIT Movie Manual; interactive Graphics Documents; The Manual of Medical Therapeutics, etc.
- *Year Books*: The Guiness Disk of Records
- *Reference Book*s: Earth Quest; World Climate Disc; interactive Periodic Table, etc.
- *Electronic Books*: Manual of Medical Therapeutics; The Electronic Whole Earth Catalogue; Microsoft Musical Instruments; Introduction to Classical Music; The Oxford Textbook of Medicine on CD-ROM, etc.
- *Electronic Newspapers/Journals*: The Times/Sunday Times/The Guardian; Times, Newsweek; Multimedia Tech for Electronic Newspapers; Integrated Multimedia Environment; Music and Multimedia Publishing; ST and Medical Publishing for Electronic Delivery, etc.
- *Multimedia Fiction*: Nowadays several Multimedia fiction books/packages are available for all levels of people. For example, The Manhole, a children fiction takes the kids to a fantasy world with talking animals and dragons where magic bean stalks grow into the sky.

GEOGRAPHICAL INFORMATION SYSTEMS (GIS)

Additional multimedia information, visuals, audio and video can be associated along with landmarks and other points of interest in a Geographical Information system?. For example, GIs multimedia application in The National Capital Planning Commission (NCPC), Washington, DC, uses online video clips and images of buildings along with their maps. In India, Bangalore Online, is a multimedia GIS applications designed with Maplnfo software. Similarly Escorts, India developed multimedia GIS for several cities in India. Number of commercial GIs reference tools are available in the market for libraries for their ready reference..

ELECTRONIC PUBLISHING

The emergence of CD-writers and recordable CDs has solved some of the problems at the libraries in storing/archiving their less used materials. Multimedia tools along with CD-writers made possible in publishing information from different sources in a most easy to use and acceptable form to the library users. Now several big libraries started publishing their special collections, image databases, OPACs, etc on multimedia CD-ROMs. It is one of the most viable alternatives to paper-based publishing.

MULTIMEDIA ARCHIVAL SYSTEM

Multimedia Archival System are mostly developed by the national museums, publishing houses, movie production companies, etc. The Design Museum located in Butler's Wharf in London has stored information regarding 250 artifacts, 40 designers, 25 manufactures and 11 monuments on Mac using Hypercard. The museum of London has over *3* million archaeological files on 7 gigabite storage space. Similarly ABC News has a very large size Mac-based video archival library for developing hypermedia applications. Project Jukebox is another Hypercard-based multimedia archival system for archiving multimedia information resources in the library.

MULTIMEDIA USE IN MUSEUM LIBRARIES

Multimedia systems allow images, sounds and text to be combined in imaginative new ways to be transmitted in digitised formats and to be stored and reproduced or networked for wide public access and use. To accelerate the multimedia digitalisation of collections, to ensure their accessibility to the public and to stress its value as a learning resource for schools and universities. Global co-operation will help museums and galleries to increase public interest in their collections and to exploit their resources for the benefit of further enrichment. The target users will be students, teachers, researchers, general public as well as curators and the end-users of the multimedia services provided by museums and galleries. Many American, European and Indian libraries are already using Multimedia in their libraries for providing information services to their users and interactive museums displays.

Examples of Indian multimedia museum guides are:

- An interactive Multimedia guide of the National Museum of Natural History designed using Director
- An interactive Multimedia guide of the National Rail Museum designed using ToolBook.

CALL NUMBER DIRECTORIES

A Call Number Directory programme was designed using Macintosh's Hypercard at the Science and Engineering Library. The Science and Engineering Library houses materials pertaining to the life and physical sciences, computing, mathematics, and nursing on seven floors. This programme helps the users in locating the information and also the physical locations of the books in different floors showing the pictures of those floors, stacks, etc.

LIMITATIONS OF MULTIMEDIA

Even though Multimedia systems have many advantages introducing such systems into offices, schools, colleges, universities, and homes is not easy task. The problems or limitations of multimedia technology are in two areas.

TECHNOLOGY

- The requisite hardware/software to setup a multimedia content creating facility is still very expensive and requires large investments.
- A wide range of multimedia software is not available to integrate, control, coordinate, manage and adapt different media for the latest human computer interfaces.
- There is a lack of support software facilitating the authoring, composition and production of multimedia content.
- Poor support technology in the area of, multimedia data and document storage and manipulation.
- Lack of proper search and pattern recognition capability for locating information from multimedia databases.
- Lack of software support technology for group decision making and cooperative work, especially in application of multimedia technology to cooperative decision making and work.
- Converting all the multimedia resources into digital multimedia and storing is difficult.
- Time being, there is no full-fledged established hardware/software multimedia technology solution for design and development of a large size realtime multimedia digital library.
- Existing distributed networks do not support real time multimedia services.

SKILLED MANPOWER

- Lack of trained manpower for the development and management of multimedia databases
- Vast amount of work required to create an hour interactive multimedia content
- Good multimedia content creation requires multi-disciplinary disciplinary knowledge, multi-technological skills and experience.

The main barrier to the widespread use of multimedia technology is the absence of standardisation among the various platforms and between hardware and software. For the time being there is no full-strength application of the multimedia information system, however, several universities are working in exploiting the full strengths of multimedia, such as natural language processing, realtime A-V content retrieval along with text and date, and implementing such a system in a network environment. The market is dominated by multimedia CD-ROMs, multimedia databases, reference tools, etc. The effectiveness of these systems will depend on various factors such as well developed software programmes, information content and development of new information handling skills. The requirements of the effective management are the support of the senior manager, the professional qualifications, knowledge about IT technology, interpersonal skills and learning models and frameworks and how to use these new resources and to be effective in the information needs of an organisation.

BASIC ARCHITECTURE OF MULTIMEDIA CATALOGUE

The multimedia catalogue must serve two roles. In its first role, the system should act as a repository for the multimedia objects and information that is gathered and generated during the various phases of the documentation process; in this role, the system interacts with the documentalists.

Its second role is the publication of the final product to the user; it should support searching, navigation and pre-viewing of the documentation, and managing the links with the content libraries. As a consequence of the different constraints relating to these two roles, an architecture based on two coupled subsystems has been selected.

The first subsystem, called the *Documentation Catalogue*, acquires the multimedia objects, and supports the documentation and validation phases.

The second subsystem, called the *Publication Catalogue*, receives the validated programmes, and supports the services aimed at the users, *i.e.* searching, navigation, previewing and links to the libraries in order to request the downloading of the content.

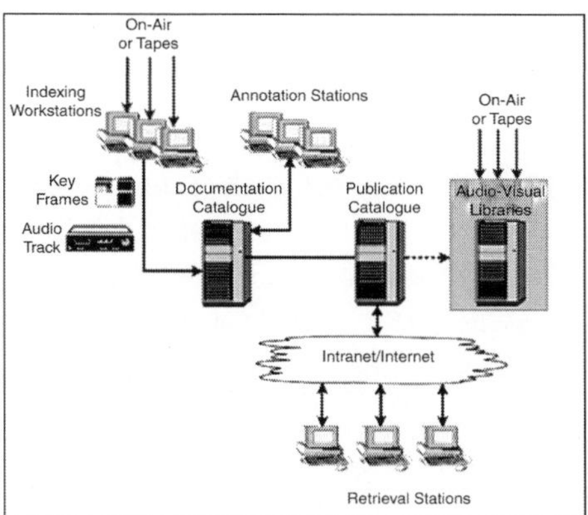

Fig. Basic Archiltecture of the Multimedia Catalogue.

Documentation Catalogue

The functions relating to the multimedia Documentation Catalogue are:

- Acquisition of multimedia objects;
- Merging of multimedia objects into programme items;
- Indexing and documentation of the programmes;
- Programme validation;
- Transferring of the validated programmes to the Searching Catalogue.

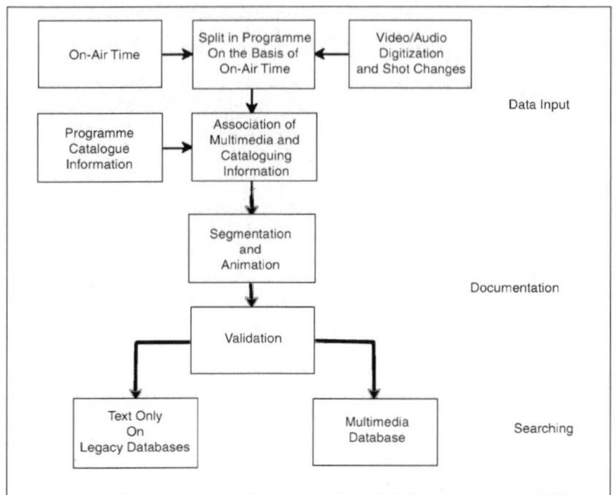

Fig. Functional Block Dlagram of the Documentation Catalogue.

Multimedia Object Acquisition

The acquisition station is based on a custom bi-processor workstation which receives at its input a composite video signal and a temporal reference, and which performs in real-time the following activities:

- Digitisation and compression of the audio;
- Detection of shot changes;
- Extraction of a keyframe for each shot;
- Association of the starting time and duration of the shot with each keyframe.

When the acquisition station is fed with on-air signals from the broadcast channels, no programme information is available at this stage.

Thus, the keyframes and audio are labelled with their acquisition time, and further processing is required to subdivide this stream into programme items. The output stream is sent to the Documentation Catalogue server.

Subdivision of Multimedia Objects into Programme Items

In the Documentation Catalogue, the continuous flow of multimedia objects is processed in order to create programme items in the database. At present, this operation is performed manually, supported by information about the transmission start and end time of each programme, automatically loaded from an administrative database. The available precision–sufficient for administrative operations–is not adequate for a completely automatic segmentation of programmes; therefore, an operator is required to refine the cut points.

This step is simplified in the digitisation chain for the legacy materials as there is very often a one-to-one corres-pondence between tapes and programmes. In this phase, a programme entity is created in the database, binding the multimedia information with some basic classification information, such as the name of the programme, the credits, identification codes of the programme, corresponding tape in the master library, etc.

Indexing, Documentation and Validation

The documentation of programmes is performed by outsourcing this work to a number of contracted companies. A general architecture has been individualised to include independent documentation islands that are connected to the Documentation Catalogue via a dedicated network.

In this way, the multimedia objects are transferred from the Documentation Catalogue to a server located in each documentation company, and then connected via a LAN to the individual documentation stations.The produced documentation is sent back to the Documentation Catalogue and added to the corresponding programme item in the database. The documentation must be validated subsequently by the archive department, before its publication.

Transferring of Programme Items to the Publication Catalogue

The validated, documented, programmes are transferred to the Publication Catalogue and then made available to the users by means of search, navigation and previewing functions.

Publication Catalogue

The Multimedia Catalogue must be able to manage the documentation relating to TV, radio, papers and photos stored in the various RAI libraries. Considering that RAI owns a huge amount of material that is increasing very rapidly, the Multimedia Catalogue would also have to be very large. A single database supporting the whole catalogue would consist of a very large number of records and would have a predictably poor performance.

Consequently, it has been decided to partition the database according to the type of material, while maintaining the capability of searching in parallel across all the partitions. The expected advantages are a large reduction in the size of each database, and a corresponding reduction in the number of concurrent users on each partition. This will lead to an increase in performance, a higher flexibility and a better scalability of the system. An additional cost to be sustained will arise from the need to maintain a distributed database which is, by its very nature, more complex than a centralised one. The user stations can be linked to the Catalogue by means of local or geographical networks, using web interfaces and standard browsers. The coding of the multimedia information has been carefully chosen in such a way that it uses minimal network resources while maintaining sufficient quality for the services provided.

Selected Technology

The documentation structure is modelled using an object-oriented approach. This structure has been mapped onto an *Object-Relational Database* (ORDB) that extends the entity-relation concepts with some features borrowed from the object-oriented technology. It is then possible to have tables of data addressed by means of the traditional SQL language, which allows for easy and efficient design and development of the searching functions, in combination with features such as user-defined data types and functions, and class inheritance.It is expected that this approach has the flexibility needed to support future releases of the system which include new requirements and new technologies. When compared with a traditional relational database, ORDB technology has proven to be very effective in the implementation of navigation functions in the media objects that make up the documentation of the programmes.

DATA MODEL

The material is logically structured according to a data model that considers a *programme* belonging to a *series* which, in turns, belongs to a *product*. The programme can be divided up into *segments* which are composed of *shots*.

These different levels are defined as follows:

- *Product*: A collection of collections, constituting a complete television programme or "title". It can also be defined as "all the programmes with the same title";
- *Series*: A set of programmes related to the same product;
- *Programme*: A media object with a unique timeline. It can be part of one or more collections, and can be sub-divided into one or more segments. A programme can also be defined as "an episode of a product";
- *Segment*: Part of a programme with a closed semantic meaning;
- *Shot*: A shot of video extracted from a programme, usually using automatic segmentation tools, according to some technical criteria, *e.g.,* a scene change, a dissolve, a wipe.

Annotations are associated with the first four levels of data, *i.e.,* the product, series, programme and segment levels. This structure is very general and can support recursive documentation that includes re-uses of the material. A typical case is shown in figure which depicts segments included within segments.

Each programme item comprises still pictures, compressed audio, formatted fields and free text. The still pictures consist of keyframes extracted from the TV programme, scaled to ¼ size and JPEG compressed.

The audio is derived from the programme soundtrack, compressed using MPEG layer-3 at 8 kbit/s. The formatted fields and free text include: the classification information, automatically downloaded from legacy databases; a minimal documenation generated in the production phase, and the annotation typed in by the documentalist during the documentation phase.

USER FUNCTIONALITIES

Search

To determine which tools the search interface for the Catalogue must offer to its users, an analyzis of user types must be performed.

At least two user classes must be considered:

- A generic user who accesses the Catalogue mainly for documentation purposes, without specialised information on its organisation;
- An expert user who is able to exploit every feature of the system, using complex queries.

Users belonging to the first class require a very friendly interface and the possibility of extending the search to many or all of the different types of material. On the other hand, users in the second class are, in the most part, professional researchers looking for specific materials to be included in new productions and therefore they need to locate the items in the shortest time, by means of comprehensive user interfaces.

Furthermore, as different documentation fields are required for different kinds of materials, a query on the whole Catalogue must be based on the subset of documentation fields that is common to all the documentation typologies.

Based on the considerations, three searching levels have been considered:

- On the documentation of all the material, *i.e.* TV, radio, paper and photos;
- On the documentation of a single type of material, *i.e.,* TV, radio, paper or photos;
- On the documentation of specific genres, *e.g.* TV fiction, dramas, magazine programmes, news, Radio news, etc.

The search at the third level is performed on all of the documentation fields, the formatted data and the free text. However, the search at the first two levels is performed only on free text and a limited subset of the formatted data. This subset contains the documentation fields available on all the material that is taken into account at that level.

Clearly, this subset is more limited at level 1 than at level 2. The search can be composed using logical operators and by looking for either the exact word, a similar word or a synonym. The searching mode is set up by the user before starting the searching operation. The result of a search query consists of the number and list of the occurrences found. By clicking on such an occurrence, the navigation interface opens and the user is able to navigate within the selected programme.

Navigation

The results of a query can be any type of documented object, *i.e.* a product, series, programme, segment or shot.

These are all entry points to a graph of related objects, interconnected either:

- Through a structural link such as from a programme to its included segments;
- From one segment to the next one of the same programme, or;
- Through an association established by the documentalist, *e.g.,* a set of news items on the same topic, or a programme and its script.

Therefore, after browsing the objects resulting from a query, the user can navigate across the graph of related objects. The user interface for navigation is illustrated in figure. On the left of the window is displayed a list of the segments included in the programme: it consists of the most representative keyframes, the title of the segment, and its duration.

Fig. Navigation Interface at the Programme Level.

At the top of the window, the Product, Collection and Programme titles are shown. The duration of the episode, as well as the production and on-air dates, are also indicated.

By clicking on the buttons in the centre of the window, a documentation area is displayed. The picture at the bottom of the window shows the index of the programme segments, organised by content. The round buttons at the bottom of the window are used for navigation. Using this interface, it is possible to display information relating to a selected segment, as shown in figure.

The page structure and the basic information relating to the Product, Collection and Programme at the navigation level are the same as for the Programme level. The keyframes in the left panel refer now to the most significant segment shots.

A selection of the most important shots is carried out by the documentalist in order to limit the number of displayed pictures and to reduce the downloading time. In any case, if required by the user, the complete list of shots can be displayed. The documentation areas associated with the segment object contain information that is specific to the segment, including segment description, video content description, participants list, location, environment, etc.

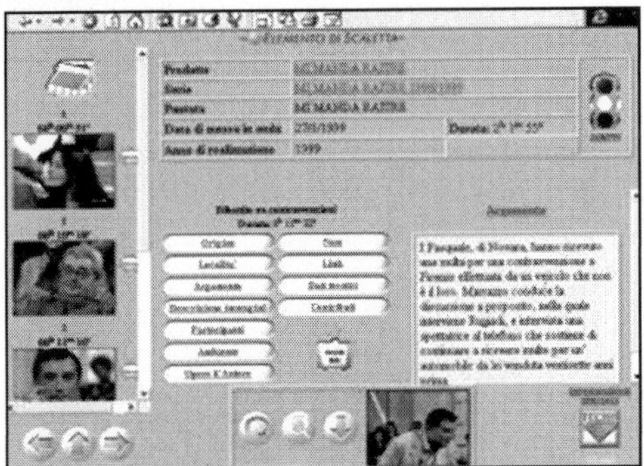

Fig. Navigation Interface at the Segment Level.

In the top right corner of the programme and segment interfaces, there is a traffic light icon. It indicates the presence or absence of legal constraints on the use of the material. Normally, the materials in the Catalogue are owned by RAI and are available for internal reuse but, occasionally, the allowed use may be constrained according to specific contracts. In the case of a yellow traffic light, the situation has to be cleared with the legal department. At the segment level, a previewing function is available. To limit the database size and keep the network occupancy as low as possible, the preview is obtained by displaying the keyframes for the duration of the relative shots, in synchronisation with the soundtrack.

"Palinsesto" Interface to Browse Undocumented Programmes

The complete documentation process, from the capturing of key frames to the uploading of the validated documentation to the Publication Catalogue, requires several days. For some genres such as news, the multimedia objects associated with the classification and broadcast date of the corresponding programme already constitute a valuable information source to some types of users.

Therefore, undocumented material is uploaded to the Multimedia Catalogue on the day following the transmission, without waiting for the completion of the documentation process. These materials can be accessed through knowing the relevant broadcast time or title. The enabled functions are: display of key frames; animation preview and display of the broadcast and classification date.

INFORMATION SOURCES IN THE LIBRARY/INTERNET

The Internet has become a big library for all kinds of information. Some information sources are available online free of charge while others are fee-based. Examples include online books, databases, journals and reference resources. Some of these are free on the Internet while others are based on subscription or purchase. MEDLINE/PubMed is a good example of a free online database while EMBASE is based on subscription.

The various categories of information sources that could be accessed through the Web:

- Reference;
- Monographs;
- Periodicals;
- Indexes and abstracts;
- Drug information; and
- Databases.

REFERENCE SOURCES

These are authoritative works that provide specific answers or information. As you go through school, you will need to use reference sources to find information about topics, locate facts, and answer questions. There are many types of reference sources, including atlases, dictionaries, encyclopaedias, thesauri, directories, almanacs, manuals, biographies, and handbooks, among others. Each type is available either in print, on CD-ROMs and the Internet. Reference information sources can be general or subject specific. For example, The Encyclopaedia *Britannica* is general while *The Encyclopaedia of Stem-Cell* Research, *The Encyclopaedia of Pain*, and *The Gale Encyclopaedia of Medicine* are subject encyclopaedias. Other reference sources such as dictionaries, atlases, directories also have both general and subject categories.

Fig. A Set of Encyclopaedia Britannicagale Encyclopaedia of Medicine.

MONOGRAPHS

A monograph is a scholarly piece of writing in form of an essay or book on a specific, often limited subject. It is a book that stands on its own rather than being part of a series. National Research Council (NRC), a monograph is a specialized scientific book. Monographs are written by specialists for the benefit of other specialists and demand the highest standards of scholarship. Most monographic manuscripts are critically reviewed and edited resulting in books that are expected to have a reasonably long shelf life. Monographs serve as an important means for conveying basic background information, such as a narrative description of a disease, path-physiology, diagnostic techniques and common therapeutic regimes etc. This trend remains true today, whether the monograph is in the print or electronic format.

Monographs can be located using bibliographies that list references of books with detailed bibliographic information (author, title, year of publication, publisher and date of publication). Bibliographies serve as tools for verification, location and selection of monographs. Today, many print sources for monographs are now in electronic formats. To locate monographs in a library collection requires using the library catalog and most libraries now have Online Public Access Catalog (OPAC). A good example is the National Library of Medicine LOCATOR plus.

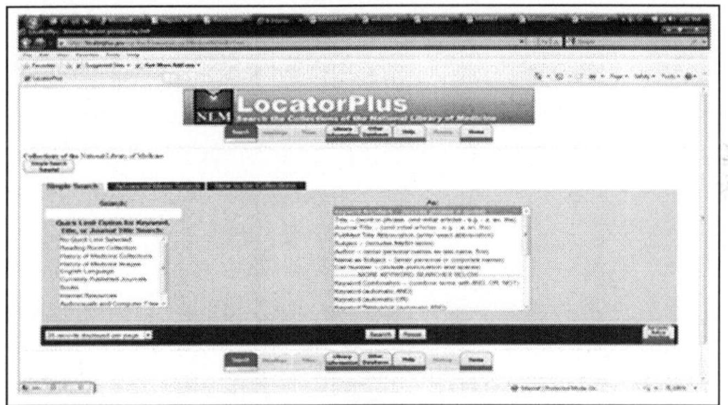

PERIODICALS

Periodicals are publications such as journals, newspapers, or magazines published on a regular basis-daily, weekly, bi-weekly, monthly, bimonthly, quarterly, yearly, etc. The information in periodicals covers a wide variety of topics and is very uptodate. Periodicals are available in both print and electronic formats. Common examples of periodicals include popular magazines (or general interest magazines), professional and trade magazines, scholarly journals, newsletters, and newspapers. The two basic types of periodicals are: popular (or general interest magazines), and scholarly.

POPULAR

Popular magazines are periodicals of non-specialist nature. The published articles are usually written by staff writers, and chosen by the editor of the publication. Magazine articles are usually shorter, written in non-technical language, and designed for the general population. Articles in popular magazines are reviewed by one or two members of staff of the organization where they are published. Popular magazines have a glossy appearance, contains many photographs and advertisements.

Examples of popular magazines are:

- O, The Oprah Magazine.
- Readers Digest.
- People.
- Time Magazine.

TRADE MAGAZINES

These are magazines that present information about a profession or a particular trade. They are written for members of a specific business, industry or organization. Trade magazines cover industry trends, new products or techniques, and organizational news written by staff or contributing authors. Good examples of trade magazines are: *The Economist, APA Monitor* and *Computer World.*

SCHOLARLY JOURNALS

Journals are written by experts or specialists in a particular field/discipline and geared towards other scholars. The purpose of scholarly publications is to report research or advance knowledge. The articles are usually longer and may contain charts, graphs, statistics, etc., as well as extensive bibliographies. The articles usually involve extensive research and in-depth studies. The writing style is more complex and the language may be technical. Examples of this type of periodical are academic journals and professional journals. Academic journals are written by members of an academic community and are reviewed by their peers while professional journals are written by member of a professional body including librarians, lawyers, doctors and nurses.

Examples of academic journals are:

- *British Medical Journal.*
- *New England Journal of Medicine.*
- *African Journal of Medicine and Medical Sciences.*
- *East African Medical Journal.*
- *African Health Sciences.*

Examples of professional/academic journals include:

- *Journal of the American Medical Association.*
- *Journal of the Medical Library Association.*
- *African Journal of Library, Archival and Information Science.*

Access to journals either in print or electronic formats is based on subscription, however; fulltext articles of some electronic journals can be accessed free on the Internet. Also, more than 7000 electronic journals are available to students, researchers, scientists, health care workers, and policy makers in Africa through the Health Internetwork Access to Research Initiative (HINARI). Using this resource requires institutional registration and login with the User Identification and Password.

NEWSPAPERS

Newspaper articles are short and written in non-technical language. They provide first-hand account of an event and so are primary sources. Newspapers come in different forms and are designed for the general public and are business in nature. Newspaper articles are usually short and written in an easy to understand language by staff reporters and reviewed by staff within the organization. Newspapers are also good sources for secondary information. However, not all information in newspapers is reliable. Newspapers are published daily, weekly or monthly. Example of newspapers include: *The New York Times, The Guardian*, and *Nigerian Tribune* etc.

INDEXES AND ABSTRACTS

Abstracts and indexes provide citations to papers dealing with specific topics in a field of knowledge. Indexes provide the essential bibliographic information needed to identify an article or other publications and usually include information about the author of the work, the source journal or other publication, volume, issue, and pagination. Abstracting tools include the same key elements but also a summary of the work usually written by the author or sometimes generated by the reviewer where an author did not submit one. Most indexing and abstracting services allow access to their content through subject and author indexes. However, each tool differs on how data is presented and the nature by which access is organized.

Examples of abstracts and indexes include:

- *Index Medicus*.
- *International Pharmaceutical Abstracts*.
- *Index to Dental Literature*.
- *Science Citation Index*.
- *Current Contents: Clinical Practice*.
- *Psychological Abstracts*.
- *Cumulative Index to Nursing and Allied Health Literature* (*CINAHL*).

Most of the popular databases searched by librarians and library users originated from printbased abstracting and indexing services. For example, the Index Medicus resulted in MEDLINE now accessible online through PubMed.

DRUG INFORMATION SOURCES

Butros and McGuinness, drug information sources cover the fields of pharmacology, pharmacy and toxicology. There are as many drug information sources as there are various specialties.

DATABASES

These are systematically organized collections of infor-mation covering different subject matters or specializing in one given subject or topic. They may be arranged in a table of contents, alphabetically, in numerical order, in an index or in subject categories. A database is made up of records. Each item in the database has one record. Records consist of smaller units of information called fields.

Common bibliographic database fields are: author, publi- c a t i o n title, article title, subject or keywords, publication date, volume, issue and page number. For example, in the MEDLINE/PubMed database, each journal citation has one record. The record consists of the following fields: author, article title, journal title, date of publication, volume, issue, page number, PubMed ID, and abstract. A digital database (8.3) is a computer programme that organizes, describes, and indexes information. It permits the user to search for specific types of information, depending upon the selected search parameters.

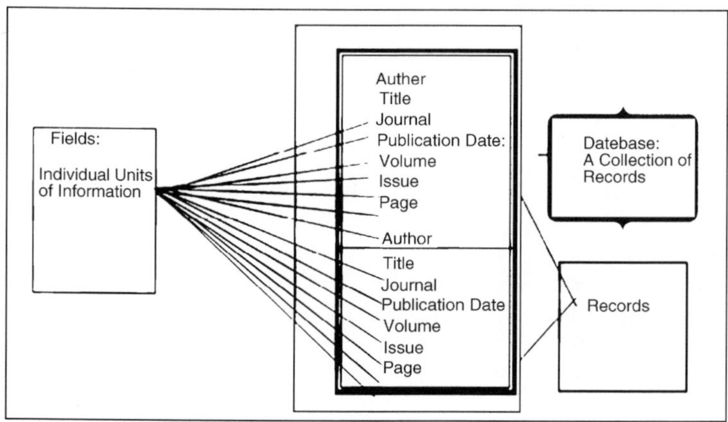

Fig. Components of a Biblographic Database

INVISIBLE OR DEEP WEB

The "invisible Web" is what you cannot find using search engines and what you see in almost all subject directories. They are gold mines of information you need to search directly. These includes all of the licensed article, magazine, reference, news archives, and other research resources that libraries and some industries buy for those authorized to use them. There is lots of helpful information locked away in databases that can never be indexed by search engines. The services that let you search this "invisible Web" or "deep Web include: Invisi-bleweb.com, Lycos Invisible Catalog, Direct search and WebData.

Examples of searchable databases containing invisible web pages valuable in academic research are:

- ipl2.
- Infomine.
- Online Bibliographic Databases:

- African Index Medicus (AIM);
- MEDLINE/PubMed;
- Cumulative Index to Nursing and Allied Health Literature (CINAHL);
- Web of Knowledge;
- Scopus; and
- EMBASE.

African Index Medicus (AIM)

African Index Medicus (AIM) is a collaborative effort between the World Health Organization (WHO) and the Association for Health Information and Libraries in Africa (AHILA). AIM gives access to information published or related to Africa and also encourages local publishing. A total of 140 journals published in Africa are indexed in AIM as of October 1, 2010. This database provides access to mainly abstracts and a few full-text articles published in African journals.

MEDLINE/PubMed

MEDLINE is the premier bibliographic database of the National Library of Medicine, Bethesda, Maryland, USA. It covers the field of medicine, nursing dentistry, veterinary medicine, the health care systems, the preclinical sciences and other areas related to the life sciences and is updated daily. MEDLINE records contain bibliographic citations from over 5,000 print and electronic biomedical journals published across the globe. It has over 12 million citations of which approximately 76 per cent include abstracts.

Cumulative Index to Nursing and Allied Health Literature (CINAHL)

Cumulative Index to Nursing and Allied Health Literature (CINAHL) CINAHL gives access to citations and abstracts for nursing and allied health information. It includes citations from over 2000 journals and abstracts are available for over 1200 titles with full text of over 7,000 records available in the database. This database also provides some coverage of biomedicine, alternative/ complementary medicine and consumer health information. CINAHL is based on subscription. However, it could be accessed free of charge through HINARI by institutions in Africa.

Web of Science

Web or science Provides access to the Science Citation Index Expanded and Social Science Citation Index. It covers science and provides technical journals in biochemistry, biology, genetics, biomedicine, genetics, microbiology, nuclear science with abstracts. It covers more than 8,000 journals. It offers current and retrospective bibliographic information, author abstracts and cited references and allows users to conduct broad-based comprehensive searches that uncover all the relevant information they need. It provides cited reference searching, the unique ISI search and retrieval feature that lets users track the literature forward, backward and through the database. It is updated weekly. Web of Knowledge (PubMed) is accessible free of charge via HINARI.

Scopus

Scopus is an interdisciplinary bibliographic database that indexes the content of more than 15,000 peer-reviewed journals from more than 4000 international publishers. It covers subjects such as the physical sciences, engineering, earth and environmental sciences, life and health sciences, social sciences, psychology, business, and management. Scopus content includes MEDLINE and EMBASE citations. Also, Scopus covers 1,000 Open Access Journals, 500 Conference Proceedings, Over 600 Trade Publications and over 125 Book titles. In addition, Scopus covers 386 million quality Web sources including 21 million patents.

Embase

Provides content to biomedical (clinical and experimental) information with extensive coverage of drug research, pharmacology, pharmacy, and toxicology, public health and mental health topics with abstracts back to 1974 and it is updated daily with pharmacological information. The database indexes more than 7000 journals, has over 18 million records. It has more than the 11 million EMBASE records from 1974 to date and seven million for unique MEDLINE records from 1966 to the present.

EVIDENCE-BASED MEDICINE (EBM) RESOURCES/DATABASES

Evidence-Based Medicine is about using information from the medical literature in making informed decision about patient care.

Many EBM databases are now accessible online including, among others:

- Clinical Queries.
- Cochrane Library.
- Clinical Evidence.
- DynaMed.
- Best Evidence.

In this module, Clinical Queries and the Cochrane Library will be discussed

Clinical Queries

This is accessible through PubMed and covers three main areas namely:

- *Clinical Study Category Query*: This filters citations to a specific clinical study category and scope.
- *Systematic Reviews:* These filter citations for systematic reviews, meta-analyses, reviews of clinical trials, evidence-based medicine, consensus development conferences, and guidelines..

- *Medical Genetics:* Filter citations to topics in medical genetics.

The Cochrane Library

The Cochrane Library is a collection of databases, published on CD-ROM and the Internet and updated quarterly, containing the Cochrane Database of Systematic Reviews, the Cochrane Central Register of Controlled Trials, the Database of Abstracts of Reviews of Effects, the Cochrane Methodology Register, the HTA Database, NHSEED, and information about The Cochrane Collaboration. The Cochrane Library has about 4,000 reviews meant for use by health care workers to enable them to make informed decisions with respect to patient care. Reviews are unique because they are both produced by, and are relevant to everyone interested in the effects of health care. Based on the best available evidence, health care providers can decide if they should fund production of a particular drug. Practitioners can find out if an intervention is effective in a specific clinical context.

Patients and other health care consumers can assess the potential risks and benefits of their treatment:

- Systematic reviews seek to collate all evidence that fits pre-specified eligibility criteria in order to address a specific research question.
- They aim to minimize bias by using explicit, syste-matic methods.
- The Cochrane Collaboration prepares, maintains and promotes systematic reviews to inform health care decisions (Cochrane reviews).
- Cochrane reviews are published in the *Cochrane Database of Systematic Reviews* in *The Cochrane Library.*

CONSUMER HEALTH INFORMATION RESOURCES/DATABASES

- MEDLINEPlus.
- National Institute of Health (NIH) Senior Health.
- New York Online Access to Health (NOAH).
- HealthyRoadsMedia.
- Toxtown.
- Toxnet.
- Household products database.

Medline Plus

Medline Plus is a product of the National Library of Medicine (NLM). Medline Plus offers information on selected, organized links to online consumer health information on hundreds of topics about diseases, conditions, and wellness issues in language you can understand. Medline Plus offers reliable, up-to-date health information, anytime, anywhere for free. You can use Medline Plus to learn about the latest treatments, look up information on a drug or supplement, find out the meanings of words, or view medical videos or illustrations. You can also get links to the latest medical research on your topic or learn about clinical trials on a disease or condition. It also includes tutorials.

Also featured are an online encyclopaedia, medical dictio-nary, audio-visual resources, and extensive links to Spanish-language health information. Medline Plus is the premier consumer health site. It should be any consumer health information seeker's first stop, and can fill the vast majority of information needs. The homepage is very well-organized; everything is accessible from there. When searching, multiple search terms automatically combined with "And". Search engine will detect misspelled words and suggest alternatives.

NIH Senior Health

This is a web site for the elderly, developed by the National Institute on Aging and the National Library of Medicine. Senior-friendly features include the ability to adjust font size and contrast, an audio option that reads text on the page aloud, and videos. Seniors with low vision, and anyone with low literacy needs, although most topics are senior-specific (*i.e.* Exercise for Older Adults). A short list of topics is easy to browse. No search option is included. Audio text reading function is very literal and function is spotty: may repeat phrases several times and/or skip words or sentences.

NOAH: New York Online Access to Health

A collaborative effort of New York librarians, NOAH provides access to selected, organized links to online consumer health information. It has a wide range of topics and extensive Spanish-language content. Non-Spanish-speaking users can navigate organized topic pages in English, and then click on "en espanol" link at bottom of page to access available Spanish language links for that topic. It is well-organized and easy to browse; browsing is often more efficient than using the search engine.

Healthy Roads Media

A collaborative effort of many different public health agencies, social services organizations, and librarians, HealthyRoadsMedia collects, creates and provides free online access to multilingual health information overviews on various topics in a variety of formats: audio, audiovisual, and written. Health topics provided in English and eight other languages: Arabic, Bosnian, Hmong, Khmer, Russian, Somali, Spanish, and Vietnamese. It is best for patients with lower literacy English and/or need for information in a language other than English. Focus is on prevention and wellness, and safety. Not all topics are available in all languages.

Household Products Database

This database links over 10,000 consumer brands to health effects from Material Safety Data Sheets (MSDS) provided by manufacturers and allows scientists and consumers to research products based on chemical ingredients. Household product database was developed by the Specialized Information Services Division at the National Library of Medicine, National Institutes of Health, Bethesda, Maryland, USA.

The database is designed to help answer the following typical questions:

- What are the chemical ingredients and their percentage in specific brands?
- Which products contain specific chemical ingredients?
- Who manufactures a specific brand? How do I contact this manufacturer?
- What are the acute and chronic effects of chemical ingredients in a specific brand?
- What other information is available about chemicals in the toxicology-related databases of the National Library of Medicine?

Tox Town

Tox Town: is designed to give you information on:

- Everyday locations where you might find toxic chemicals.
- Non-technical descriptions of chemicals.
- Links to selected, authoritative chemical information on the Internet.
- How the environment can impact human health.
- Internet resources on environmental health topics.

Tox Town uses colour, graphics, sounds and animation to add interest to learning about connections between chemicals, the environment, and the public's health. Tox Town's target audience is students above elementary-school level, educators, and the general public. It is a companion to the extensive information in the TOXNET collection of databases that are typically used by toxicologists and health professionals.

Toxnet

Toxnet is a database on toxicology, hazardous chemicals, environmental health, toxic releases and other information resources from the Toxicology and Environmental Health Information Programme. Developed by the U.S National Library of Medicine.

INTERNET PORTALS, DIGITAL ARCHIVES AND INSTITUTIONAL REPOSITORIES

- Health Internetwork Access to Research Initiative (HINARI) African Journals Online (AJOL).
- PubMed Central (PMC).
- *Bioline International (BI):* Through this site you can search through free and open access medical journals.
- *Biomed Central*: Open Access (OA) journal publisher that allow readers

free access to published full text journal articles while authors pay fees to get published.

- *Scientific Online Library (SciELO):* An AO publisher that gives access to full text articles.
- *Directory of Open Access Journals (DOAJ):* Gives you free access to online journals related to your subject area.
- Loughborough University's Institutional Repository.
- *Google Scholar:* While regular Google can be a helpful tool, sometimes you just need scholarly results, and that's just what this tool does, paring down results to the most reliable and academic sources.

INFORMATION SOURCES ON SOCIAL NETWORKING APPLICATIONS

In recent years social networking applications popularly known as Web 2.0 are now being used as a means of communication, especially in sharing and dissemination of information. Libraries are also using this media to reach out to their clients.

Common Web 2.0 applications that have become sources of information include:

- Facebook;
- Blogs;
- Twitter;
- MySpace;
- YouTube; and
- RSS.

4

Management Information Systems

INTRODUCTION

Researcher has defined a Management Information System as:

- the process and structure used by an organisation to identify, collect, evaluate, transfer, and utilise information in order to fulfil its objectives. It is a system that provides management with information to make decisions, evaluate alternatives, measure performance, and detect situations requiring corrective action.

The implementation of performance assessment in academic libraries is an essential part of good management practice. Although she had reservations about the current Management Information Systems in university libraries because, for example, few academic libraries had produced a statement of their objectives, she still believed that Management Information Systems could contribute to effective management of library activities.

The four main objectives for Management Information systems have been defined as:

1. To facilitate the decision making process in the library by providing the managers with accurate, timely, and selective information that assists them in determining a specific course of action.
2. To provide for the objective performance measurement and assessment of selected relevant areas of the library. The areas are to be determined during strategic planning.
3. To provide pertinent information about the library's internal and external environments.
4. To provide information on alternative strategies and contingency plans.

The purposes can only be implemented if people look upon Management Information Systems as an integral part of the framework of management in the academic library and not as a peripheral system which has been installed for the benefit of an individual or a single department.

- There may be subsystems within the larger system, which may be branch libraries, or departmental divisions such as cataloguing, acquisitions or circulation, but they must still be seen as integrated parts of the whole, and must function as such. In the systems approach, however, the library organisation must be seen as an organic whole, with information as its lifeblood and in which each part of the system is integrated by the flow of information throughout.

An integrated Management Information System is very important because it can be used to provide supporting information to determine:

- *Efficiency*: is the library doing things right.
- *Effectiveness*: is the library doing the right things.
- *Competitiveness*: is the library heading in a direction which is consistent with the environment.

Any discussion of the Management Information System must lead to consideration of the inputs data, processing data and the outputs data. Inputs to the management information system consist of both internally and externally generated library data. External information covers factors such as legislation, politics, trends in society, changes in technology, user demand, and comparative statistics for other, similar institutions. Internal data is that derived from administrative routines and transactional information. Administrative routines include those related to personnel, finance, acquisition, cataloguing, processing of materials, binding, building services, maintenance services, etc.

Output measures will include data of circulation, general user satisfaction, etc. All service points will need to be monitored so that internal performance comparisons can be made and the contribution of each service point are the overall objectives of the organisation assessed. In term of library managers' needs, a variety of inputs is evidently needed. It may be necessary to process information in different ways for different levels of decision-making needs, and different types of output reports will be needed to meet those different needs.

Selection of appropriate data elements for inclusion in a Management Information System assumes that:

- Clear goals and measurable objectives have been developed for the library,
- For each data element there is rationale for how it will be used or in what combinations with other data elements it can be used to determine success towards the accomplishment of objectives, overall library effectiveness, or performance measures for specific library services/operations, and
- The library can, in fact, collect reliable and valid data for a particular data element.'

The data in a management information system also needs to be processed to turn it into meaningful information for library management. For this reason, management information systems require an appropriate data processing system. Data processing is the capture, storage and processing of data for the purpose of transforming it into information useful for decision making.

In recent years, data processing for management information systems in business and industry has increasingly been undertaken by computers:

- A modem MIS will always rely to some extent on computer technology, although a computer is not a requirement. The reality of the 1980's would indicate that a computer is a necessity for the most sophisticated systems.

In libraries, in contrast, the development of the use of computer has been:

- Modular, in the sense that it is based on a single library operation such as acquisitions, serials, control or cataloguing. The more general applications of management information lay hidden, as it is often seen only as a departmental resource.

This need not necessarily have been so. An early prediction of the advantages of information produced by computers was made in 1979 by Tague, who suggested that computers should produce information for control at both macro and micro level in libraries.

However, in 1986, Brophy, having analysed eight large computer systems used in British libraries, noted that:

- Automated library systems seem to be primarily about control at the micro level. Moreover, they produced management information which was relatively crude, highly structured and very much a system by-product.

The needs of individual managers tended to be overlooked, especially when the design of MIS was in the hands of computer personnel.

- Too often, management information has been produced as an afterthought following computerisation. Most computerised issue systems, for example, were never designed to produce management information although librarians have often struggled over the data generated by these systems in an attempt to derive some meaningful information about issue patterns.

Technological changes have helped to ease this problem. As opposed to the use of mainframe and mini-computers, 'the advent of the microcomputer now provides an alternative to the dependence on large-scale centralised computer systems. Computer power can now be deployed cheaply to different parts of an organisation to allow for local processing of data.'

Computers should be easily able to provide four types of report: periodic reports, exception reports, on demand reports, and predictive reports. Periodic reports provide routine, statistical information in detailed or summarised form. Exception reports highlight areas requiring managerial attention and would focus on those that have been overlooked. On demand reports provide a response to a particular non-standard question. Predictive reports give forecasts and provide comparisons based on statistical manipulation of data.

The principal requirement of the outputs of academic library management information systems is that they should be of interest to:

- The relevant committee - the members wish to know how the library service is performing and whether the institution, is getting value for money.
- The chief financial officer - his role is primarily custodial, and he wants to be assured that there is no overspending and that money is used for the purpose intended.
- The chief librarian - who wants to know how services under his control are performing in accordance with plans, targets and budgets.
- The managers of individual sections or services—who want to have data on the operations and performance with plans, targets and budgets.
- Outside organisations requesting library perfor-mance data on a regular basis.

In these ways, the outputs of management information systems become information for decision making.

In general, management information is:

- 'The right information in the right form at the right time, so enabling the manager effectively and effici-ently to do his/her job.'

The value or quality of management information is determined by three factors. They are:

1. The content of information: Information is the substance of communication, but to be information rather than data or noise, it must be meaningful, relevant and new to the receiver.
2. The form or presentation of the information: Information should be presented in a style and format readily understandable by the manager. This means that the producer of information must be aware of the recipient's knowledge of technical terms, numeracy/literacy levels, his individual characteristics, the characteristics of the group with which he works and so on. These and other factors help the information producer to form an idea of the perception level of the manager and increase the likelihood of producing understandable information capable of being used which, it will be recalled, is the only way information can create value.
3. The timing of its presentation: Information which is produced must be communicated to the manager in time to be used. Delays in data gathering, processing or communication can transform potentially vital information into worthless waste paper.

In the planning process, information should support the decision making process. Since one of the major problems facing academic libraries is the impact of changes in available financial support, the Colleges of Further and Higher

Education Group (CoFHE) of the Library Association has been considering the categories of management information required for making decisions concerning the budget.

They concluded that these are:

- Information about the institutional identity of the library.
- Information about the target group.
- Information about the collection resources.
- Information about the financial resources.
- Information about library personnel.
- Information about facilities and equipment.
- Information about various programmes and functions.

CoFHE also considered the requirements for collecting management information, and suggested the following guidelines:

- The information sought must be worth the costs of collecting it - direct and indirect.
- Consider sources of information already available within the institution before setting up mechanisms to collect it.
- Keep the collection of information relevant, *i.e.,* remember the purpose - 'to support the budget request.'
- Remember to consider qualitative and quantitative data as both can be relevant.

MANAGEMENT INFORMATION SYSTEM VS. DECISION SUPPORT SYSTEM

Researcher identified four major problem areas of management information systems. They are:

1. Output is undiscriminating.
2. The information is not analysed for a purpose.
3. The system is not user-friendly.
4. The information which is given by MIS may not be acceptable.

Decision support systems can be seen as an extension of the idea of management information systems to provide a wide range of information in a more flexible and interactive way. They are designed to support decision making needs of management rather than act a useful by-product of transaction processing systems.

The special feature of a decision support system is that it solves a major problem of management information systems, *i.e.*, the poor communication between the system and the users, library managers. Decision support systems have interface outputs which are more live than those of management information systems.

The main interfaces in decision support systems are:

- Regular reports which provide information on parts of the system, which are predetermined by the system's users.

- Event-centred reports in which a report is generated only when a predetermined event has occurred. This will usually be the result of an exceptional condition, which is signalled by the system.
- *Ad hoc* reports which are generated in response to a stimulus by the system user to report on a condition which is not normally monitored.
- A query language which enables the user to interface directly with the system and to test changes in conditions experimentally. This is usually performed with 'goal-seeking' and 'what if techniques.

Beside the interface output, a decision support system also provides the report formats which may be required by the system's user, ranging from simple one-off designs to sophisticated presentations for senior managers. They are:

- *Standard reports* containing details prompted by the system user but in a format determined by standard software.
- *Tailored reports* containing information determined by the user and in a format designed by the user.
- *Tabulations* enabling the user to examine a range of statistical data rapidly, in either a standard or tailored format.
- *Spreadsheet format* allowing the user to transfer data from the system into a separate format which can be manipulated in a statistical layout.
- *Graphic presentations* providing a method of transmitting a trend analysis rapidly, and in a user-friendly manner.

Like management information systems, the data input into decision support systems can be external or internal data concerning the library. The three levels of influence on decision making can be isolated:

- Information from the library's operations.
- Information from the parent organisation.
- Information at the national and regional level.

The differences between a management information system and a decision support system lie not only their features, but also in their users. Management information systems tend to be used by lower and middle management because of their ability to assist in making structured decisions. In contrast, decision support systems tend to be more useful to top management because they can help with decisions on unstructured issues. Where they exist, decision support systems appear to be mainly used at the strategic management level.

CHANGES IN LIBRARY AND INFORMATION CENTRE MANAGEMENT

Due to fast-paced technological change and new skill requirements, information professionals are increasingly required to renew their skills and practice in order to gain an awareness of technological advances. As a result, the profession itself exists in a state of flux alongside these emerging technologies, with traditional roles being increasingly subsumed by new skills and working environments, and, therefore, job descriptions. Thus, information professionals are now expected to be aware of and capable of using and demonstrating emerging ICTs. There is a need for additional training to augment the traditional skill and knowledge base with a competency in ICT use. Information professionals must be flexible, and adopt traditional skills to incorporate the requirements of technological advances.

Given the current situation, wherein ICTs are being continuously updated or introduced and traditional formats are being replaced or supplemented by digital formats, it seems likely that there will continue to be a need for regular training for information professionals. There is also an increased focus on communication skills, with more people involved in the electronic information environment. Information professionals are being called upon to work closely with ICT users and providers - including IT staff - and to work in collaboration with others in the profession. Some groups of users lack the necessary IT skills to obtain quality information and information professionals will therefore be called upon to act as both educators and intermediaries.

Given these circumstances, information professionals are required to have additional teaching and communication skills. Thus, it is vital for those in management positions to recognise the imperative of *continuing professional development* (CPD) and ensure that the staff is proactive in maintaining up-to-date levels of expertise. The significance of CPD in this milieu has been acknowledged by both the United Kingdom's *Chartered Institute of Library and Information Professionals* (CILIP) and the United States' *American Library Association* (ALA).

Certain active roles are necessary for change management to:

- *Establish the quality goals of the library:* Library and Information Centres (LICs) should aim to establish the quality goals for qualitative service to its user community.
- *Provide the resources to their library:* LICs should provide all necessary resources suitable in the ICT era to manage the LICs in a better way.
- *Provide the quality-oriented training to the library staff:* New generation library staff are almost trained with ICT applications to LICs but old staff and others who are novices in such applications need quality training because without quality training library staff are unable to provide automated services.
- *Stimulate quality improvement in the day to day activities of library:* This is the age of competition. Like other organisations, to survive the LICs, top management should stimulate the staff for quality improvement in the day to day activities of LICs.
- *Review progress of the library activities:* Higher management should review the progress of library activities to maintain the quality and quantity of assigned job to the staff.

- *Give recognition to library staff:* Top level management should recognise the operational level library staff for quality performance, without which they will be demoralised to perform the job in a better way.

With the change in environment the objectives need to be revised to face the challenges of future. Over a period of time, due to the impact of technological advances, research and development, economic, social and political factors, the objectives also tend to change. To adopt these changes, it is essential to state objectives and functions of information system in changing context. For this purpose the following steps should be followed.

Structure Related Changes

The structure related changes in libraries and information centres may include:

- *Change in the work design:* The work design of a traditional library is not similar to modern automated library, so a change in the work design is compulsory for the success of automated library.
- *Change in the basis of departmentalisation:* There are various departments in university and research libraries. In case of automated library, book acquisition, classification and cataloguing, circulation, serial control assignments are being done through computer with specific software instead of doing manually. Besides these departments, modern library has other departments like barcoding, RFID tagging, OPAC/web-OPAC, e-journals, e-books, CD-ROM, digital library, touch screen kiosk, server maintenance etc.
- *Change in the number of operation levels to perform various activities, routine work of library staff:* As there is a major change in the processing and service departments a change in the number of staff in the lower level or operational level management has become essential.
- *Change in the plans, programmes, policies and procedures to and improving integration among various sections:* Due to changse in the pattern of service; plans, programmes, policies and procedures and integration within various departments it is very essential to cater to the service in a better way.
- *Change in the span of management and levels of management for effective co-ordination mechanism and flow of task:* Since the nature of job of modern automated library is more complex than traditional library, it is very difficult to manage large number of operational level staff under one middle level manager. In view of this span of management should be narrow and levels of management should be changed because top and middle level management have to be directly linked with every

department to perform each department's functions in a better way as well as for effective co-ordination mechanism with every department.

- *Change in line-staff and functional authority, work group relations between people and functions to improve their ability:* Line positions are responsible for accomplishing the organisation's primary objectives; they have final authority to make decisions. Staff positions, on the other hand, provide suggestions and advice for the line positions but cannot, theoretically make decisions for the line positions. An organisation seeks to keep authority for decision making in the positions accountable for results and to preserve a clear chain of command from the top to the bottom of the organisation. But in the automated library system there should be no hurdle between line and staff position because anyone who is aware about a particular system can give his advice. It helps to improve the work group relation as well as the ability of the all levels of management.

Structural changes affect relationships among the organisational positions and in the interactions among internal departments, the reporting mechanism, interactions of all sections in the library and the functional relationships.

Changes for Technological Advancement

The technology refers to the sum total of human knowledge providing ways to do the things in a better way with the help of techniques. It may include inventions and techniques affecting the ways of doing things.

Thus, technology related changes may include:

- *Use of new machines and equipments for developing new services or modifying existing services:* Many new machines and equipments, *e.g.*, computer, server, barcoding equipments, RFID tools are necessary for developing new services or modifying existing manual services. So the awareness about the use of new machines, equipments and tools is very essential.
- *The procedure of doing things which may result in change of work process:* The methods and procedures of doing new tasks should be changed in context of old library system. So that the work process is not disrupted.
- *Introduction of technological devices like computers and computer related technologies:* Introduction of technological devices like computers and computer related technologies is necessary for automated library. Without computers and related technologies, we are unable to cater to services in automated library system.
- *Change in the existing techniques for making or doing the things in effective way or adoption of new techniques for creative work:* Automated library is ICT oriented and some technique is involved in every work.

So existing techniques of traditional library management should be changed and adoption of new techniques is very essential to carry out every task and service in automated library environment.

- *Change in the methods of using new tools equipments and products:* In the traditional library system, there are only a few equipments like fumigation chamber, catalogue cabinet, book rack, cardex, journal display rack, etc. But now computer terminals, server, barcoding equipments, RFID tools, etc., equipments and products are being used, so it is very natural to change the methods of using new tools, equipments and products.

The change in the technology affects the nature of work and activities, organisational structure, the processes and the people's behaviour.

Task-related Changes

Technology related changes determine the ways to complete the task effectively and efficiently. Task related changes helps to achieve major gains in terms of cost, service and time.

Task related changes may include:

- *Identifying the steps involved in performing tasks:* It is very necessary to organise meeting with library staff at all levels to identify the steps to perform the tasks effectively.
- *Task identification:* Every task should be identified to depute the staff who is efficient in that work. So, proper task identification is the key factor to perform the task properly and to serve the user community in a better way.
- *Significance of task related changes in attaining the organisational and institutional objectives:* As the nature of library has been changed so it is very significant to change the task which is relevant in changed atmosphere to attain the organisational and institutional objectives.
- *Identifying the skills and abilities required for the changed task:* It is very natural to identify the skills and abilities required for the changed task and to assign the specific job to the specific staff that is suitable for that particular job.
- *Improving both quality and quantity of work/ service:* For the satisfaction of our customer we should improve our quality as well as quantum of day to day work/service.
- *Bringing cost-effective solutions through maximum use of available resources:* Cost-effectiveness is concerned with the value. It asks, "This is what the service costs. Is it worth it?" So effectiveness of the resources is the key to maximum use of available resources.
- *Improving the work performance:* Quality training of staff is very essential to aware the task of each and every personnel effectively which improves the work performance.

People-related Changes

Change in any factor has an impact on human resources and human behaviour.

In the context of Library and Information Science, the people-related categories include:

- *The library staff:* In case of library staff, it requires the corresponding changes to be made in the skills, abilities and the performance of the employees.
- *New investment in training and development activities so that employees acquire new skills and activities:* New skills and activities are required in automated library system so new investment in training and development is essential. Library can get the fund from UGC for this purpose by making a systematic and comprehensive proposal
- *Socialising employees into the organisational structure so that they learn the new routines on which organisational performance depends....':* Top management should meet with middle and operational level management to become aware about the every bit of work with theory and practical and to assign the job to every personnel as well as time required for this purpose. Through socialising the employees organisational efficiency can also be increased.

Accordingly the change may also include –

- *Change in skill levels of the workforce:* Skill levels of each and every employee should be changed to cope up with new task.
- *Change in the training programmes to improve performance levels:* Training programme should be organised in a scientific way to sensitise the employee about every practical aspect of work and service. So change in training programmes is essential to improve performance levels of the staff.
- *Change in attitude and values:* Change in attitude and values is a must for better performance in work and service in the changed library environment.
- *Change in behaviour and interaction pattern:* As the library scenario has changed from traditional to automated one, behavioural and interaction pattern regarding work and service should also be changed.
- *Change in technology requires different skills of the operator:* Presently, library is technology controlled. To cope up with this change, the library personnel requires different skills to carry out their own task because it is very difficult to work properly for a unskilled staff.
- *Change in the structure requires change in their position, their authority, responsibility, etc.:* Due to shift from traditional to automated library, structural change is required. For this purpose positional, authoritative and responsibility change is necessary for better performance.

- *The readers:* Readers/users/customers are our prime focus. To serve the right user to the right information at the right time, we have to organise our resources systematically through which they can collect their information himself/herself. Such a systematic arrangement helps us to work and serve the users with less human resources.

Any change in the processes demands that it should be communicated to the readers to enable them to adjust to these changes. Readers are ultimately getting the benefits of all the technological advances, procedures, services, activities as well as other resources for their satisfaction in the libraries and information centres.

Changes in Library Policies

Change in the objectives and functions of the library and information system by the planning body would directly impact the existing plans and policies of the library. Accordingly, change in plans and policies become essential. The developmental plans and policies should be in conformity with the objectives and functions of library and information system as well as the institution it serves.

Changes in Objectives and Functions of Information System

The information system in the changed environment shall aim at:

- *Ensuring maximum use of all available resources:* Top management should ensure maximum use of all available resources through cost-effective solutions.
- *Promotion and development of all units in the library:* In the automated library, to cater the service to the users in a right way, it is very essential to develop all units in a proper way.
- *Better communication of ideas to achieve the objectives in an ever changing environment:* To communicate every new ideas to all levels of management is essential to achieve the objectives in constantly changing environment of library work and service.
- *Minimising the time, cost and efforts involved in all the activities, processes and functions:* Top level management should plan with with staff at middle and operational level for proper coordination of every function with minimum time, cost and efforts because duplicity of activities, processes and functions increases the time, cost and efforts.

In order to achieve the newly stated objectives as per the requirement of changing circumstances, certain functions are to be carried out. These functions may relate to adoption of latest technologies, use of modern tools and techniques, updating professional skill, ability and knowledge through education and training, future prospects of change in goals, objectives and functions, etc.

Librarians will need to be ready for competition and prepared to find new ways to make their skills and services distinct from those offered by the competition from media companies, publishers, internet companies, intermediary service providers and also from technologists parking on traditional library territory with technical names for old fashioned library ideas.

PROCESS OF MANAGERIAL CHANGE IN LIBRARIES AND INFORMATION CENTRES

The various steps involved in a planned change are:

- *Identifying need for change:* In the changing scenario of library, it is very essential to identify every need of users for effective planning and execution.
- *Elements to be changed:* It is very natural that the elements in traditional library and automated library are different. So top level management should foster awareness about every element of change and communicate the relevant elements to every unit.
- *Planning for change:* Every organisation/institution plans the total work procedures for proper execution. So, for the sake of efficiency all the steps for success in the changing scenario.
- *Assessing change forces:* It is very essential to assess the change forces for success of the new project/assignment.
- *Change actions:* Each and every action should be changed for proper functioning of every unit for better work and service.
- *Feedback:* This is very important aspect of every organisation/ institution. Without feedback system, an organisation/institution cannot assess their customer needs and information seeking behaviour as well as their satisfaction level.

Above steps in a planned change can be applied for managing the changes in libraries and information centres.

Identifying Need for Change

Various external and internal factors necessitate change in libraries and information centres. This change may be made in staff, library building or internal layouts with infrastructural facilities, the hardware and software requirements, activities and services, etc.

While identifying the need for change, the following should be considered:

- How the change will have an effect on the system, space, staff, services, activities, etc.
- What will be the frequency and nature of change.
- How it will impact use of information sources for study, research and development.
- How it will impact users information requirements.
- How it will have an effect on the procedures, policies and programmes.

Identification of need for change depends on:

- Readers' expectations;
- Changing objectives of libraries and information centres according to changing environment;
- Policies and programmes to be implemented to achieve these objectives; and
- New challenges created by change in technology.

These steps will determine the rationale why change is essential and if change will be made, whether it will create problems or not?

Elements to be Changed

What elements of the libraries and information centres should be changed is to be decided for managing the change. It will be decided on the basis of the need for the change as well as the objectives of the change. The identification of need for change will determine the base for why change is essential whereas this step will specify what elements in the system are to be changed.

Generally change is required in the structure, technology, hardware and software requirements, database design, IT infrastructure, skills of the staff, and nature of library services, etc. The nature and extent of change in the elements will further depend upon the nature of problems being faced by the libraries. Sometimes a change in one element may require change in another element, *e.g.,* a change in any activity from manual to machine may require change in staff and their skills but at the same time change in the structure of the libraries may also be required.

Planning for Change

Planning for change includes deciding in advance about:

- When to bring change.
- Who will bring change and
- How to bring change, etc.

In the libraries and information centres change is usually required in the structure, technology, staff and services. Careful planning for bringing change in these elements is essential because "Planning looks at how the librarians and information scientists can develop the means to locate the resources which are most relevant to the need of users community, integrate these resources into their infrastructure, adopt the necessary technology and finally to anticipate the future trends in changing circumstances".

Accessing Change Forces

Various internal and external forces enable us to bring change. To manage the change effectively, it becomes necessary to ensure the co-operation of the people to create an environment in which change will be accepted by all. Change force, both internal and external, is an important consideration to anticipate and respond properly for the problems in the existing system.

Success in managing the change is possible only when we assess change forces and their impact on the efficiency and effectiveness of the existing system. If the effect of these change forces can be accessed, it becomes possible to take necessary actions for change.

Actions for Change

A distinguished social psychologist, Kurt Lewin, developed what he called 'Action Research' which happens to be a more motivational approach and a more evolutionary one.

According to him 'since most change efforts flounder because carefully expected plans are ignored or sabotaged', this first step is critical:

- Seek change when the people who are going to have to effect the changing are distressed and feel they have a problem.

The next step involves getting them to accept some procedure for exploring how the problem can be solved.

The manager . . . gets the department to establish a study or mini research project on the problem:

- What kind of information is needed?
- Who will collect it?
- Who should analyse it and how; what is secret and what can be openly discussed?

The manager may have to help to get the project underway. It may require some outside technical aid, a survey, a review of old records, interviews with people in the departments.

This step means the manager must:

- Get consensus on what kinds of data and what method of collection and assessment the group will accept as valid for evolving a solution to its problem.
- Make feedback then, the critical element; it becomes a catalyst to the people who will have to change, emphasising the discrepancy between what they believed and the reality of the situation.
- Aid people in coping, skill transfer, experimenting with new methods.
- Then the cycle is repeated.

Usually, the initial efforts won't be roaring successes; there will still be unresolved problems, and some innovations won't work as planned or hoped.

So the group which is the focus of change is encouraged to continue:

- Research/study the work flow problems – by collecting data.
- Evaluate and feedback.
- Consider further innovations.

- Get help in implementing these.
- Then check how these are working.

The manager's role is one of felicitato, so that the individuals will be motivated to change, in contrast to being told to change; Further, the process is, or ought to be, a continuing one'. The Lewin model has suggested that every change requires three steps – "the first step is unfreesing - individuals who will be affected by the impending change must be laid to recognise why the change is necessary. Next, the change itself is implemented. Finally, refreesing involves reinforcing and supporting the change so that it becomes a part of the system.

These steps can also be effectively applied in library and information centres to manage the change. At first step, the library staff as well as the reader community have to be informed about why change is essential to improve efficiency of services. At second step, they have to be made aware about new methods of working, new procedures adopted, their expected roles in changed environment, etc. We have to conceive them to recognise the basic purpose of change and ensure that they fit into the new organisational change for the benefit of all. At third step, integrating change into actual practice, the staff as well as readers has to adapt to the new environment with improved performance. They have to be protected from reverting back to the old and traditional behaviour.

Feedback

Feedback is essential to ensure that changed pattern is going to achieve the objectives with minimum time, money and energy and determine whether follow-up action is essential to ensure success of change in management. The impact of change is to be measured in terms of attainment of objectives, improvement of services, readers' increased satisfaction, employee motivation and increased level of efficiency and effectiveness of each activity, product and service.

CHANGE MANAGEMENT STANDARDS

- All substantive changes to the IT Environment must adhere to the XX change Management process. A substantive change has the potential to affect the ability of users and systems to interact with each other.
- All changes must conform to the published guidelines that dictate the 'look and feel' of the XX web environment.
- All web page content changes must have the approval of the web page owner prior to change implementation.
- All changes to the production systems within IT will have a corresponding set of documentation that describes the change, the business reason for the change and the disposition of the change. This includes emergency and exception changes.

- The risk and/or impact ratings of the requested change will determine which of the four phases of the change workflow will be required to promote the change into production. For 'minor' changes only Analysis and Implementation will be required.
- Anyone with a valid XX Notes access will be able to enter a change into the Change Request process. Only authorised approvers will be able to accept a change request into the Change Management process.

STATUS OF CHANGES

The following status codes are used to reflect the status of a change request:

- *Open* – The change has been received and accepted but has not been assigned
- *In-Progress* – The change has been received, acknowledged and assigned. Work is in progress to fulfill the change request.
- *Approved* – The business and technical assessments have been completed and the change has been approved and committed to the change scheduler.
- *Rejected* – The change has been rejected and will be routed back to the Request for Service process and sent back to the customer with an explanation and a recommended course of action.
- *Closed* – The change request has been closed.
- *Canceled* – The change request has been canceled.

TYPES OF CHANGES

The Change Management Procedure applies to all types of changes related to the XX IT environment.

The following is a description of each of the types of changes that can take place and the rules that apply to each:

- *Application Changes:* Changes to any application code that is running on or linked to by any hardware or software in the XX IT environment. These changes are typically made to enhance the function or performance of or to fix a known error in the IT application environment. These changes cannot be implemented without approval of the owner of the application and cannot be requested by any programmer other than the one assigned to the programme. Assignment of Risk Category Level of the change is to be a joint effort of both the owner and the Change Implementer.
- *Hardware Changes:* All XX IT and IT support equipment installations, discontinuances and relocations are controlled by the Change Management Procedure. This activity can be requested by anyone but must have the approval of the Operations Manager.
- *Visual Image Changes:* Changes to the 'artistic' presentation of web pages are not required to make entries into the Change Management

system. Changes to 'Active' areas of the web page are required to use the XX Change Management procedure.

- *Software Changes:* The criteria for entering a software change into the Change process are based upon the effect that the changes may have on the IT support resources. If the changes affect the system, users or the support staff there is a requirement to enter it into the Change process. If the change is made for the exclusive benefit of the requester and if failure could not affect anyone else, that change would be exempt from the Change Process. For example, a change made by a programmer affecting a procedure or a programme under development on a test application requires no entry. However, when stand-alone test time is required on a production system, a change request form is required.
  - Typically, software changes would include changes to the Operating System, Vendor supplied Programme Products, e.g., Visual Studio, Java, etc., or common application support modules. However, during the last two and first five workdays of each month changes are restricted to emergency and critical necessities as determined by the Director of Information Technology.
- *Network Changes:* All installations, discontin-uances and all relocations of equipment used for IT teleprocessing communications are entered into the change process. This includes all routers, switches and telephone lines as well as Personal Computers if they are connected to the network.
- *Environmental Changes:* Environmental changes normally involve the facilities associated with the IT Installation. These facility changes include items such as air conditioning, chilled water, raised flooring, security, motor generators, electricity, plumbing and the telephony system for voice and data. For example, when there is a planned weekend power outage initiated by the local power company this information is submitted to the Change Management Process a minimum of two weeks prior to the scheduled outage and communicated to management, staff and the user community.
- *Documentation Changes:* All procedural changes to the standard operating procedures will be implemented through the Change process. Also, all permanent deviations from the published schedule time for running of production applications will be communicated through the Change Management system.

CHANGE LEVELS

The following guidelines for definition of Change risk levels are provided for consideration during the planning cycle. It must be clearly understood that these requirements are the minimum for each of the defined levels. The Requester may wish to plan additional lead times, documentation or reviews to insure that targets can be met and planned implementation schedules can be achieved. All changes are tracked, correlated and used for management reporting, statistics, trending, etc., to identify when and where additional resources should be provided.

For any change that fails, the Change Requester must enter an explanation in the comments section of the Change Record for that change and notify the Change Coordinator. The Change Coordinator will then close the change with the appropriate close status. If the change is to be attempted at a later time, the Change Requester should re-enter the change with the new date. Changes that cause a Platform outage will be reviewed at a Quality Measurement Meeting.

LEVEL E CHANGES

Emergency changes are those changes that are vital in order to ensure that IT's committed service levels are maintained. An Emergency change should not be used in order to bypass the appropriate lead-time for a change that has been entered into the system.

Exception changes are those changes that are a result of a business need and must be installed prior to the required lead-time. These types of changes proceed to the implementation phase when the requester's manager and the Director of Information Technology acknowledge that an Emergency or an Exception situation exists and authorise the modification planned. These changes will be post-reviewed to assure successful implementation, along with identification of any external impacts or new requirements. Post-review will also evaluate the reason for the Level E change request and try to determine a way of eliminating this requirement in the future. The post-review will also evaluate if, in fact, the change addressed a real or a perceived emergency condition. In all cases, the review must determine if additional action is required, what that action should be and who will be responsible for the action. Documentation requirements for Emergency changes are the same as any change. The Requester is responsible for meeting all requirements for the change documentation within one week of the implementation.

For non-application changes:

- Is the change needed to restore immediate service to the end user.
- Is the change necessary to fix an existing problem immediately.
- Is this a change that must be installed immediately but the need for it was not recognised early enough to be approved through the regular process.

For application changes:

- Must this change be done immediately to fix problems for jobs that

ABENDed during the previous night or are required to run in order to bring up on-line systems.

What Types of Management Approval is Required for Level E Changes

Approval required by:

- Director of Information Technology or her designee.
- Change Management Process Owner or his designee.
- Manager of the user department requesting the change.

Depending on the scope and impact of the proposed change, approval by one or more of the following individuals may be required.

- Operations Manager.
- Application Development Manager.
- Network and Technical Services Manager.

LEVEL 4 CHANGES

A Level 4 Change would have a major impact on IT services if a problem occurs during install. The install time is lengthy and the backout is very difficult or impossible. Level 4 Change Requests are to be entered into the Change Management Data Base at least thirty business days prior to the planned implementation date. The Requester or representative for a Level 1 change is required to attend the Change Communication meeting immediately prior to implementation so that any questions or concerns may be addressed.

Whenever a Level 4 change must be expedited to address a critical timing situation, a special meeting must be held. To expedite a Level 4 change, all parties that may be affected by this change must be present or represented at the special meeting. It is the responsibility of the change requester to arrange the meeting and assure attendance by the required groups or individuals. If the required groups or individuals cannot be assembled, the change cannot be expedited and an escalation will be required.

How do you know that the Change Falls Under Level 4

For non-application changes:

- From the end user's eyes, is it possible for the change to have a major impact on services if problems occur.
- Is the change visible to all end users.
- Is this a high-risk change.
- Is this the first time this change has been done.
- Is the change difficult or impossible to backout.
- Is it extremely difficult to install the change.
- Does the change involve a lengthy install time.

For application changes:

- Would failure of the job being changed stop the flow of all jobs for critical files or an application system.

What Types of Management Approval is Required for Level 4 Changes

Approval required by:

- Change Review Board.
- Manager of user department requesting change.

Depending on the scope and impact of the proposed change, approval by one or more of the following individuals may be required.

- Operations Manager.
- Application Development Manager.
- Network and Technical Services Manager.

LEVEL 3 CHANGES

A Level 3 Change may impact a large number of end users. It is a high-risk change that requires a significant effort to backout. Level 3 Change Requests must be entered into the Change Management database fifteen business days prior to implementation. All Level 3 changes will be communicated via the Change Management reporting system. The requester or representative for a Level 3 change is required to attend the Change Communication Meeting immediately prior to implementation so that any questions or concerns may be addressed.

How do you know that the Change Falls Under Level 3

For non-application changes:

- Will the change be visible to a large number of end users.
- Is this a high-risk change.
- Has the change been done only infrequently?
- Will a significant effort be required to backout the change.
- Is it difficult to install the change.

For application changes:

- Would failure of the job being changed stop the flow of jobs for non-critical files or applications.

What Types of Management Approval is Required for Level 3 Changes

Approval required by:

- Manager of user department requesting change.
- Network and Technical Services Manager.
- Change Review Board.

LEVEL 2 CHANGES

A Level 2 Change is not transparent, but is minimal in risk and impact. It is the responsibility of the Requester to notify any areas of a potential impact. The change is a Level 2 if it requires an IPL of a system, subsystem or the restart of a critical component on a production system. Level 2 Change Requests must be entered into the Change Management database prior to the Scheduled Change Window being requested. The Requester or representative for a Level 2 change is required to attend the Change Communication meeting immediately prior to planned implementation so that any questions or concerns may be addressed. All Level 2 changes will be communicated via the Change Management reporting system and will be tracked and reported by the Change/ Problem Coordinator.

Examples of Level 2 changes:

- Single fixes—APAR, PTF, etc.
- Low usage programme product upgrades, installations.
- PARMLIB updates which require an IPL to implement.
- Regular maintenance updates to system or application libraries.
- Hardware Preventative Maintenance.
- Data management to critical volumes.

How do you Know that the Change Falls Under Level 2

For non-application changes:

- Will the change have only minor impact on services provided to the end users if problems occur.
- Will the change be visible only to a small group of end users.
- Is this a moderate risk change.
- Is the change relatively simple to install.
- Has the change been implemented successfully a number of times before.
- Does it require only a moderate effort to backout the change quickly.
- Will it require only an IPL, recycle of major application or reloading of an NCP to implement or backout.

For application changes:

- Is this the first time the job has been installed.
- Must this job be fixed to run tonight.

What Types of Management Approval is Required for Level 2 Changes

Approval required by:

- Manager of user department requesting change.
- Change Review Board.

LEVEL 1 CHANGES

A Level 1 Change has little or no external visibility, no external dependencies or no operator intervention. There is no associated risk or impact with the change, either to the system if the change is incompatible or to the Requester if the change implementation is delayed. The change does not require an IPL or recycle of an application to implement or backout. Level 1 changes are entered into the Change data base and will be communicated daily to any affected areas where impact or interest can be identified outside of the Requester's own area.

How do you Know that the Change Falls Under Level 1

For non-application changes:

- Will the change have only minimal or no impact on services provided to the end users if a problem occurs.
- Is the change familiar or common to those who will implement it.
- Is the change reliable and low risk.
- Is the change easy to backout if a problem occurs.
- Can it be backed out without an IPL, recycle of a major application, or reloading of an NCP.

For application changes:

- Would failure of the job stop just this job.
- Is this a low priority job.

What Types of Management Approval is Required for Level 1 Changes

Approval required by:

- Manager of user department requesting change.
- Change Review Board.

ASSIGN CHANGE IMPLEMENTER FLOW

Description:

- The Assign Change Implementer flow begins once a change request has been documented and selected for the change management process. During this workflow, a change record is assigned to an appropriate owner, the change record is updated with this assignee information, and the change is sent to the assignee.

Scope Inclusion:

- All changes reviewed by the Change Review Board.

Scope Exclusion:

- Changes not accepted by the Change Management process or Changes not reviewed by the Change Review Board.

Goal:

- To ensure that change requests are assigned to appropriatc implementers.
- To ensure that the change management workload is allocated by area of expertise.
- To balance workload within an area of expertise.

Start Trigger:

- Initial change record.

Stop Trigger:

- Initial change record is assigned to an owner.

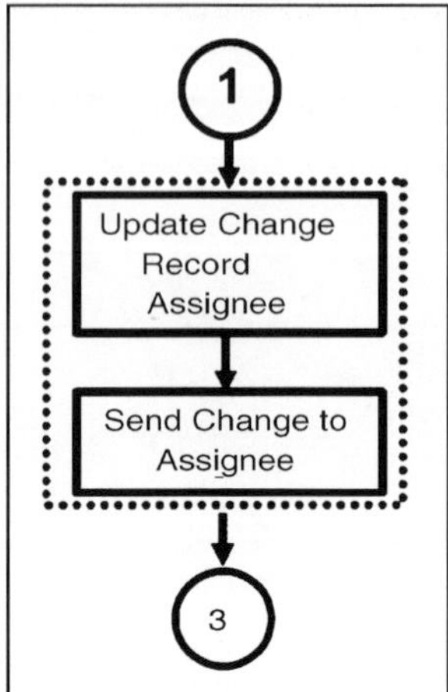

Fig. Workflow Diagram for Assign Change Implementer

Workflow Details for Assign Change Implementer (fig. 2.1):

- *Update Change Record Assignee:* Assign the change an owner based on the classification of the change.
- *Send Change to Assignee:* Place the assignee information into the change record and send an e-mail notification to the assignee.

ENTER CHANGE REQUEST FLOW

- *Description:* The Enter Change Request flow begins when a change request is submitted. In this activity, all required information about the change and supporting documentation is entered into the Change Management system. The change request should be submitted in accordance with the time frame required by the initial impact assessment.
- *Scope Inclusion:* All changes, including software, hardware, control mechanisms, configurations, environments, facilities, databases, business applications, processes, and procedures.
- *Scope Exclusion:*
  - — Development activities that produce the actual change content.
  - — The coordination of sets of changes.
  - — Testing of the change package.
- *Goal:*
  - — To introduce changes into the environment with minimal disruption to information technology and its users.
  - — To communicate such that all affected users are aware of changes.
  - — To log all changes into the change management system.

— To ensure all pertinent change information is collected.
— To ensure all changes meet lead time criteria.

- *Start Trigger:*
  — Change Request.
- *Stop Trigger:*
  — Fully documented and approved change request.

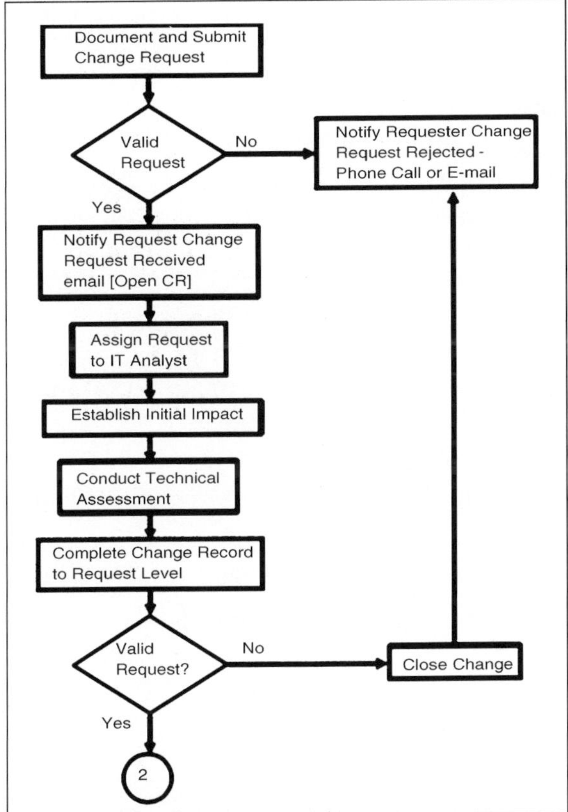

Fig 2.2 Workflow Diagram for Enter Change Request

Workflow details for enter change request (see fig. 2.2):

- *Document and Submit Change Request:* Collect system change request and begin preliminary review of the change.
- *Valid Request:* Determine whether or not to submit change request into change management system based on whether the request form has a managers signature, it is within IT responsibility, and filled in correctly.
- *Notify Requester Change Request rejected – phone call or e-mail:* If change request is rejected, provide a form of notification.
- *Notify Requester Change Request received – e-mail:* If change request is approved for the change management system, a change record is

opened and a change number is assigned. A notification is auto-sent to the change requester by Peregrine.

- *Assign request to IT analyst:* Assign the change request to an initial analyst to review the change record.
- *Establish Initial Impact:* Determine impact of the change to the customer community. This will include times when service is not available, testing time, new procedures, new support requirements, and any other impact that may occur as a result of the change.
- *Conduct Technical Assessment:* Determine the feasibility of the change from a technical perspective. This assessment will include the amount of resources, level of knowledge, and skills necessary for the change.
- *Complete Change Record to Request Level:* Based on initial impact and technical assessment, determine the type and category level of change, and complete all descriptive fields. Additionally, the completeness of the change success criteria is validated.
- *Valid Request:* Based on the initial assessments, determine whether to perform this change. This decision is based on the change conforming to the strategy, resources being available, and whether or not it is already being worked on.
- *Close Change:* Mark change record as closed when it doesn't pass validation requirements.

MONITOR CHANGE CALENDAR FLOW

Description:

- The Monitor Change Calendar flow determines the scheduling for changes to be deployed. During this workflow, changes are penciled into a calendar, and the schedule is monitored for changes that are completed or have run out of time in their scheduled change deployment window. If time has expired for a change then it can be escalated and rescheduled based on escalation standards.

Scope Inclusion:

- Changes that are formally put into the change calendar.

Scope Exclusion:

- Changes that are not formally put into the change calendar.

Goal:

- Monitor the change calendar for changes that have not been completed and have run out of time for the purpose of change escalation.
- Allow for changes to be rescheduled.
- Allow for changes to be removed from the change calendar upon completion.

Start Trigger:

- A change request has been assigned an owner and has been sent to that assignee.

Stop Trigger:

- A change is complete and removed from the calendar.

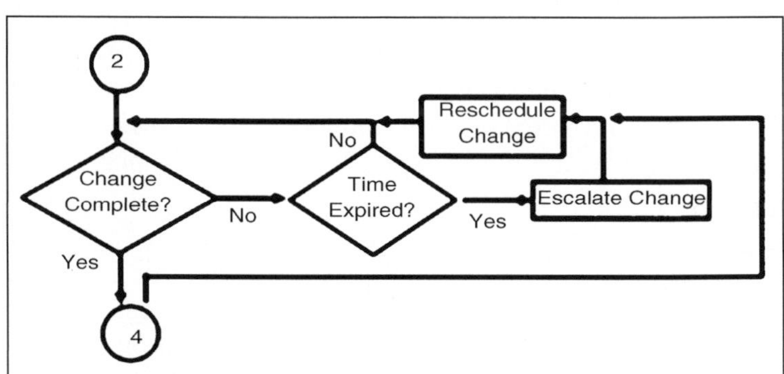

Fig. Workflow Diagram for Monitor Change Calendar

Workflow Details for Monitor Change Calendar (fig. 2.3):

- *Change Complete:* Monitor the change calendar for change work that has been completed.
- *Time Expired:* Determine whether a change record that is incomplete has run out of time.
- *Escalate Change:* Reclassify the change to a higher change category level if time has expired.
- *Reschedule Change:* Update the calendar with a schedule for the change after it has been escalated or if the change package is incomplete.

PERFORM ASSESSMENTS FLOW

Description:

- The Perform Assessments flow involves conducting both a business and technical review of the change package. The assessments determine if the change package is complete and can therefore continue through the change management process.
- Specifically, the perform business assessment flow involves validating the impact of the proposed change on XX from a business perspective, evaluating the completeness of the success criteria and communication plan and reviewing the backup/ backout/ recovery plans. The assessment looks at the proposed timing of the change and ensures that the customer's management has given the agreement necessary for the change to be approved and scheduled. Standards, business requirements, and SLAs are reviewed and a recommendation is made to approve, reject, or reschedule the change.

- The perform technical assessment flow reviews the completeness of the change plan, test plan, backup/ backout/ recovery plans, platform impact assessment, estimated install time, etc., from a technical perspective. The change success criteria are validated and the impact of the change to the environment is reviewed to ensure it has been accurately evaluated. Technical standards are enforced and a decision is made to approve, reject, or reschedule the change.

Scope Inclusion:

- All documented changes with a change category that requires a formal business or technical assessment.

Scope Exclusion:

- Changes with change categories that specifically do not require formal business or technical assessments.

Goal:

- To ensure that all factors have been taken into consideration in terms of the business aspects of the change.
- To ensure that all factors have been taken into consideration in terms of the technical aspects of the change.
- To ensure that everything required to deploy the change and to maintain service is included in the change request.

Start Trigger:

- Fully documented change record.

Stop Trigger:

- Assessed change.

Workflow Details for Perform Assessments (fig. 2.6):

- *Business Review of Change Package:* Review the change package for the following points:
  - — Ensure that the business requirements will be met.
  - — Verify existence and completeness of backup/ backout recovery plans.
  - — Verify existence of test plans, including the testers names and expected results.
  - — Ensure that the change conforms to business standards and policies.
  - — Determine whether the change conforms to service level agreements.
  - — Review communication plan for change.
- *Technical Review of Change Package:* Review the change package for the following points:

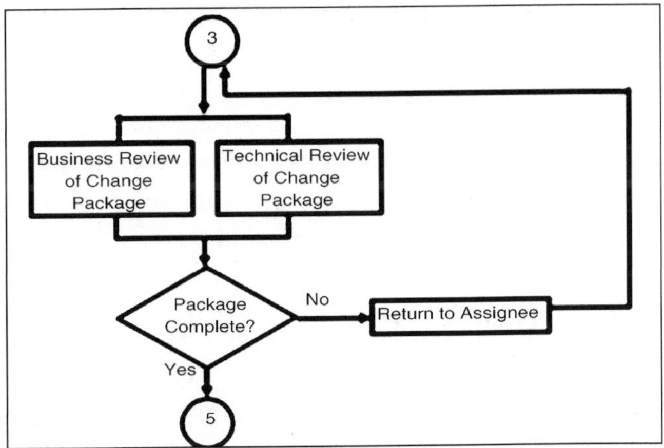

Fig. Workflow Diagram for Perform Assessments

— Determine the impact on the technical environment.
— Ensure that the change conforms to technical standards.
— Verify the completeness of the change plan.

- *Package Complete?:* Make a decision on whether the package is complete based on the results of the business and technical reviews.
- *Return to Assignee:* If the package is determined not complete than the change is returned to the assignee and can be rescheduled.

APPROVE CHANGE FLOW

Description:

- The Approve Change flow is initiated as soon as both the business and technical assessments have been completed. If the change is approved, it is passed on to the next sub-process to finalise scheduling. If the change is rejected or determined to be rescheduled, it may be sent back to the business or technical assessment subprocesses once the necessary actions are taken. All parties that have been involved to this point in the process should be notified of the approval, rejection or rescheduling.

Scope Inclusion:

- All changes that have been forwarded for approval from a business and technical perspective and whose change categories indicate the requirement for formal approval.

Scope Exclusion:

- Changes with change categories that specifically so not require formal approval.

Goal:

- To ensure that appropriate approval is obtained for change requests.
- To ensure that the change record is properly updated.

- To minimize service interruption.

Start Trigger:

- Completed change record with business and technical review including recommendation.

Stop Trigger:

- Approval for change deployment.

Workflow Details for Approve Change:

- *Final Change Review:* Final review of change prior to acceptance and scheduling.
- *Accept Change:* Based on the result of the final change review, determine whether to go ahead with or close the change.
- *Close Change:* If it is decided not to continue with change, then change record is closed by change coordinator.
- *Notify Requester Change Request rejected – phone call or e-mail*

LIBRARY SKILLS AND MANAGERIAL CHALLENGES

Our skills and background as librarians can both help and hinder our managerial exfforts. If we think consciously about these linkages, we can learn to become more effective in any managerial position.

Positive connections include:

- *The ability to collect and analyse information:* Throughout your managerial career, you will need to utilize these skills in activities ranging from creating a budget, to strategic planning, to writing a marketing plan.
- *The urge to share information:* Any organization benefits from the free flow of information; close-mouthed managers foster inefficiency, rumors, and resentment.
- *The ability to organize knowledge:* Again, this will be useful in activities as large as strategic planning and as seemingly small as keeping updated and organized personnel files.
- *The tendency to build networks:* No manager can "go it alone," and librarians' propensity to share information, stories, experiences, and acquired knowledge with one another will stand you in good stead here.
- *The belief in the principle of equity of access and treatment:* As useful when it comes to staff as when dealing with library customers.

On the other hand, tendencies you need to be careful of as a library manager include:

- *The notion that "the patron is always right:"* When you extend your wish to make life comfortable for your patrons to bending over backward to make life easy for your staff, you run the risk of not pushing your people to their fullest.

- *The wish to avoid conflict:* Studies and personality tests consistently show that librarians tend to tip the introverted and conflict-avoiding side of the scale. This is a generalisation, but watch for these tendencies in yourself and be willing and able to step in to manage conflicts among your employees and with your patrons.
- *Emphasis of the philosophical over the practical:* Library school tends to foster a black-and-white worldview of philosophical idealism; managers eventually need to learn to compromise.

Additional linkages will be emphasized in the appropriate chapters, but always be open to understanding the ways in which your background as a librarian affects your work as a manager. Make a conscious effort to manage as a librarian. Overall, remember that you are a *library* manager, and that the ways in which you manage your people and institution need to be true to the principles and practices of librarianship. Ultimately, working effectively as a library manager demands developing a new way of thinking and behaving, while remembering your roots as a librarian or building a background in librarianship.

MAKING THAT TRANSITION

As you adjust to your management role, the first transition from managed to manager can be the hardest. As a non-management employee, you may have been provided with an orientation, directions, and fairly explicit instructions on your day-to-day duties when settling into a new position. As a manager, you may be thrown into a new job with little direction or instruction on how to proceed; management positions are often largely what you make of them. Although you will have a broad outline of your administrator's, board's, or institution's expectations, part of your job will actually be to define your own specific responsibilities and role within your department, library, or section.

Even after the first transition or two gives you an idea of what to expect, the transition into any managerial position can be tricky throughout your career. Transitional periods are inevitably stressful for both you and your new staff, as everyone involved is dealing with a fairly major change and needs to renegotiate relationships and work patterns. But while your staff members' daily work will most likely remain relatively constant, providing them with an underlying stability to draw upon while weathering the changes your arrival brings, you will face the additional task of redefining yourself as a supervisor, a department head, or an administrator. The first few months in a managerial position can be critical in establishing your credibility, settling comfortably into your new role, and setting out your management style and strategies.

This transitional period, while difficult, also presents the opportunity to begin as you mean to continue, to build relationships and alliances with your staff, supervisors, and colleagues, and to lay out your vision for your department, section, or organization. It is always harder to switch gears later than to chart your course from the outset. Take time, however, to get to know your staff, their personalities, their strengths, and their weaknesses before launching into a major change initiative. In some ways it can be especially difficult to take over a position from a previous manager who seems to have run the zoo in a less than optimal manner. Library staff will have developed an understandable mistrust of those in a management role.

Much of your time at the outset may be spent undoing the damage your predecessor left behind, rather than in moving forward with your own initiatives and ideas. As one manager survey respondent notes: "Be aware that your staff may not trust you or your motives at first." This can be frustrating, so work on maintaining your own energy and enthusiasm. New library managers often come in brimming with ideas, but need to have the willingness first to learn the library's organizational culture and to lay the groundwork of trust needed for their initiatives' success. Also think about the ways in which succeeding an ineffective manager can actually work in your favour.

Any moves you make may lead to improvements—and there will be a general predisposition towards change. If you were promoted from within, having suffered with the rest, you will also have insight into what not to do when you move into a management role. Another manager survey respondent even explains her theory of management as: "Having seen library management done badly, I try to think: what would my old boss have done–and do the opposite." One staff survey respondent suggests: "Never forget what it's like to have a bad boss, and don't turn into one yourself." If you have experienced a history of incompetent or ineffective managers, though, it may take you some time to overcome your own distrust of management and realise that you are now one of "them". Librarians who are promoted into a managerial position from within will find that their former coworkers will have particular preconceptions and expectations for their behaviour as a manager, based on past conversations and behaviour as an employee. Your former colleagues may no longer be quite sure how to interact with you. Oregon State University Librarian for Systems Applications says that: "the biggest surprise for me was that people I had worked with for more than five years viewed me as a different person simply because I had become a manager."

They would sometimes agree to concepts that I presented, even though in reality they had very different views on the issue. I found this disconcerting because I wanted and expected them to express their honest opinions. As any manager, your relationships and interactions with non-managerial staff members will inevitably change. Katharine Salzmann, Archivist/Curator of Manuscripts, Southern Illinois University at Carbondale, explains:

"I don't know if it was exactly a surprise, but the biggest adjustment I had to make was simply realizing that I was a 'boss.' I wasn't fully prepared for the role and how people's expectations of me would change, or how my working relationships with individuals would change."

This is not to say that you cannot have good, friendly working relationships with your staff members, but your relationships as manager and managed will tend to take on a different flavour than that of your relationships with your professional peers. You need to consider how important it is to you to be liked, as opposed to being respected as a manager. If you have tended to find most of your friends through work, you may need now to extend that circle outside your institution's walls. If, on the other hand, you come from the outside to assume a management position in a given library, your first step before defining any new goals will be to familiarize yourself with the institution's existing mission and organizational culture, as well as with the people who will be working for you. You will need to settle into your new environment and to give people a chance to settle into the inherent change your arrival brings.

You will of course have your own theories, ideas, and priorities–as well as responsibility for those imposed from above and outside. If you appear to be swooping in with a completely new agenda, however, you will undoubtedly meet with fierce resistance from existing staff. People need a compelling reason to move out of their comfortable routines, and need to feel as if they are a part of any change. Make it a point to learn from and work with your staff from the very beginning.

Realise also that the fact that your administration made the decision to hire from the outside rather than promote from within may mean that it is consciously looking for new perspectives and fresh ideas. Capitalize on this desire for change by enlisting administrative, institutional, and/or board support for your initiatives from the outset. Your goals have a greater chance of success if they receive consistent support throughout the management hierarchy of your organization. Successful management is undoubtedly more complicated than just "doing the opposite" of what your previous less-than-competent boss used to do.

A good first step, though, as you begin defining your role as a manager, is to think back to all of your experiences as someone who has been managed, inside or outside of a library environment. Identify both the role models you do, and those you do not, wish to emulate. Debbie Hackleman notes that "in some cases I learned by observing others–both what worked well and what I would choose to do differently. Observing negative examples is often quite useful." Of course, it is always easier to identify negative experiences and to dwell on what not to do. This is a useful beginning, and you should always keep your previous managers'–and your own– missteps firmly in mind. Dwelling on the negative, however, fails to provide us with a solid foundation for deciding what *to* do, for making the decisions that help propel both our careers and institutions forward, and for establishing our own management style. The next task, therefore, involves deciding where to go and how to begin. Before implementing any changes, you will need to identify the goals for your institution, section, or department, within the larger goals of the organization, larger institution, or system.

You need to provide yourself and your staff with a larger context for your work, in order to successfully define both what you do and why you do it. Lastly, realise that, in any management situation, you will also be compared to your predecessors. Whether comments tend to run along the lines of: "That's not how Ms. X used to do it," or: "We're so glad not to have to waste our time pleasing Mr. Y anymore," it will take staff some time to settle in and become accustomed to your way of managing things. Remember, you are not the first person to ever face this transition— and, if you should ever leave your position, your staff will be equally as glad to explain to your successor just what she is doing differently. Do not get hung up on people's tendencies to bring up the past; libraries are long-lived institutions, and each library's history includes a long line of managers and management styles. Focus on carving out your own place and creating your own part of your institution's history.

WHAT A LIBRARY MANAGER DOES

The ways in which library managers spend their time of course vary among institutions and different levels of management—and in a sense, this is what this entire book is about! But there are some similarities among the roles and responsibilities of most managers. The basic job of any manager is to direct her resources and people towards accomplishing the defined goals of the institution. Higher-up managers may be responsible for defining these larger goals; section or department managers may set goals for their part of the whole in terms of the larger mission of the library; and libraries, as service institutions, need overall to define and to prioritize these goals in terms of the needs of their patrons or customers. As a library division manager at the Josephine County Library System, Oregon, explains: "Fight for the patrons, and every decision that is made should be made because it will make it easier for the patron." Any traditional managerial activity fits into this broad definition. You supervise and evaluate library staff in order to ensure that they work effectively to provide the services your patrons need and expect.

You keep the technology and facilities in your institution humming along so that customers have a comfortable, safe, and useful place to work, as well as the tools to meet their informational needs. You help create a culture of customer service, realizing that your approach and that of your employees goes a long way towards creating an atmosphere in which you can effectively serve your community. The way in which you manage people largely defines their attitudes towards their work, which in turn defines how smoothly the organization runs. You hold the authority to make decisions within your institution, and are responsible for making those decisions in the way that will best accomplish institutional goals. You are responsible for ranking the importance of various activities in terms of these goals, for prioritizing goals themselves, and for allocating resources to best accomplish library goals.

INFORMATION TECHNOLOGY USE IN LIBRARY MANAGEMENT SYSTEM

The IT revolution has also embraud the library system. A massive and rapid computerization process throughout the levels of the library system has made IT an integral part of the library management scene in many countries all over the world. The incorporation of IT into the day-to-day activity of libraries has a strong impact on virtually every aspect of their management processes. Although there is no agreed definition of IT, the term "IT" includes three main components – *management information system* (MIS) or *decision support system* (DSS), hardware, and human factors. A management information system is the set of structure and procedures that govern the collection, processing, analysis, presentation and use of information within an organization.

IMPACT OF ICTS IN LIBRARIES

Technology is changing the nature of libraries and librarians, and it continues to exert a major influence on the strategic direction of libraries in society. Today the library services are transitioning from local traditional collections to global resources provided on demand via the most advanced networking technologies.

DIGITAL DATA STORAGE IN LIBRARIES

Digital data storage media for storing digital data are constantly being developed, improved or superseded, and any discussion of them here can only be taken as description of the current situation i. e., optical discs, magnetic media, other media for digital data storage. The concept of the "digital library" evolved out of potential for digitization of all forms of media: print, image, sound, complex data sets, and computer simulations of non-time-bound sequences, otherwise not demonstrable events, etc., and retrieving them in context of multiple networked information systems.

The digital library often serves as a multidimensional catalogue or index to bring together the resource discovery information of every resource that was topically, creatively, or by reason of other connections generatively related. A digital library does not only consist of digitized and digitally born information resources, but also of electronic metadata on non-digital objects. Digital Data: Considerable attention is now being paid to the possibility of converting the intellectual content of items in library collection into digital data by electronic means and storing it on magnetic tapes or discs. Both textual and pictorial information can be converted. For example by using optical character recognition devices which convert texts into their digital code equivalent, or by using scanners to convert text or, more usually, pictures into an analogue form.

Text can also be input by keyboarding. In addition to information already in another format being converted to digital format, much information is now originated in digital form and may appear only in that form in the library. Digital data have considerable advantages. They can be rapidly duplicated and speedily transmitted without deterioration through electronic communications networks to whatever the user is working. Storage: It is a mainly technical requirement, although new media may complicate storage decisions and costing. Today's large digital repositories use multiple level of mass storage media and mechanical robots to locate and mount the media.

Phases of Digitization: Undoubtedly, digital media will have to co-exit with print media. Different kinds of collection could be digitized at different times depending on the priorities of the library. To start with, any one type of collection, for example, important out of print publications could be made available in digital form. Feedback of its usage can be sengut and analyzed. In the next phase, another type of data could be converted into digital form. Digitization Process: Digitization is a process of converting paper documents to electronic format. Scanning process does the conversion.

Digital information can be transmitted and received anywhere in the world where the infrastructure to send and received is in place. Due to the implementation of the IT, the librarian need to be well aware of the technical issues, potential problems involved, trained manpower available, the hardware required, document management systems, *optical character recognization* (OCR) technology for implementing digitization of the collection and services. As been know the concept of digital library is growing very fast globally. It is a welcome trained that various institutions and professional societies are involved to provide opportunities for the library and librarians to upgrade and enhance the professional knowledge about digital library. Various important aspects like digital libraries issues, architecture, electronic publishing, collection building, storage, organization, transmission of digital information, creation and use of hypertext and hypermedia system, networks and their implications, manpower development etc. We are in the early stage of a transmition from a print-based to a digital society.

The latest technologies offer cheap computer processing power, cheap mass storage, inexpensive and ubiquitous access to high speed networks and retrieval devices give us the ability to create, to manipulate, to storage and especially to transfer large quantities of information in digital form at low costs. Digital information can be stored on any medium that is able to represent binary digits 0 and 1.

Conversion from the conventional storage to digitized format required discrete analysis as the primary function, based on user electronic storage and retrieval system. Some of the common digitized storage media that are presently used world over are the Hyper books, CD-ROM, Multimedia. New media are constantly being developed. Some that are still in experimental stages or have been only very recently introduced are digital videotape, digital audiotape and digital paper.

CREATING NETWORKS WITH GROWING REACH

It involves rapid advances in two technologies – digital storage and processing of information and satellite and optical fibre transmission of information– are creating new and faster ways of storing, handling, distributing and accessing information. These innovations enable the processing and storage of enormous amount of information, along with rapid distribution information through communication networks. For example in 2001 more information can be sent over a single cable in a second than in 1997 was sent over the entire internet in a month.

Linking computing devices and allowing them to communicate with each other creates networked information systems based on a common protocol. Individuals, households and institutions are linked in processing and executing a huge number of instructions in imperceptible time spans. This radically alters access to information and the structure of communication extending the networked reach to all corners of the world.

TECHNOLOGICAL TRANSFORMATIONS

Today's technological transformations are intertwined with another transformation, globalization and together they are creating a new paradigm – the network age. These transformations expand opportunities and increase the social and economic rewards of creating and using technology. They are also altering how and by whom technology is created and owned, and how it is made accessible and used. Technology is not inherently good or bad the outcome depends on how it is used.

SOME INITIATIVES IN IT SECTOR

The Department of Information Technology has setup Community Centre (CICs) at 487 blocks in the seven North Eastern States 9 Arunachal Pradesh, Assam, manipur, Meghalaya, Mizoram, Nagaland, Tripura) and Sikkim to provide connectivity at the block level and thus promote application of Information Technology for accelerating socio economic development of the region.

INFORMATION TECHNOLOGY ACT

The Government of India has created the necessary legal and administrative framework through the enactment of the Information Technology Act, 2000. While on the one hand it seeks to create the public key infrastructure for electronic authentication through digital signatures.

DIGITAL LIBRARY

Digital Libraries are a form of information Technology in which social impact matters as much as technological advancements. Future knowledge networks will rely on scalable semantics, to automatically indexing the community collections so that users can effectively search of billion repositories.

NATIONAL INFORMATION CENTRE (NIC)

It provides informatics services for decision support to government offices/ bodies at national, state, district and block levels. It offers network services. NIC also provides video conferencing facilities.

LIBRARY MOVEMENT AND ISSUES IN INDIAN DIGITAL LIBRARIES

India has a glorious history of 5000 years with a rich heritage of philosophy, language, religion, art and culture. The Nation has 428 languages with 1600 dialects out of which 13 are extinct. These languages have several classical scriptures in their Scripts. These scriptures are scattered and preserved in different libraries of the country.

Creating a digital library of available classics and establishing federated look-ups to these collections are burning issues of the day. The Indian Digital Library Initiative (IDLI) has been triggered out of Digital Library Initiative (DLI) of United States. Both the Indian collections and the environment are totally different from the one United States has. A fresh look to the existing problems should be given.

TECHNOLOGICAL ISSUES

World has witnessed impeccable technological advancements. There are digital library suites can be used directly for creating digital collection. But much of the development is in English and European languages as the computer was first used by them only. But off late, market for other scripts is also felt by IT giants and hence Unicode as character representation standard is introduced. Unicode is still being evolving as it promises to cover all the world scripts and signs. The country has a big share in IT industry of the world. But little has been done for the languages and scripts of India.

An Optical Character Recognitions (OCR) software in any Indian script is yet to be developed. The tests are on the way at Indian Statistical Institute, Kolkata and Centre for Develop-ment of Advance Computing (CDAC), Pune. A product named Chitran-kan by CDAC, Pune is available for use in Devnagari but the product has limited variety of font support and is still in testing phase. The Indic scripts are off child of Brahmi script which is not in practice anymore. The derived scripts of Brahmi like Devanagari and other Indic scripts have complex rende-ring principles when it comes to representation of characters in machine.

Complex character glyphs are rendered depicting features like bidirectional and dynamic composition. It is difficult to create rendering engines of this kind for all the Indic languages but major work has been done in this area. The work is in progress to integrate rendering plug-ins with web browsers for creating web sites in Indian scripts. With Devanagari and other major scripts the task has been achieved and now-a-days one can see many web sites in regional languages. One of the important problems Indian IT community facing today is about sorting the words of one language. There are scores of examples of same kind in Sanskrit. It is because of these reasons it is very difficult to generate index for any Indic document.

Besides, there are no good corpora available in public domain which can be taken as sample for experimentation and testing. This has also influenced the search algorithm. Unlike search algorithms of English, search algorithms in Indian languages are yet to be evolved. What is available today as Indian language search is only pattern matching. The work is still at preliminary level because of the complexity of the languages. It is easy to work with Sanskrit for the purpose as it has morphological rules for construction of words but addressing the same is difficult with other Indic languages (Hindi, Oriya, Tamil etc.) as they don't have such kind of rules for word construction.

The Stemming algorithms like Soundex and Metaphone are yet to be developed by any of the Indian languages. To get a feel, if one searches for Hindi word (correctly spelt as means Back) in Google, gets only the former Hindi string in search result. An application of stemming algorithm would have brought the correct later one in the search results. Similarly, there are n-gram techniques of string search which are warranted to be tested with Indic text.

Though the metadata is not a potential problem but due to uncontrolled growth there is lot of disparity in use of metadata standards. Many of the libraries have drafted their own metadata set not confirming to the International standard. This has happened in the case of distributed digitization centers at the initial stage. Though, an awareness has been aroused among the professionals to use International standard, but, still it is very difficult to convert non-conforming one's to the standard form.

With the use of codified data a standard metadata scheme can yield an efficient cross-lingual information retrieval. This technique of cross-lingual information retrieval has been demonstrated in the system named "Brass" developed at Documentation Research and Training Centre. Such infor-mation retrieval systems can supplement automatic translation projects to some extent, as there is not significant development in machine translation of Indic languages.

BEHAVIOURAL ISSUES

The Government of India must look forward to pool the knowledge base of the country. Phase-wise pooling of available knowledge resource of various libraries in the country must be encouraged. This requires funding to various libraries for digitizing the documents of their collection. So far, much of the funding for the purpose is made through United States through Million Book Project. Though, the project has been initiated with novel interest, unfortunately, keeping control over the whole project appeared little difficult. Besides, many of the technological challenges specific to Indian context are new to the American environment need to be addressed. It looks better to initiate test-beds in first phase with the objective to demonstrate technological capabilities.

Some centres can be identified from different language speaking states and accordingly funded for developing technical capabilities in a limited time frame. Unfortunately, the present growth of digital libraries in the country is unplanned which has resulted in bad models or instances with just scanned images. The first phase of the National Digital Library Movement could have been better utilized only to understand the underlying difficulties and the possible solutions. The second phase of the project could have been funded for building the live digital collections for use and receive feedbacks.

The required changes and modifications could be further implemented nationwide. There are several libraries with unique collection of its kind. With the third phase such collection can be digitally preserved as well as universal access to the documents could be insured. It has been observed that many of the libraries having unique and rare collection are scared of going online because they think of loosing the physical presence of users in the library. This behavioural difficulty must be addressed in order to ensure universal accessibility including the digital preservation at national level.

Conditional Issues

A multilingual country like India has several conditional constraints hindering the overall growth of digital libraries in the country. There are representation in the literature from all states and languages. It is easy to map the script due to common origin from Brahmi but it is equally difficult to convey the meaning in different languages. It can be easily observed that in different parts of the country people know more than one language with having one script. For example, it is very common to see Brahmins reciting hymn in Sanskrit (a language) written in their mother script.

In such cases mapping of characters can be very handy. Since writing is known to Indians from 3000 BC and paper is invented only in AD. 104. Apart from that the printing technology reached very late to India. Hence, it was very late when Indians started using paper. Many of the ancient writings are on stones, leaves, clay tablets, tree barks, cloth etc. Anything before, AD 1600 is hand written which is difficult for machines to read. Some of the objects are so brittle that they can only be handled using special means. There is abundance of such material in the country.

INDIAN SCENARIO

India is witnessing a strong move for developing digital libraries around the country. Some are in public domain like LDL of Documentation Research and Training Centre, Bangalore and Digital Library of India. Some are with restricted access like, Nalanda Digital Library of National Institute of Technology, Calicut. As far as, the English literature is concerned there are editable text available over web but when it comes to Indian language only scanned images of the documents are available for display supplemented by metadata. The experiment has been done with many of the Open source software and results are positive. Some test beds can be found at Documentation Research and Training Centre site but still much has to be done.

5

Quality Concept in Library Services

The library is an organization to offer reference and information services to its users. Library service is the combination of the services-process and its delivery. In a library, the service offered from acquisition section, technical section, maintenance section etc. are the processes carried out there and thereafter delivered to the users. The quality should start from the acquisition section, which should be carried uniformly to circulation section. A user who had an unpleasant experience from the library will tell it to many people, but a good experience will be told to very few. Therefore it is very necessary for librarian to understand the users, what they want, how they want, and when they want the documents and information.

HOW TO IMPROVE THE QUALITY IN LIBRARY SERVICES

In this information age it is very easy to make a quality based library if the parent body or concerned authority assist financially as well as collectively. It is very necessary for the librarian and its parent body to look forward for the present and future generation to cope up with international phenomena. A user must be educated with proper technology to use the library effectively.

He or she should have knowledge of what facilities and services are available in the library and information centre and how to access those efficiently and effectively. To improve the service quality the user satisfaction survey is a tool that provides both quantitative and qualitative data. It is an important part of libraries for process and performance measurement.

Main steps to measure users' satisfaction are:

- Conducting sample survey.
- Data collection.
- Process and analysis of data.
- Interpret and present the data.
- Finding out result.

With the help of the result the librarian can take new steps for development of library. The regular survey will enable the library to understand the changes in users satisfaction and to plan the services accordingly.

The Users' Satisfaction is based on Many Factors Like

- A source of up-to-date information, knowledge, accessing facilities and assistance.
- The library should organize its facilities visible to the users; otherwise they may not have it and get dissatisfied.
- *Accessibility:* The library resources and services should be easily accessible. Books should be arranged in shelves in proper classified order, so that the users can locate books quickly. In case of electronic library the electronic database like OPAC will help the users to find out the books in stacks.
- *Tangibles:* The tangibles of libraries, namely the building, furniture and other physical facilities, collection, staff, machines etc. should be sufficient and appropriate and useful for the users.
- *Courtesy/Friendliness:* The library staff should be very courteous and friendly with the users.
- *Physical Appearance/Atmosphere/Cleanliness/Comfort:* The appearance of library, its facilities, collection, staff and services should be attractive and pleasant. A Welcoming atmosphere should be must. Furniture, floor, racks, documents etc. should be neat and clean.
- *Process-Reliability/Communications:* The processing part of the library should be dependable and efficient that suffices the expectations of the users. The way of communication, assistance and guidance also greatly affect the satisfaction of the users.
- *Some Useful Criteria to Measure Users' Experience in a Library are:*
  - Speed of services delivery (Access time, location, processing, etc.);
  - Value added services such as Xerox service, CAS, SDI etc.; and
  - Technology used.

It is observed that if something goes wrong that can be very easily learned from the users, so the users' complaints can be taken as good measure of user satisfaction.

Steps for Staff to Meet the Users' Needs

- Being responsible for the total service quality to the users both the Technical staff and frontline staff in the library should serve the users.
- Services must be provided to the users in a most effective way.
- Providing maximum benefits to the users form collection and facilities.
- Stay close to users: Library can not understand users' needs, tastes, interests etc. without listening to them, and services without users' interest will be a mere wastage.
- Users must be treated well, informed well and acknowledged well about the services to the users.

KINDS OF INFORMATION SERVICE

Information service, in the most general sense, is the process of assisting library users to identify sources of information in response to a particular question, interest, assignment, or problem. Sometimes referred to as reference service, the *Reference and User Services Association* (RUSA) of the American Library Association defines reference transactions as "information consultations in which library staff recommend, interpret, evaluate, and/or use information resources to help others to meet particular information needs". These reference transactions can take place in person or via the telephone, e-mail, or virtual reference technologies.

Librarians are also creating Web sites, answer archives, and links to answers to "frequently asked questions" all designed to anticipate user questions and help people find information independently. Traditional reference desk service continues to be highly valued by library users in many settings, but the newer forms continue to grow in popularity. Consequently, it is all the more important that librarians understand the range of enquiries that can be expected, allowing them to provide a full and ready answer, regardless of the form in which the query arises.

ANSWERING REFERENCE QUESTIONS

In light of the immense diversity and range of possible questions, being approached by a patron with a reference need can seem like a daunting prospect. Indeed, much of the difficulty of information services arises from uncertainty about the kind of service or breadth of information called for by a given question. Categorizing reference questions by type is a useful way to make sense of such concerns. Three common types of information service are ready reference questions, research questions, and bibliographic verification. *Ready reference questions* such as "Where was Abraham Lincoln born?" "Who won the 1992 World Series?" "What is the capital of Nicaragua?" or "Where can I find a copy of the United States' Declaration of Independence?" can be readily answered using one or two general reference sources.

The librarian may be tempted to tell the user the answer to simple ready reference questions. Yet here the old saying that "giving a man a fish feeds him for a day while teaching him to fish feeds him for a lifetime" is proven true. No matter how simple they seem initially, ready reference questions provide the possibility of teachable moments. Whenever possible, librarians should lead users through the process of looking up the information rather than simply providing the solution.

Librarians who assist users with ready reference enquiries on a regular basis sometimes choose to create a "ready reference" section of the most commonly used resources either in print or on the library's Web site to answer quick questions. Typically, such sections include a general all-purpose encyclopaedia, dictionaries, almanacs, and handbooks. Care must be taken to keep the sources uptodate and to avoid depending so heavily on this subset of the collection that other sources are overlooked by library users and librarians.

Librarians may find that ready reference questions have diminished due to the ease of answering basic questions through online information portals such as Google. Nevertheless, ready reference remains a cornerstone of information services, and librarians should be primed to provide it at any time. *Research questions* are more complex, may take much longer to answer, and typically require multiple sources of information. These questions often require the user to consider a variety of sources and viewpoints and to subsequently draw conclusions.

Sometimes questions that initially seem like ready reference questions are far more complex as previously hidden facets of the user's enquiry are revealed. Here, the variety of possible sources increases with the complexity of users' questions. Librarians should, for example, guide the user in the use of bibliographic sources, citations, and the back-of-the-book bibliographies. Likewise, users with complex questions may need to be taught how to find or request the full text of articles for which only citations are given in a search of electronic databases, allowing them to move beyond cursory surveys of the literature.

Research questions, especially if the user is unable to fully articulate the nature of his or her query, require librarians to ask questions of their own, trying to get at the nature of the request before setting out to help the patron answer it. The librarian may, for example, have to determine how much information is needed, what level of information is needed, and what other sources have already been consulted. Information services call for mutual engagement, especially with more complex questions.

Reference librarians should never be passive participants, pointing the way to an answer. Instead, they should play the part of dynamic guides, joining users on their journeys to knowledge. Naturally, the extent of such engagement may vary from one circumstance to another. Different types of libraries tend to have their own standards for how long librarians should spend with users on research questions. Many public libraries recommend that users be given five or ten minutes of personal assistance and then asked to return if more help is needed.

A university library may have a similar standard, or depending on the institution, may be able to invite the user to make an appointment for more in-depth research assistance. Some libraries may suggest that users call or e-mail ahead of their visit so the librarian can be prepared to offer the best possible assistance. Other libraries, including special libraries, may only be able to provide a basic level of help during the first visit. Libraries may refer users to other libraries with more specialized materials in the area of the user's research or may offer to call back if additional information is found.

Finally a library user may seek *bibliographic verification* when he or she has already obtained the information needed but must verify the sources. Sometimes this service is a matter of fact checking, whereas on other occasions users may have completed their research but lack full citation information. As users increasingly depend on electronic databases for information, compiling and formatting bibliographic citations becomes easier. Verifying and citing material found on Web pages is more difficult since the information needed for the citation is not always easy to find.

READER'S ADVISORY SERVICE

Reader's advisory service, sometimes considered a type of information service, is the quest to put the right book in the hands of the right reader. Librarians are increasingly expected to provide an answer to the dreaded question, "Can you help me find a good book?" Fortunately, as demand has increased, so too has the ease of providing this service. Although there is no substitute for one's own knowledge or experience, many new technologies serve to make the reader's advisory far easier than it was in the past. Many online databases, for example, have functions that automatically recommend other books for those who like a given title. Others have searchable lists of works by genre, helping readers match their favourite books to others like them.

As always, however, remember that reader's advisory, like other reference work, is predicated on the interaction between librarian and library user. Asking directed questions, listening carefully to the users' responses, and tailoring assistance accordingly is the basis of excellent, truly helpful service. The reader's advisory service is generally associated with public libraries and tends to be employed primarily by those looking for fiction. In academic libraries, it is far less common as users rarely come in searching for a mystery to read. Even so, reader's advisory may be needed to help lay researchers looking to deepen their knowledge of a particular field.

A patron who has read and enjoyed Stephen Ambrose's *Undaunted Courage*, but is troubled by allegations about Ambrose's questionable accuracy and academic honesty, may want to know the titles of books about the Lewis and Clark expedition that are both reputable and engaging. Successful reader's advisory librarians are skilled at asking users questions that enable them to assess users' reading level, language, or educational background. They must know a great deal about various genres of fiction and nonfiction and be intimately familiar with their library's collection. Significantly, it is important that they be able to convey their expertise in a friendly and conversational manner.

INFORMATION LITERACY

User instruction, which is now usually referred to as *information literacy*, may range from showing an individual how to use the library's online catalog and basic print reference sources to formal classroom sessions about conducting research in the library. The basic component of information literacy includes demonstrating how, when, and why to use various reference sources in an integrated way that will capture the user's attention at the teachable moment. In today's educational settings, the ease of using electronic resources often results in a failure to teach more traditional research strategies. While finding superficial information has grown easier, in-depth information has become increasingly obscure for many students.

In the library too, approaches to instruction may vary and librarians often question whether to simply answer questions posed by users or to teach users how to employ the available resources. This may be contingent on the mission or purpose of the library. Academic institutions may call on their librarians to help students understand how to engage effectively and independently in the research and information evaluation process. Public librarians, by contrast, may try to teach users about reference sources in a more informal manner as they lead users to the answers they seek.

Thus, while instruction is always an important part of reference work, the degree to which they go about providing it is highly contingent on the circumstances. In any case, all reference librarians must be skilled at helping users find information and answers quickly and be ready to teach users how to use the reference sources that are available. The best reference librarians develop an intuition for when to be information providers and when to be bibliographic instructors.

In some libraries, only specific, designated librarians are charged with conducting library instruction courses. Nevertheless, an increasing number of librarians are required to participate in their libraries' bibliographic instruction programme, and library school graduates are expected to be capable of teaching basic classes on the use of library resources. As should be clear, even those librarians not charged with providing formal instruction have the opportunity to teach those they serve.

MEASURING QUALITIES OF LIBRARY SERVICES

The important measuring tools and techniques are:

- TQM (Total Quality Management).
- SERVQUAL.
- LibQUAL.

The TQM is one of the techniques used for the improvement and maintenance of quality or performance of the library. It is to provide the right information to the right users at the right place and time and also at the right cost.

The most important components of TQM in a library are:

- Benchmarking.

- Performance Measuring and Monitoring.
- Qualification and experience of staff.

Benchmarking is a process of comparing the operations, products and services of a library with a library doing quality processes and offering quality products and services to the users. Performance measurement is necessary to identify the problems, if any and find out new ways for improving the products or services. It requires both qualitative and quan-titative data.

The major performance indicators of the library functions are:

- *Acquisition:* Efficiency, effectiveness, cost productivity.
- *Classification:* Accuracy, Time factor, cost.
- *Cataloguing:* Efficiency, Time effectiveness.
- *Technical Processing:* Efficiency, effectiveness, cost productivity.
- *Collection Management:* Efficiency, ease, accessibility, effectiveness.

Quality of service depends on quality and experience of staff. The TQM supports user education, sufficient and convenient technical infrastructures. SERVQUAL is the most popular assessment tool of service quality. It is designed by the marketing research team of Berry, Parasuraman, and Zeithaml. SERVQUAL evolve a set of five dimensions to assess the service quality-

- *Tangibles:* Appearance of physical facilities, equip-ments, personnel, and communication materials.
- *Reliability:* Ability to perform the promised service dependably and accurately; giving correct infor-mation asked.
- *Responsiveness:* Willingness to help users and provide prompt service making new information available.
- *Assurance and Empathy:* Knowledge and courtesy of employees and their ability to convey confidence to users. It involves politeness, friendliness, skill to provide information.
- *Access:* It means there are adequate staff and equipments as well as hours of operation. Location of library is central and convenient.
- *Communications:* It involves understanding the users' needs precisely, provision of user education, teaching library skills to users, the use of language understandable to different categories of users.
- *Security:* It involves physical safety within the library, and keeping library dealings secured.

LibQUAL + is a library service quality measurement tool based on the SERVQUAL models of assessing service quality. It is standard survey instrument used in many libraries.It is a tool measuring users' perception of service quality and identifies gaps between desired, perceived and minimum expectation of services. LibQUAL +TM 2002 is the latest version to listening the users

USERS' EXPECTATIONS: QUALITY OF SERVICES

- Modern building and furniture are required for a good library.

- A good library provides excellent facilities and services.
- Required books and journals in adequate number will be available with attractively displayed in a good library.
- In a good library, the staff will assist the users for locating a document.
- Accurate information and proper records will always be available in a good library.
- The staff of a good library will have sufficient knowledge to answer user's questions.
- Easy accessing and convenient working hour should have in a good library.

USERS' PERCEPTION: QUALITY OF SERVICES

- My library has modern building and furniture.
- My library provides me excellent facilities and services.
- Necessary books and journals in adequate number are available displayed attractively in my library.
- My library assists the users for locating the documents needed.
- Accurate information and proper records are always kept in my library.
- The staff of my library has proper knowledge to answer my question.
- My library is easily accessible with convenient working hours.

FACILITIES IN A QUALITY BASED LIBRARY

Physical Facilities:

- Good library is easily accessible.
- Good layout for a good library.
- Sufficient Space, lighting and ventilation.
- Clean, tidy and hygienic.
- Cozy and comfortable furniture.

Library Collection:

- Good collection of textbooks, journals, reference books, online journals, ebooks, etc. is needed in a good library.
- Good library displays new arrival of books in separate shelves.
- Good library offers open access to the collection.

Library Staff:

- Staff in a good library should be experienced with knowledge of modern technology.
- Staff should help the users to locate the documents needed and do their works in time.
- Sufficient staff to run the library.

Technical Processing:

- Good library acquire new documents in time.

- Shelf arrangement and rectification is a never ending process in a good library.
- Good library has proper catalogue or database for collection (OPAC etc.).
- Good library has prompt processing, charging and discharging system.

SERVICES IN CENTRAL LIBRARY, IIT GUWAHATI

The Central Library, one of the important central facilities of the Institute, currently has about 85,000 volumes, including textbooks, reference books, conference proceedings, back volumes, standards, and non-book material such as CD-ROMs, audio tapes, video tapes, slides. The Library also subscribes to about 484 current periodicals. All operations of the Library are automated with the help of an integrated library software package (LIBSYS). The database for the entire collection has been created and available through On-Line Public Access Catalogue (OPAC) to the users via campus network. Now this facility is also available through Institute's Intranet as a Web enabled OPAC.

The Library is a member of INDEST consortium (Indian National Digital Library in Science and Technology Consor-tium), under the aegis of the MHRD, provides online access to few important science and engineering abstracting database services, such as COMPENDEX and INSPEC, MathSciNet, SciFinder Scholar, Web of Science etc and several full-text journals and Indian Standards. The Central Library Intranet Page provides the IP based online accesses to these resources. Opening hours is from Morning 8 a.m. to 11 p.m. Average number of users in library is 200 per day.

USE OF PUBLIC LIBRARY SERVICES

Expert assessment of the nation's health care system suggests that it is slow in translating knowledge into practice and that patient care is not keeping abreast of advances in basic research. The American Medical Informatics Association recently proposed a plan for improving health care delivery. The plan focusses on clinical decision support, which "encompasses a variety of approaches for providing clinicians, staff, patients or other individuals with timely, relevant information that can improve decision making, prevent errors, and enhance health and health care."

The National Library of Medicine (NLM) can make a substantial contribution to improving national health by making a wide range of biomedical resources readily accessible to advanced information technology. There is a large, and growing, amount of online health-related information. Some resources are in the form of text readily accessible only to humans; examples include MEDLINE/PubMed and ClinicalTrials.gov. Other information is structured and includes biomedical vocabularies, clinical and molecular biology knowledge bases, and model organism annotation databases. Within NLM, examples include the Unified Medical Language System and Entrez Gene.

There are also several specialised biomedical databases, for example the BIND database and PharmGKB, as well as commercially curated drug databases, such as Micromedex DRUGDEX and DrugDigest. The growth of online information resources for biomedicine is outstripping access applications that could allow users to maximally exploit those resources. In order to take full advantage of available resources, the Library needs to provide services beyond traditional information retrieval.

Emerging research provides the underpinnings for developing applications that accommodate the growth in online information. Advanced applications manipulate information, not just text, and provide visualisation of results and interconnections among multiple sources. Some research concentrates on extracting information from text. Other emerging systems focus on using the information extracted; examples include automatic summarisation, question answering, and knowledge discovery.

METHODS AND PROCEDURES

We discuss issues involved in constructing a Biomedical Knowledge Repository and illustrate an emerging Web application that exploits a preliminary version. The SemRep and Sem Gen natural language processing systems will be used to extract information in the form of semantic predications consisting of arguments and a predicate that represent relations between concepts asserted in text. Information in biomedical structured resources will be converted into a common format and all information will be integrated into the repository. Finally, a significant aspect of this project is the development of applications that exploit the Biomedical Knowledge Repository.

Extracting Predications from Text

Two programmes developed at LHNCBC will initially be used to extract semantic predications from ClinicalTrials.gov narrative and MEDLINE/PubMed citations for the repository. SemRep was devised to apply to the clinically oriented research literature, while SemGen addresses the genetic etiology of disease.

SemRep

SemRep is a rule-based symbolic natural language processing system developed for the biomedical research literature. As the first step in identifying semantic predications, SemRep produces an underspecified syntactic analysis based on the SPECIALIST Lexicon and the MedPost part-of-speech tagger. The most important aspect of this processing is the identification of simple noun phrases. In the next step, these are mapped to concepts in the Metathesaurus using MetaMap. Syntactic analysis in table, for example, contains Metathesaurus concepts and semantic types for the sentence in table.

Table. SemRep Analysis

Sentence	Phenytoin induced gingival hyperplasia	(1)
Syntactic analysis	[[head(noun(phenytoin)), metaconc('Phenytoin' :[orch,phsu]))], [verb(induced)], head(noun(['gingival hyperplasia')), metaconc(' Gingival Hyperplasia':[dsyn]))]]	(2)
Semantic Network	'Pharmacological Substance' CAUSES 'Disease or Syndrome'	(3)
Semantic Predication	Phenytoin CAUSES Gingival Hyperplasia	(4)

SemRep relies on structures to translate syntactic structures into semantic predications. One aspect of this processing is 'indicator' rules which map syntactic elements to predicates in the Semantic Network. Argument identification rules then find syntactically allowable noun phrases to serve as arguments for indicators. If an indicator and the noun phrases serving as its syntactic arguments can be interpreted as a semantic predication, the following condition must be met: The semantic types of the Metathe-saurus concepts for the noun phrases must match the semantic types serving as arguments of the indicated predicate in the Semantic Network.

For example, in the structure given in table, the indicator *induced* maps to the Semantic Network relation in table. The concepts corresponding to the noun phrases *phenytoin* and *gingival hyperplasia* can serve as arguments because their semantic types match those in the Semantic Network relation. In the semantic predication produced as output, the Metathesaurus concepts from the noun phrases are substituted for the semantic types in the Semantic Network relation.

SemGen

SemGen was adapted from SemRep in order to identify semantic predications on the genetic etiology of disease. The main consideration in creating SemGen was the identification of gene and protein names as well as related genomic phenomena. For this SemGen relies on ABGene, in addition to MetaMap and the Metathesaurus. Since, the UMLS Semantic Network does not cover molecular genetics, ontological semantic relations for this domain were created for Sem Gen. The allowable relations were defined in two classes: gene-disease interactions and gene-gene interactions.

Other Systems

The information submitted to the repository by SemRep and SemGen could be supplemented with output from other natural language processing technologies that produce relationships. Phenotypic information from clinical narrative could be made accessible with the NLP system described by Friedman *et al.*. For molecular biology phenomena, several systems use syntactic templates and shallow parsing to produce a variety of relations, including gene and protein functions, protein interactions, and protein modifications such as phosphorylation. Friedman *et al.* use extensive linguistic processing for relations on molecular pathways, while Lussier *et al.* use a similar approach to identify phenotypic context for genetic phenomena.

Converting Structured Data into a Common Format

Since, relations in structured resources are already represented in some kind of formalism, their conversion to a common format is somewhat easier than extraction from text. However, the challenges in normalising such knowledge are not unlike those encountered with textual data. In both cases, knowledge extraction involves syntactic issues and semantic issues.

Various formalisms are used to represent structured data, including relational databases, tables, graphs, etc. Currently, no universal conversion mechanism is available. Moreover, the semantics of the data is often implicit or limited, for example, to short column names in a database schema. The objective of the conversion is the creation of 'normalised knowledge'. This effort, in the context of knowledge management, is somewhat equivalent to term normalisation. Knowledge normalisation ensures that the same entity referred to in different resources is ultimately identified in such a way that it is recognised as a unique thing. Knowledge normalisation forms the basis for information and data integration.

Description of Resources

Over the past twenty years, NLM has developed many knowledge resources, from various perspectives. Terminological resources such as the *Unified Medical Language System* (UMLS) result from the integration of many existing terminologies and ontologies, represented in a common formalism–UMLS' Rich Release Format—and partially normalised. While synonymous terms are grouped together as names for a given concept, synonymous relationships are typically not identified as such.

Nevertheless, with some 8 million relations, the UMLS Metathesaurus constitutes an important resource, providing mostly hierarchical relations and co-occurrence relations. Another source of structured knowledge is represented by the many databases available under the umbrella of the NCBI's Entrez system. While some databases such as MEDLINE/PubMed and *Online Mendelian Inheritance in Man* (OMIM) are mostly textual resources, many other NCBI databases contain predominantly structured information.

Entrez Gene, for example, is a gene-centric resource in which a record provides gene properties such as names, associated diseases, function, sequence, etc. While numerous links have been created across the resources in the Entrez system for navigation purposes, such links typically require human interpretation and therefore cannot be used for knowledge discovery purposes in high-throughput systems. Finally, structured databases and knowledge bases are also available outside NLM.

One example of large, publicly available genomic resource is represented by the genome annotations for the major model organisms. Here, the existence of a controlled vocabulary—the Gene Ontology—has contributed to developing unified functional annotations, integrated in systems such as the Mouse Genome Database and the Saccharomyces Genome Database. In the clinical domain, the various knowledge bases of drug information constitute important resources about drug-drug interactions, drug kinetics and metabolism, and indications and contraindications. DRUGDEX, produced by Micromedex, is an example of such a resource.

Representing Normalised Knowledge

One of the strengths of the World Wide Web is that it relies on textual information, easily created and interpreted by humans. This is also one of its principal limitations. The absence of explicit semantics prevents agents from being able to make sense of the information on the Web. This is the motivation of the Semantic Web, which aims at creating a vast collections of integrated and interoperable resources.

There is an obvious parallel between the Semantic Web and the Biomedical Knowledge Repository we propose to create. The technologies developed for the Semantic Web offer possible solutions to some of the challenges we face, including selecting a formalism for normalised biomedical knowledge and identification issues for biomedical entities. It is worth noting that some of these issues are still actively being debated in the Semantic Web community, especially in the Semantic Web Health Care and Life Sciences Interest Group.

Formalism

Many of the resources produced by NLM and other organisations are available in XML, the eXtensible Markup Language. However, the semantics of XML is limited. In addition to XML, the World Wide Web Consortium (W3C) has produced the specifications of other formalisms for representing resources.

Collectively know as Semantic Web technologies, these specifications define the building blocks of the Semantic Web. Of particular interest to us is the Resource Description Framework. RDF extends the capabilities of the extensible markup language XML as it enables many-to-many relationships between resources and data. The resulting structure is a graph in which the nodes are resources or data and the edges are relationships.

The basic unit in RDF is therefore the equivalent of a triple, similar to a relation in the UMLS Metathesaurus or a predication extracted by SemRep. RDF integrates limited inference rules, enabling, for example, the definition of subclasses and subproperties.

Some extensive resources such as UniProt have already been converted to RDF. The BioRDF task force of the W3C Semantic Web Health Care and Life Sciences Interest Group currently investigates methods whereby existing biomedical resources can be converted to RDF.

Such methods include XSLT, GRDDL and DB2RDF, among others. The *eXtensible Stylesheet Language Transformation* (XSLT) uses a stylesheet approach to converting XML to RDF. GRDDL specifies associations between markup languages–including XLM–and RDF. Finally, DB2RDF is used to convert databases to RDF.

Identification Issues

In order for RDF triples to form a graph–and for integrated knowledge to be interoperable-entities and relationships must be identified consistently and unambiguously. For example, if the disease *Neurofibromatosis 2* is identified by the code *SNOMEDCT:92503002* in one resource and by the code *MESH:D016518* in another, the RDF triples involving *SNOMEDCT:92503002* and *MESH:D016518* will not come together as expected unless both resource are converted to the other annotation system or mappings are created between the two systems.

For example, the UMLS Metathesaurus could be used to convert or bridge between MeSH and SNOMED CT, in this case through the concept *C0027832*. The predications extracted from the literature by SemRep already use UMLS codes to identify biomedical entities. From a technical perspective, several technologies have been developed by various communities to implement identification mechanisms for RDF.

There are three major identification mechanisms:

- LSID (Life Science Identifier), promoted by the Life Sciences community. Examples of applications using LSID include Taverna and resources created by the BioPathways Consortium;
- Solutions based on the HTTP protocol, promoted by the W3C; and
- ARK (Archive Resource Key), promoted by the Digital Library community.

There are important differences among three mechanisms regarding location independence, backward compatibility, resolution mechanism and versioning. It is unclear at this time what mechanism would suit our needs best.

Pilot Project: Converting Entrez Gene to RDF

As a proof of concept, we converted the Entrez Gene database into RDF. The entire Gene database in its native ASN.1 format was downloaded by FTP from the NCBI web site and later converted to XML using the programme gene2xml provided by NCBI. Using the *eXtensible Stylesheet Language Transformation* (XSLT) approach, we mapped the element tags of the XML representation to more intuitive relationship names manually, and used them during the automatic conversion to RDF. Finally, we stored this RDF version of Entrez Gene in the Oracle 10g relational database management system, which provides support for storing and querying native RDF data. The conversion process is illustrated in figure.

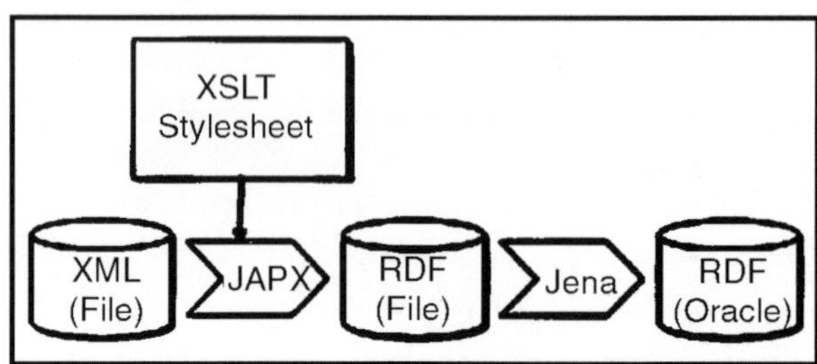

Fig. Overview of the Conversion of Enrez Gene from XML to RDF

Mapping XML Element Tags to RDF Properties

While XML data can be mechanically converted to RDF, the resulting RDF graph would be of limited interest because the semantics of the properties is most often implicit in XML and needs to be made explicit. Starting from one typical Entrez Gene record, we identified all its XML element tags, corresponding to the properties of the gene, as described in the Gene record.

Examples of such properties include *<Genetrack_geneid>* and *<Genetrack_update-date>*, indicating the identifier and the update date of the gene record, respectively. A total of 124 unique elements tags were identified. Because XML element tags represent gene properties, they were transformed into predicates in RDF. For example, *<Genetrack_geneid>* becomes *has_unique_geneid* and relates the gene record to its unique identifier in the Gene database. Note that the RDF property now conveys the notion–implicit in the XML representation–that the identifier is a unique identifier, corresponding to a primary key in a relational database. Converting XML elements to RDF properties requires familiarity with the structure and content of the original record structure and is a key component to the mapping process. After eliminating redundant and superfluous XML element tags, 106 unique RDF properties were created. The mapping of Entrez gene XML element tags to RDF properties is specified formally using the XPath language and constitutes a stylesheet. This stylesheet is specific to the conversion of the Entrez Gene database.

Converting XML to RDF through XSLT

Once the stylesheet is created, it can serve as an auxiliary file for existing programmes realising the XML to RDF conversion. In other words, the major interest of this approach is that no specific code is required for the conversion, because the transformation logic resides entirely in the stylesheet. We used JAXP, the Java *Application Programming Interface* (API) to XML, to implement the conversion. The resulting 411 million RDF triples were then loaded in a store using Oracle 10g using the Jena API.

Lessons Learned, Issues and Challenges

This experiment confirmed the feasibility of converting a large resource from XML to RDF. It also showed that the issues are not technical, but rather lie in the necessity of making explicit the relationships represented implicitly by element tags in XML. This step requires the manual intervention of a domain expert. In our experience, it took less than a week for one person familiar with both bioinformatics and stylesheets to formalise the mapping between XML element tags and RDF properties.

Although the stylesheet created is specific to the Entrez Gene database, it is expected that part of the expertise acquired during this transformation can be applied to transforming other NCBI resources. The major unresolved issue concerns entity identification. If the RDF graph resulting from the conversion of Entrez Gene is to be integrated with clinical or bibliographic information, the diseases associated with genes must be represented not as literals as they currently are, but by their identifiers in the corresponding clinical and bibliographic controlled vocabularies, or with the *concept unique identifier* (CUI) in the UMLS Metathesaurus. Only after such mapping will the RDF graph integrating Entrez Gene and, say, the Metathesaurus, support queries such as *Find all genes associated with neurodegenerative diseases*. The knowledge required in this cases comes in part from Entrez gene and from UMLS.

Integrating Predications: Biomedical Knowledge Repository

The Biomedical Knowledge Repository can be understood as a specialised version of the Semantic Web. It consists of an extensive collection of predications, represented in a common format, processable by computers. Biomedical terminologies and ontologies provide the concepts involved in the facts. Logical reasoners extend the capabilities of the repository by inferring new knowledge. Each fact in the repository is annotated with metainformation regarding its origin, making it possible for applications exploiting the repository to select facts of interest in a given context and for a particular task. Once it is fully populated, the Biomedical Knowledge Repository is expected to comprise several hundred million facts, collected from hundreds of sources.

Origin of the Predications

The Biomedical Knowledge Repository (BKR) comprises predications form three major sources: extracted from the biomedical literature by NLP programmes such as SemRep, converted from existing structured knowledge bases, and contributed by users. In our vision of the BKR, NLM not only contributes to populating the BKR, but also makes it available to the community as a framework for researchers to deposit their predications.

Predications resulting from experiments, from alternative processing of the literature, and inferred from other predictions, for example, can be contributed by members of the community and made available to others. One measure of success of the BKR would be for it to become a standard repository for the knowledge created through biomedical research experiments. In order to maintain the consistency and integrity of the BKR, its developers would have to follow guidelines regarding formalism of the predications and identification mechanism for biomedical entities.

Metainformation Associated with the Predications

Just as few users need all the vocabularies in the UMLS Metathesaurus for a given purpose, it is unlikely that all predications will be equally useful for a given task, such as question answering. Instead, a mechanism supporting the selection of relevant sets of predications is needed.

The metainformation associated with each predication enables this selection and may include the source of the predication, the method of extraction, the date of extraction, in addition to the usual metadata associated with MEDLINE/PubMed citations for predications extracted from the literature. Researchers contributing predications to the BKR will be requested to annotate them with similar metainformation. Another form of contribution to the repository is to provide not predications, but annotations to existing predications. Such a contribution represents a form of collaborative curation of the repository by the community, similar to the framework developed by the SWAN project for the Alzheimer research community.

Storing the Predications

Several technological solutions, called RDF stores, have been developed for storing information in RDF format, generally implemented on top of some storage system. One such open source RDF database is Sesame. More recently, traditional database management systems have started offering direct support for native RDF triples. For example, version 10g of the Oracle system supports RDF in addition to the relational model. Since, we need to store large amounts of both RDF and traditional information, we started experimenting with Oracle 10g while converting Entrez Gene to RDF last summer. Preliminary results are encouraging although we might face optimisation issues.

Querying the Predications

Analogous to SQL for relational databases, SPARQL is the language for querying RDF. Like SQL, SPAQRL queries have a SELECT and a WHERE clause. However, in a SPARQL query, the WHERE clause follows the pattern of a RDF triple in which at least one element of the triple is replaced by a variable. In the BKR, the predications to be queried would first be selected based on their annotations. For example, a typical query supporting multidocument summarisation would be as follows.

Select all predications from MEDLINE/PubMed returned by a PubMed query on *metabolic syndrome*, restricted to citations from *JAMA*, *Am J Cardiol.* and *J Hypertens.*, published between 2004 and 2005. Additionally, select those predications from the UMLS Metathesaurus and Entrez Gene having at least one node in common with those from the literature.

Integrating Predications

The query example presented above illustrates the interest of integrating knowledge under a unique framework. First, there is a unique namespace for all knowledge in the BKR. As suggested, largely rely on the UMLS for identifying biomedical entities.

Second, once integrated into a graph, the predications can serve as a basis for inferencing, creating additional knowledge along the way. This represents an advantage over traditional database and information retrieval approaches. Finally, complex rules can be written to implement additional reasoning. For example, it is possible to restrict queries to those redundant predications asserted in more than 2 sources and for which the frequency of occurrence is above a certain threshold.

Estimated Size of the Repository

Once fully instantiated, the Biomedical Knowledge Repository is expected to comprise several hundred million predications extracted from the literature, terminological resources and structured knowledge bases. Assuming an average of ten predications is extracted from the title and abstract of each MEDLINE/ PubMed citation, we can expect about 150 million predications from MEDLINE/ PubMed.

The UMLS Metathesaurus records about 9 million relations, either symbolic or statistical. Some seven million functional annotations for the major model organism databases are recorded in the Gene Ontology database. Finally, our conversion experiment with Entrez Gene yielded over 400 million RDF triples. In this experiment, the objective was to systematically represent in RDF all the information present in the original XML file. In fact, part of this information would become metainformation in the context of the BKR, resulting in a significantly smaller number of triples to be actually contributed to the repository.

Exploiting the Repository: Semantic Medline Web Portal

As a pilot project to exploit a preliminary version of the Biomedical Knowledge Repository, we are developing a Web portal, called Semantic Medline, for managing the results of PubMed searches. The portal is designed as a Java-based Web application that seamlessly integrates PubMed, SemRep processing of the results of the search, automatic summarisation, and, finally, visualisation of the results, with links to the underlying citations and relevant additional knowledge in the UMLS Metathesaurus, the Genetics Home Reference, and Entrez Gene. Realtime access is achieved by pre-processing text from MEDLINE/PubMed abstracts and other sources with SemRep/SemGen and storing the results in a database.

Background

Several recent systems visualise the results of information identified in text as a way of providing users with enhanced access to the information retrieved. Results are often represented as a graph of interrelated relationships. The Telemakus project is based on relationships identified by hand and is meant to enable knowledge discovery through interactive visual maps of linked concepts among documents. Jensen *et al.* constructed literature networks of genes found relevant in gene expression data analysis.

Analysis is based on co-occurrence of genes in MEDLINE/PubMed abstracts. Van der Eijk *et al.* use various relations for literature-based discovery. The relationships represent co-occurrence of MeSH headings associated with MEDLINE/PubMed citations by a mapping programme. Feldman represent several gene-related relations in a graph. The relations were extracted with a type of underspecified natural language processing. Finally, Tao *et al.* visualise genomic information across both structured and textual databases.

Implementation

Semantic Medline is implemented as a three-tier, Java EE-based Web application. The three-tier architecture allows for the separation of user interface, application logic and data storage, providing improved performance, easier maintenance and scalability. We leverage mature open-source technologies in the development to the extent possible. The prototype runs in a Tomcat servlet container on an Apache Web server. It has been developed using the Apache Struts Web application framework. This framework encourages the use of *Model-View- Controller* (MVC) paradigm to provide a clean separation of application model, navigational code, and page design code through the use of Java Servlet API.

The controller is a Java servlet that mediates the application flow; the model comprises Java classes that represent the functionality of the semantic tools and the view is JSP pages that contain dynamic content. A MySQL database is used to store Semantic Medline data, which includes semantic predications extracted from MEDLINE/PubMed abstracts and ClinicalTrials.gov clinical study texts as well as a subset of UMLS Metathesaurus data. The database tables are prepopulated from plain text files that contain SemRep/SemGen output and Metathesaurus data using Perl scripts. Hibernate *object/relational mapping* (ORM) tool is used to programmatically access the database. We use such Hibernate features as database connection pooling and query caching for increased performance.

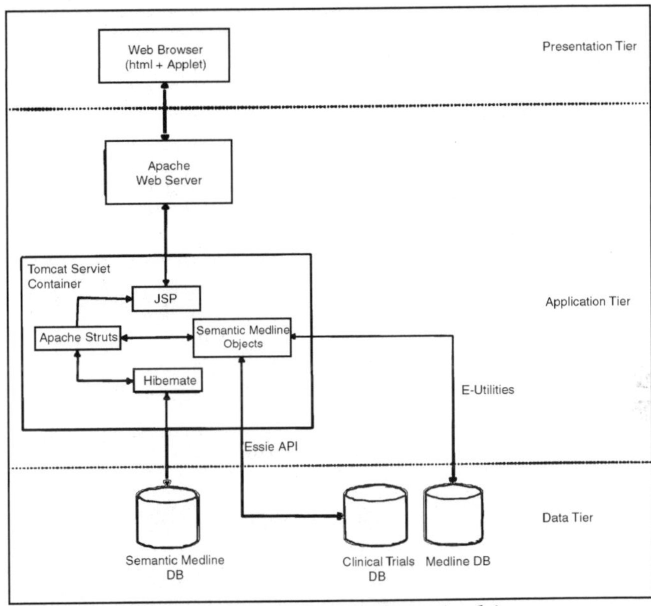

Fig. Semantic Medline System Architecture

Using Semantic Medline

MEDLINE/PubMed contains more than 16 million citations drawn from nearly 4,600 journals with biomedical relevance. Searches often retrieve large numbers of items. For example, the query 'diabetes' returns 207,997 citations. Although users can restrict searches by language, date and publication type, results can still be large. For example, a query for treatment for diabetes, limited to articles published in 2003 and having an abstract in English finds 3,621 items; limiting this further to articles describing clinical trials still returns 390 citations. It is difficult for a user to effectively exploit the information in this many citations. Semantic Medline addresses this difficulty by allowing users to summarise the results of searches focused on one of several points of view, including diagnosis and treatment of disorders, drug interactions and adverse events, genetic basis of disease, and pharmacogenomics.

A clinical scenario based on a summary focused on drug interactions illustrates the potential use of Semantic Medline for taking advantage of the research literature in clinical practice. In a hypothetical situation, a patient presents with peptic ulcer and tests positive for *Helicobacter pylori*. The clinician has tried several standard regimens including two different triple regimens: and; however, the patient still tests positive for *H. pylori*.

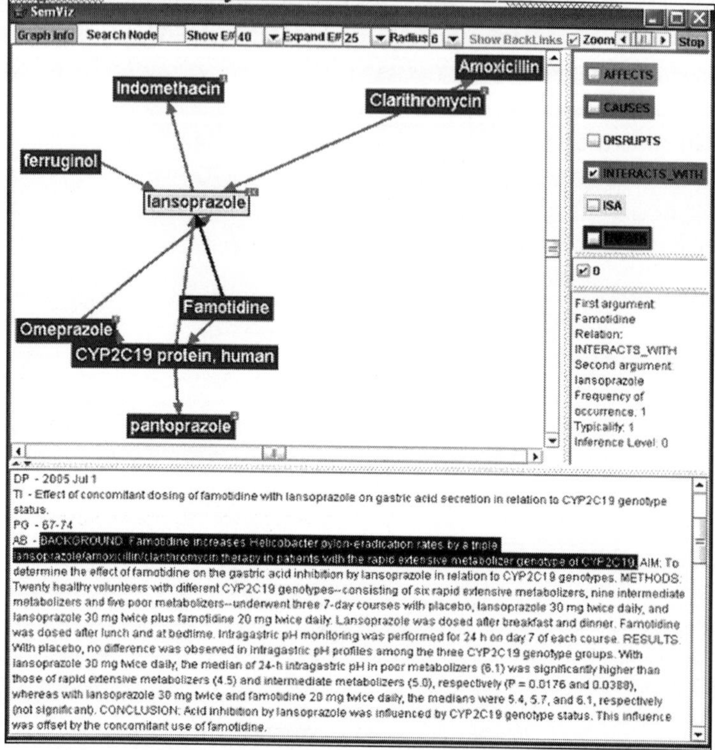

Fig. Summary of 564 MEDLINE/PubMed Citations for Lansoprazole

In order to gain insight from recent research, the physician uses Semantic Medline to issue a PubMed search for lansoprazole. SemRep extracts 5,971 predications from 564 citations returned by this search, and automatic summarisation for drug interactions involving lansoprazole condenses the final list of predications to 182, which are visualised by the system as the interactive graph in figure. Figure provides an informative overview of recent research on lansoprazole represented as predications asserting INTERACTS_WITH. Each predication is linked to the MEDLINE/PubMed citation that generated it.

Table Medline/PubMed Citations

PMID	Title
15963082	Effect of concomitant dosing of famotidine with lansoprazole on gastric acid secretion in relation to CYP2C19 genotype status
15710002	Concomitant dosing of famotidine with a triple therapy increases the cure rates of Helicobacter pylori infections in patients with the homozygous extensive metaboliser genotype of CYP2C19

Of interest for this case are two predications in the graph: 'Lansoprazole INTERACTS_WITH Famotidine' and 'Famotidine INTERACTS_WITH

CYPC19 Enzyme.' SemRep extracted the first predication from a citation with title seen in the first line of table and the second from a citation with in the second line.

Both citations discuss the salutary effect of combining famotidine with lansoprazole. In the second citation, which reports on a randomised controlled trial, the authors realised between 63 per cent to 100 per cent eradication of *H. pylori* with the addition of famotidine to a standard triple therapy and conclude that this is a promising option for patients who phenotypically are extensive metabolisers. If the patient in this hypothetical scenario falls under this category, it would be a potentially valuable regimen to pursue.

EVALUATION PLAN

We intend to follow a multifaceted evaluation plan, focusing evaluation activities on specific aspects of the project.

Evaluating Extraction

For this project, effectiveness of information extracted from text crucially depends on the accuracy of SemRep and SemGen. We have performed linguistic evaluation across a wide variety of predicates that includes the clinical as well as the genetic domain.

Among the predicates evaluated were Treats, Prevents, Location_of, Causes, Isa, Interacts_ With, Affects, Disrupts, Process_of, Part_of, Manifestation_ of, Associated_With, Inhibits, Stimulates and PREDISPOSES. Recall on the extraction of semantic propositions with these predicates has ranged from 41 per cent to 74 per cent and precision from 68 per cent to 84 per cent. Previous evaluations have been reported in and as suggested, continue this evaluation paradigm.

The framework for evaluating knowledge extraction from terminological and structured knowledge bases is not as well established as the evaluation of relation extraction from text. However, several aspects are particularly important. The rules used for the conversion need to be reviewed independently by several experts for a given knowledge base and integrated across databases in order to ensure consistency of the extraction of the relationships. Key to the consistency of the graph is also the mapping of literals to concepts–the nodes in the RDF graph and their consistent representation by identifiers from authoritative sources.

Evaluating Integration

Ideally, the graph resulting from integrating knowledge from several sources is consistent both structurally and semantically. Therefore structural techniques based on graph theory and semantic approaches similar to reasoning services created for description logics are expected to play a central role in evaluating the quality of knowledge integration in the repository.

However, the UMLS Metathesaurus, while resulting from the integration of a much smaller body of terminological knowledge, is already not always structurally or semantically consistent. Like the Metathesaurus, the Biomedical Knowledge Repository will allow contradictory predications to be represented as long as they occur in the original information sources. However, consistency is expected to be found at both structural and semantic levels on limited subsets of the repository.

Evaluating Applications

When evaluating applications such as automatic summarisation, it is useful to compare results against curated resources. Standard measures of performance can be calculated with respect to the reference standard chosen. For treatment of disease, the British Medical Journal clinical evidence concise is one alternative.

For drug interactions and adverse events, Micromedex DRUGDEX, DrugDigest, and the First DataBank's National Drug Data File can be used. A more ambitious method, requiring human experts, is task-based evaluation. Ultimately, user-centred evaluations such as the one described by McKeown must be considered.

PROJECT SCHEDULE

- *Year 1:* Pilot study, processing all of MEDLINE/PubMed, integrating Entrez Gene
- *Year 2:* Integrating UMLS and other NCBI resources
- *Year 3:* Annotating predications, opening the BKR to collaborative development and use
- *Year 4:* Fully integrated ALS system available

PROJECT RESOURCES

This project relies on a range of existing competencies and resources and has the potential to federate research energies throughout the Lister Hill Center. In addition to the efforts of the two core component projects, Semantic Knowledge Representation and Medical Ontology Research, the success of this project relies on collaboration with the Indexing Initiative, the Lexical Systems Project, and ClinicalTrials.gov.

The effectiveness of applications drawing on the repository could be strengthened by providing links to Visible Human images where appropriate. In order to accomplish the goals of this project additional staff and equipment are required: staff for creating and populating the repository and servers for providing effective access to the repository. Initially, PubMed and ClinicalTrials.gov will be processed by SemRep and SemGen and the predications extracted will be stored in the repository. Dedicated servers are required to process PubMed for this project.

TECHNOLOGICAL INNOVATIONS IN IMPROVING LIBRARY SERVICES

Once librarians were considered only the custodians of the library collection, but the change in information media from print to electronic has shown the new sunrise in the life of librarians. The basic aim of a library is to meet the teaching, learning, scholarly-research and other information needs of its faculty, students and research scholars and that too effectively and with efficiency. Medical library and information professionals ensures that health care providers have access to reliable, relevant, accurate, up to date and timely information that enhances the quality of health care.

The migration of information from paper to electronic media has changed the whole nature of research. With the easy availability of office computers and the transformation of media, the popularity and usage of digital and virtual libraries has been increased. World Wide Web has totally changed the meaning of a library. Physical presence has been decreased rapidly with the invention of virtual library. There is a universal assumption that man was born innocent or ignorant and should actively seek knowledge. "Information seeking is thus a natural and necessary mechanism of human existence". Information seeking behaviour is the purposive seeking for information as a consequence of a need to satisfy some goal. In the course of seeking, the individual may interact with manual information systems or with computer-based systems.

Information seeking behaviour involves personal reasons for seeking information, the kinds of information which are being sought and the ways and sources with which needed information is being sought. Information seeking behaviour is expressed in various forms, from reading printed material to research and experimentation. Scholars, students and faculties actively seek current information from the various media available in libraries, *e.g.* encyclopaedias, journals and more currently, electronic media. In this era of 'E', a sea change can be seen in the information-seeking behaviour of the users of library. In the phase of print media, users had no choice except going to the library and search for the material in books, journals and archives for hours. Search was very time consuming in print phase. Changing needs of users have changed the role of a librarian, which has transformed a librarian into information professional. Librarians have always acted as a link between knowledge source and its users.

In this era of 'E', librarians are playing the role of an electronic middleman. They are now helping the readers in the best possible way by using the latest technology and searching techniques. Users are being connected to the information resources via Internet for hyper-links and for many more options and choices for advance search. The change in the information-seeking behaviour is the result of the invention of E-resources. Readers felt relaxed with this invention and inclination towards these resources was natural.

There are many types of E-resources like Ebooks, E-journals, various open sources, gateways and databases. Chronologically we can divide these resources specifically journals as, in-print journals, on-line journals free with print, only on-line journals, on-line databases. In the era of 'E', readers demand has become significant as they ask for an article or topic in place of a book or journal and at the same time they prefer to search online databases to fulfill their needs. With the invention E-resources quantity and quality of research both have been affected. Different search techniques are undertaken by library users to search and locate relevant information. To understand how users of libraries search and locate relevant documents, we librarians, need to understand the search techniques and what resources and sources of information they generally use and require. Information professionals and users both suffer from the problem of exhaustive information, from a wide range of sources and shortage of time to find, manage and evaluate.

Sometimes users search internet indiscriminately without knowing the facts. Here librarian plays an important role by making the users aware of the importance of the evaluation of the retrieved information by guiding them, how to retrieve, what to retrieve and how to further use that retrieved information, which is called evaluation of information. The challenge posed by the information explosion is being successfully met by electronic information sources. Further this information explosion, diversity of user need, financial crunch and impossibility of self-sufficiency has led to the formation of consortia at local, regional, national and international level.

OBJECTIVE

The main objective of this study is to know the changing needs and information-seeking behaviour of the users and further various methods and resources being adopted by the librarians to fulfil these needs, which is the result of various technological innovations. Information seeking is a fluid and situation dependent activity where a seeker's actions are influenced by access to information, perceived quality and trust in the information source. This reminds the necessity of regular study and development of information system and management information services in North Indian Medical Institutes.

This work intends to study followings in libraries as a prototype of North Indian Medical Institutes:

- To examine information seeking behaviour of library users of North Indian Medical Institutes.
- To study the problems faced by the library users of North Indian Medical Institutes while seeking and using information.
- To explore the role of the library consortia's for providing service to the library users.
- To review the use of E-databases in this era of information explosion.

HYPOTHESIS

In this study it is hypothesized that:

- Physical visit to the libraries has been declined.
- Preference of users has been shifted to online documents from print one.
- Lack of knowledge about IT is the main problem the user face in the information searching process.

METHODOLOGY AND SCOPE

There are many ways to get information. The most common research methods are: literature searches, talking with people, focus groups, personal interviews, telephone surveys, mail surveys, e-mail surveys and internet surveys. A survey has been conducted on North Indian Medical Libraries through a questionnaire to know the changes in the information-seeking behaviour and needs of the users in this era of 'E'. So the medical professionals who were enrolled as member in the various medical libraries of Chandigarh and adjoining areas were considered for the study in hand. Further it can be stated that there were about 720 active library users of these libraries, so these users were taken as the subject for the study.

Through the stratified random sampling technique 72. Questionnaire method was used as it can be completed in one of the two basic ways. Firstly, respondents were asked to complete the questionnaire with the researcher not present and thus data was collected from 72 medical professionals, out of which 33 were students and 39 were senior residents, Assistant professor and professors. Secondly, respondents were asked to complete the questionnaire by verbally responding to questions in the presence of the researcher. This variation is called a structured interview and this method was applied on 28 librarians to know their observations.

FINDINGS (USERS)

Visits to the Library

Twenty-nine respondents (40 per cent) reported frequently visiting a medical library, 18 (25 per cent) rarely visited and 24 (33 per cent) never visited; one respondent did not answer this question. Respondents in their first year reported frequent visits to the library more often than those did in their second year. In the overall group, those who never or rarely visited a library indicated that E-resources are not sufficient; documents that they needed were not available or libraries were not needed because of the Internet.

So the main observation regarding visit to the library is that students visit library more frequently in their initial years of college/ institute. Overall group of users prefer to search Internet as they are not satisfied with the available E-resources in their library. They only visit the library after making sure that this required information is available in the library. This service is being provided through WEB OPAC in most of the libraries today. So hypothesis 1 stands proved.

Preference of Information Sources

Most respondents reported performing database searches independently. Among those who did their own searches, MEDLINE and PUBMED was the bestknown and most frequently used database: only 1 of 72 respondents did not know of MEDLINE. HINARI is being used by some users but the main problem with this database is that site is very slow. When asked about criteria for selecting references, the most important feature was free full-text availability with the demand of online database and formation of consortia. Regarding access to the full text, few respondents said they visited a library to check document availability and ordered articles through a library. More than half of respondents preferred electronic tools for literature searching. Yet most indicated they preferred to print documents rather than read them online. Respondents were further asked about their preferences about the form of the document. An online database is the most preferred format (39 per cent) in contrast to the print only format that is the least preferred one (10 per cent). This observation directly shows the shift of the preferences of the users from print to the online formats. It is strongly supported by the findings in which online journals and databases have become the most preferred form of document as 75 per cent users need only online resources in form or the other. Further users prefer taking print of the required information as they feel discomfort in reading directly from the screen. So hypothesis 2 stands proved.

Problems in Information Seeking

Several problems were identified in the information searching process. Many respondents found difficulties in choosing among the large number of documents retrieved in searches and lack of time was also noted as a problem. Common obstacles in the information-seeking process identified by respondents include lack of time, doubt about the existence of relevant information, retrieval of too much information and difficulties with navigation and searching. Since latest innovations have made the search easier with the latest options like E-mail alerts, send articles etc., but problem in information searching still persists due to the lack of knowledge of I.T. So the hypothesis no. 3 also stands proved.

OBSERVATIONS (LIBRARIANS)

According to the librarians, Internet search engines, E-print services, author Web sites, full-text databases, electronic journals and print resources are all used to some extent by most of the users. Convenience remains the single most important factor for information retrieval. Speed of access, ability to download, print and send articles are top advantages of electronic journals for all groups. All these services and facilities are possible with the application of IT.

These observations reaffirm that important opportunities remain for librarians and libraries in providing both access to information resources and educating clinicians in how to effectively utilize such tools. Determining the relevance of a document or source is solely an individual's perspective, so the library or librarian is not a determining factor in differentiating sources. It would, however, be advantageous for a library to know and have the relevant material available for use. Library users expect their libraries to obtain new electronic resources while simultaneously maintaining or growing traditional print collections until the electronic resources are fully stable. Libraries are expecting to do this with no additional funding. Research has also concluded that information sources like electronic databases are of fundamental importance in a clinical environment giving their direct contribution to decision making in health issues, often making the difference in patient survival. Increasing demand of E-databases can be met with the formation of consortia only, as E-databases are the main feature of consortia these days. Important observation is that these databases have become addiction for the users.

Library Consortia

Information explosion, diversity of user need, financial crunch and impossibility of self-sufficiency has led to the formation of consortia at local, regional, national and international level. A library consortium is an association of a group of libraries to achieve mutually the common objective. Working in an atmosphere, which is fully affected by *Information Communication Technology* (ICT), librarians are mastering the use of electronic resources to better understand and meet the information needs of the users and further train them in using new searching tools for better search.

Consortia provide the following common benefits to the libraries involved:

- Access to otherwise un-subscribed reading materials.
- Scope for electronic archives.
- Getting deep discounts through joint pricing negotiations.
- Developing common resources databases.
- Effective document delivery system.
- Enhanced search facilities
- Better scope for developing a union catalogue among participating libraries.
- By forming consortia, librarians are contributing to the economy of their country by saving Government revenue to a great extent. Following are some of the big and successful consortia's of India.

E-DATABASE

Understanding the user needs play an important role in growing the libraries and librarians; otherwise the library profession may grey in future. To meet the increasing and advanced demands of the user, consortia are playing an important role. Secondly to avail full fruit of consortia a very sincere suggestion to library professionals is to be in touch with whole of the new technology, bridging the libraries through I.T and ICT. One should know the inside out of all the E-databases and involved I.T application.

An E-database is an organized collection of information, of a particular subject or multidisciplinary subject areas; Information within an Edatabase can be searched and retrieved electronically. Edatabase can be full-text or bibliographic. Full-text databases contain the whole content of an article such as citation information, text, illustrations, diagrams and tables. Bibliographic databases contain only citation information of an article, such as author name, journal title and publication date and page numbers. There are many Edatabases and all these databases have various features of searching techniques and tools, which are being used by the librarians to help the users in finding best information in less time.

Some of the popular medical E-databases are mentioned below:

- Academic Search Premier:
  - BMJ
  - MEDLINE
  - OVID
  - PROQUEST
  - PUBMED
  - SCOPUS
  - WEB OF SCIENCE
  - HINARI

Almost all the reputed publishers have come up with the Edatabases like Oxford University Press, American academy of Pediatrics, Cambridge University press and many more. All these e-databases can be considered as the latest technological innovation in the field of information.

6

Quality Management Approaches in Library Services

INTRODUCTION

Having different characteristics, library services require special approaches of quality management that go beyond the simple adoption of manufacturing techniques for a product. Quality management related to library functions can be viewed in three phases: before service, during service, and after service. Library services ultimately focus on satisfying the information needs of customers. Before services are provided, the technical service departments should have required books and information resources collected and value-added to enhance their value to the customers. Therefore, the customer-oriented library should regard technical services as resource development system to ensure that every customer has resources properly acquired, organised, displayed or accessed. Having direct contact with customers, the public services should be regarded as information service delivejry system and focus on providing information to customers accurately, promptly, and responsively to help customers solve problems, and build up customers' knowledge and ultimately enhance their productivity.

Administrative management should be regarded as the service support system to coordinate and allocate resources as well as provide support for technical services and public services to satisfy customers' needs, and to evaluate service performance periodically and to continuously improve service quality. Figure shows the quality management approaches and techniques associated with the stages of service delivery in libraries.

Resource Development System

Largely concerning itself with backstage activities, a resource development system is the off-line preparation for public services and has no direct contact with customers. For services in which the customer need not be present, the service transaction can be de-coupled and standardised. For example, acquisition is considered to be a customised service. Convenient access to Web-accessible public access catalogue, however, has weaned customers from present interaction with live librarians to interaction via online purchase request and, consequently, only routine order preparation and commu-nication is required.

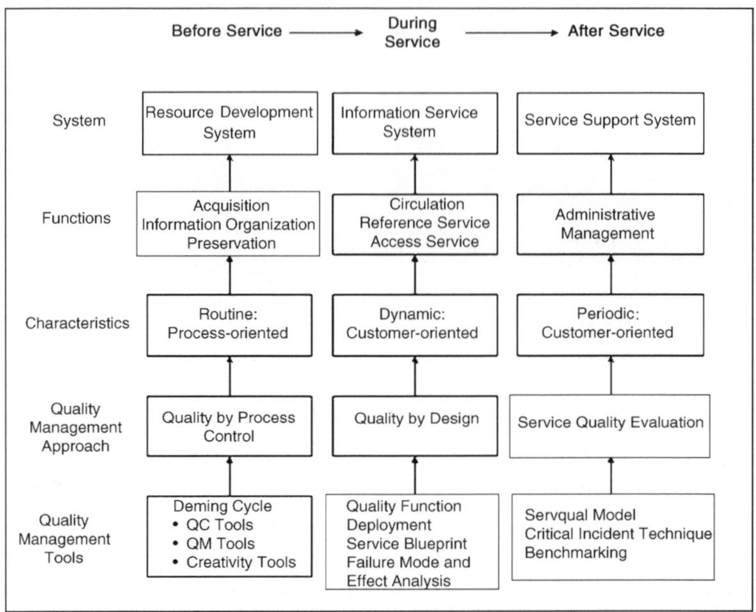

Fig. Framework of Quality Management Approaches in Libraries.

Most activities related to technical services have technical and procedural standards to follow, accounting for why each function is characterised by a high routine and process-orientation.

International or domestic rules govern the cataloguing, classification, and information organisation. In addition, standardised practices also exist for acquisition and preservation, *e.g.* how order requests are to be formulated and transmitted.

In fact, many practices in technical services are standardised by actual work routines and formalised based on a detailed and systematic study during library automation. Therefore, the quality management of a resource development system should emphasise the concurrent control of process to ensure that all books and resources have been accurately collected, accessed and valueadded appropriately. Quality by process control is the best quality management strategy for a resource development system.

Deming's PDSA cycle, together with the seven quality control tools, the seven quality management tools, and the seven creativity tools can be applied in technical services to improve service quality. The PDSA Cycle is focused on satisfying customer needs. This requires an attitude of putting the customer first and a belief that this principle is the object of one's work. Implicit in the

Deming PDSA approach is that improvement in quality results from continuous, incremental turns of the wheel.

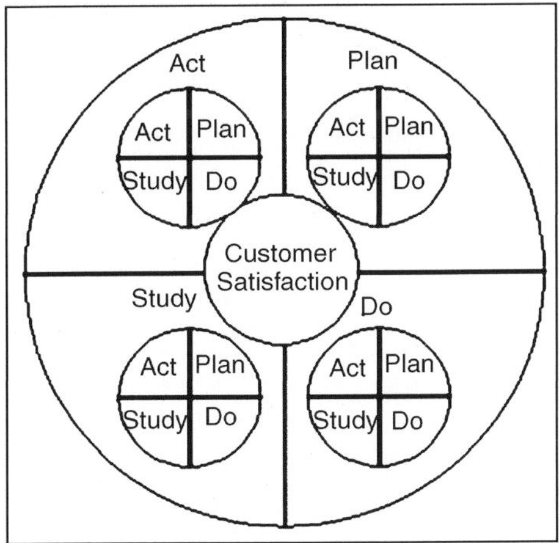

Fig. The Deming Circle

Seven simple tools — cause-and-effect diagrams, run charts, scatter diagrams, flowcharts, Pareto diagrams, histograms and control charts — have been termed the Seven Quality Control. In the early 1970s, as Total Quality Control (TQC) expanded to service and administrative areas, it became clear that the 7QC tools were not always appropriate. So, the seven new QC tools or the seven management tools – affinity diagrams, interrelationship digraphs, tree diagrams, matrix diagrams, prioritisation matrixes, process decision programme charts, and activity network diagrams–were developed under the leadership of Nyatanni. Among these the affinity diagram is a tool for organising language data. After ideas are brainstormed and written on cards, they are grouped together with similar ideas. A header card is created which captures the meaning of each group of ideas. This is a creative, right brain, activity.

The Seven Creativity Tools are problem definition, brainstorming, brainwriting, creative brainstorming, word and picture association, advanced analogies, and the morphological chart. While the original seven QC tools are oriented towards the analysis of quantitative data, the seven management tools and seven creativity tools are designed to handle unstructured, verbal information in group-base problem-solving or decision- making processes. All these tools can be used separately or complementarily. For example, the acquisition department can use control chart to evaluate the performance of dealers, and build partnership with the best dealer.

The serial department can use the cause-and-effect diagram not only to analyse the causes of missing issues but also use relation diagrams to control the order status of critical serials to ensure the completeness and promptness of serials collection. In addition, the Pareto diagram can be used in the cataloguing department to collect the data on bibliographic verification and copy cataloguing for further analysing the feasibility of enhancing productivity and shortening the processing time.

INFORMATION SERVICE SYSTEM

The information service system is a service delivery system that has direct contact with customers. In circulation, access and reference services, the customer often serves as the co-producer and works with the librarians and the library system to produce a final product which enhances knowledge, skills, or promotes the enjoyment of leisure activities. The service encounter is always initiated by the customer. Therefore, the major function of an information service system is dynamic and customer-oriented. Because of direct interaction with public service librarians, customers require the service to be done right the first time and to be consistent every time.

Consequently, quality by design is the best quality management strategy for information service system. Quality management tools that can be applied are quality function deployment, failure mode and effect analysis, and service blueprinting which is specially designed for effectively managing the service encounter. Reference service has direct encounters with customers, and the service quality depends highly on the performance of the reference librarians and their interactions with customers. Therefore, the design of reference service can adopt the techniques of quality function deployment.

Library activists proposed a modified framework of quality function deployment for reference service. There are four phases to facilitate communicating service requirements from the customer to the activities related to quality management of reference service delivery. The first phase is to identify the customer's needs and requirements. The second phase is to define the service requirements and design the co-service system so that the right quality is built in from the very beginning of service design.

The third phase consists of process planning which is a matter of selecting the co-service process "best" producing what the customer needs. Phase four involves the planning of the quality management activities. It emphasizes translating reference processes into quality management activities in order to ensure quality both before and during the reference encounter. The first task of applying QFD to reference services is to identify customer needs, which are descriptions in the customer's own words of the benefits they want the reference services to provide. The opinions posted on the library web site or BBS, customer complaints, records of reference interviews, previous user studies, and so on, will all contribute to the list of customer needs.

In reference services, the primary customer needs might be categorised as "good employees", "right answers" and "nice environment". In order to manage the customer needs, the primary needs need to be structured into a hierarchy. For example, the primary need for "good employee" might be elaborated as "good attitude" and "good skills" in serving customers. And the "good attitude" is subdivided into "kind and polite", "does not have to wait", "assists users in looking up information" and "properly dressed".

Each customer need is, then, to be met in terms of professional terminology – that is, service requirements. For example, the words "kind and polite" express the customer's concept, but librarians need these words translated into their vocabulary in order to actually build a service delivering standards and quality management activities. In delivering reference service, "kind and polite" may be described in terms of the responsiveness, approachability, attentiveness, and courtesy. The service requirements of reference services translated from customer needs might be grouped into answer, process, and environment, using an Affinity Diagram.

For example, the quality of answer might be evaluated according to two perspectives – results and sources. And the quality of source might be evaluated according to the indicators of credibility, acceptability, accessibility and availability. After the service requirements have been identified and prioritised, the most important requirements must be linked to reference process to design the co-service system to satisfy the customer needs.

Circulation and access service is the major contact between the customer and the library, and is usually the starting point for customers to use all other library services. With information networks, most customers can remotely access the webpac or search networked databases. After identifying the availability of certain books or documents, the customer is physically present in the library to check out those books or photocopy the required documents. If the collection or documents needed by the customers are unavailable, the customers can also apply for an interlibrary loan or document delivery service. Encounters between the customer and library are integral and continuous, with each customer possibly encountering many points of services and interacting with varying service facilities and librarians.

Therefore, the circulation and access service should be designed by integrating all of the service points to provide seamless services to customers. The service blueprint is a customer-focused service process analysis tool. Figure gives an example of a typical service blueprint for access service. A service blueprint is a detailed map or a flow chart of the service process. However, creating a flow chart can only depict the workflow of internal operations from the perspective of the librarian.

Such a flow chart neither provides understanding of the interaction between the librarian and the customer; nor can it integrate these encounter points with related activities that support these encounters. Therefore, the concepts of "line of interaction" and "line of visibility" are used in a service blueprint to improve service encounters. Consequently, the service delivery process can be simultaneously viewed from the perspectives of the librarian and the customer. The line of interaction differentiates actions performed by the customer from actions performed by the librarians. Customer actions are placed above the line.

Actions performed by the librarians are located below the line. These actions are charted on the service path proceeding from left to right. Along the line of interaction, the encounter points, *i.e.* the points in the service process where the customer receives the access services, can be easily specified. The line of visibility in a service blueprint distinguishes those processes that are visible to the customer from those that are behind the scenes.

This concept facilitates the understanding of the interconnection between "below-the-line" and "above-the- line" service processes and the recognition that the latter processes where the customers' experiences directly depend on the former processes that customers do not experience.

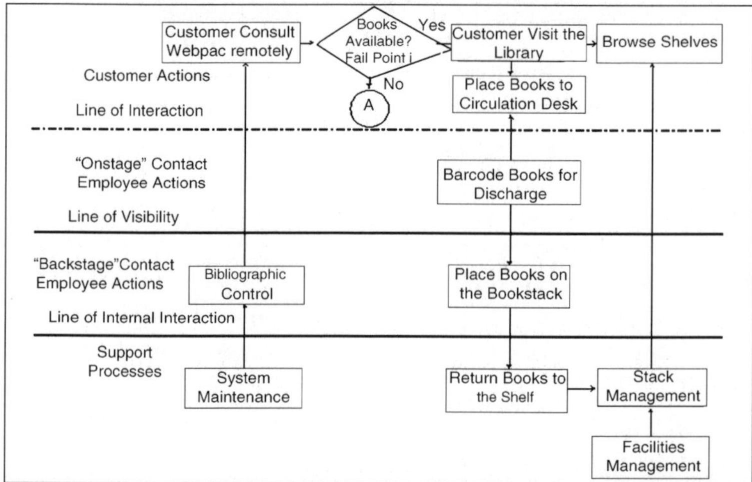

Fig. Framework of Service Blueprint - A Case of Access Service.

The blueprinting exercise also provides librarians with opportunities to identify potential fail points and, then, use the failure mode and effect analysis to design "foolproof" procedures to avoid such an occurrence, thereby ensuring the delivery of high-quality services. The purpose of failure mode and effects analysis is to identify all the ways in which a failure can occur, to estimate the effect and seriousness of the failure, and to recommend corrective design actions. An FMEA usually consists of specifying the following information for each critical component: failure mode, cause of failure, effect on the product or system within which it operates, corrective action, and comments.

SERVICE SUPPORT SYSTEM

The performance of a customer-oriented library should be evaluated on the basis of quality and quantity. Quantitative evaluation in terms of output measure is the basic element of a statistical report, which is mainly prepared for accountability not for improving service. Meanwhile, customer satisfaction significantly contributes to improving service quality. Based on the evaluation results, the service support system should allocate resources to those services that customers deem as having low satisfaction.

In practice, the SERVQUAL model, critical incident techniques and benchmarking can be used to evaluate and improve service quality in library services. Parasuraman, Zeithaml, and Berry developed a multiple-item scale called SERVQUAL for measuring the five dimensions of service quality. A score for the quality of service is calculated by computing the differences between the ratings that customers assign to paired expectation and perception of each of twenty-two statements. This instrument has been designed and validated for use in a variety of service encounters.

In addition, many investigators have adapted the SERVQUAL measures to evaluate the service quality of libraries. Critical incident techniques can be used to analyse the service encounters between the customer and librarians. Customers and employees are interviewed separately to describe their experiences of the service experience. By doing so, the cause of success or failure of the service encounter can be analysed; the critical factors of service encounters can be identified as well.

Correspondingly, staff training and development courses can be designed to enhance the capacity of librarians and library instruction. Moreover, information literacy prog-rammes can be designed to equip the capacity of customers. For every quality dimension, some organisations have earned the reputation of being "best in class" and, thus, a benchmark for comparison. Benchmarking, however, involves more than comparing statistics. It also includes visiting the leading organisation to learn firsthand how such outstanding performance has been achieved.

QUALITY MANAGEMENT APPROACHES

Quality management approaches can be categorised broadly into three stages according to the evolution of management control. Management can implement control before an activity commences, while the activity occurs, or after the activity has been completed. Consequently, three types of control are feedforward, concurrent and feedback. The most desirable type of management control is feedforward control that is future-directed and takes place in advance of the actual activity.

Feedforward control is advantageous because it allows management to prevent anticipated problems rather than having to cure them later and to avoid wasting resources. Concurrent control, as its name implies, takes place while an activity is in progress. When control is enacted while the activity is being performed, management can correct problems before they become too costly.

The most conventional means of control relies on feedback. The feedback control takes place after the activity.

However, a disadvantage of this approach is that the damage will have already occurred by the time that the manager has the information to take corrective actions. Consequently, feedforward control is the most economic approach and can meet the requirement of customers, followed by concurrent control and feedback control, respectively. Interestingly, quality management approaches developed and applied to assess and improve product quality can be related to types of management control from the perspective of an open system. Quality management approaches were originally developed as being product-oriented. Feedback control, an inspection-based quality control approach, was introduced to detect inferior products at the after-production stage. Realising that quality could not be improved by merely inspecting the finished product, subsequent efforts switched the emphasis of quality management from inspection to process control: from feedback control stage to concurrent control stage.

The underlying premise regarding quality in the concurrent control stage is that quality is equivalent to meeting or exceeding customer expectations. Manufacturing products that reflect the diverse needs of customers, is more of a function of good design than of good control of a process. Therefore, quality management has gradually shifted to emphasis on the design phase: from concurrent control stage to feedforward control stage.

Quality by Inspection

The inspection-based system was perhaps the first scientifically designed quality control system to evaluate quality. The system is applied to incoming raw materials and parts for use as inputs for production and/or finished products. Under this system, some quality characteristics are examined, measured and compared with required specifications to assess conformity. Therefore, the inspection-based system is a screening process that merely isolates conforming from non-conforming products without having any direct mechanism to reduce defects. Reducing the damage to final products, sampling plans were developed to control product quality. Although an effective technique, a quality control system based on sampling inspection does not directly achieve customer satisfaction and continuous improvement. Producing fewer defects through process improvement is the only means of reducing defects.

QUALITY BY PROCESS CONTROL

Defects inevitably add to the production cost and waste resources. Therefore, a business strives for zero defects. The quality management system based on sampling inspections has been replaced by the approach of continuously improving the process. This concept, as pioneered by Deming, moves from detecting defects to preventing them and continuing with process improvement to meeting and exceeding customer requirements on a continuous basis. The continuous cycle of process improvement is based on the scientific method for addressing problems, commonly referred to as the Deming cycle.

Deming's approach consists of four basic stages:

- A plan of what to do;
- Do or carry out the plan;
- Study what has done; and
- Act to prevent errors or improve the process.

The planning stage consists of studying the current situation, gathering data, and planning for improvement.

Related activities include:

- Defining the process, its inputs, outputs, customers, and suppliers;
- Understanding customer expectations;
- Identifying problems;
- Testing theories of causes; and
- Developing solutions.

In the do stage, the plan is implemented on a trial basis to evaluate a proposed solution and provide objective data. The study stage determines whether or not the trial plan is working correctly and if any further problems or opportunities are identified. In the final stage, act, the final plan is implemented and the improvements become standardised and implemented continuously. This process then returns to the plan stage for further diagnosis and improvement.

The Deming Cycle can enhance communication between the staff involved and help employees to use the wheel to improve processes. Some of the specific tools used to improve processes are control charts, process capability studies, seven tools, seven new tools, and seven creativity tools. However, the appropriate tools must be applied for the specified purpose. For example, cause-and-effect diagrams and process flow charts could be more appropriate during the planning stage of the Deming wheel, whereas control charts may be most appropriate during the stage of checking.

QUALITY BY DESIGN

The Deming approach shifted the focus of quality management a step back from inspection to process control. The approach of quality by design makes a further step back from process to design. By definition, Quality by design implies that quality must be built in early in the development and design stage. By doing so, the final product can satisfy the customers.

Two important techniques for designing quality products are:

- Quality function deployment (QFD) and
- Failure Mode and Effect Analysis (FMEA).

Quality function deployment is a structured approach that:

- Identifies and ranks the relative importance of customer requirements;

- Identifies design parameters that contribute to the customer requirements;
- Estimates the relationship between design parameters and customer requirements and among different design parameters; and
- Sets target values for the design parameters to best satisfy customer requirements.

A QFD matrix is frequently used to translate prioritised customer requirements into identifiable and measurable product specifications and engineering requirements to reduce functional variation and costs, thereby facilitating the decision-makers in making designrelated decisions. Many investigators have successfully applied QFD in product and service design. Failure Mode and Effect Analysis is a methodical approach to examine a proposed design for possible ways in which failure can occur.

FMEA consists of:

- Identifying and listing modes of failure and the subsequent faults;
- Assessing the probability of these faults;
- Assessing the probability that the faults are detected;
- Assessing the severity of the consequences of the faults;
- Calculating a measure of the risk;
- Ranking the faults on the basis of the risk;
- Attempting to resolve the high-risk problems; and
- Verifying the effectiveness of the action by using a revised measure of risk.

In addition to providing preliminary information on reliability prediction, product and process design, FMEA helps engineers identify potential problems in the product earlier, thereby avoiding costly changes or reworks at later stages. Closely scrutinising quality management reveals that many techniques are based on experience derived from manufac-turing tangible products. Whether or not quality management practices can be transferred to a service industry delivering intangible services has received considerable attention.

Many investigators confer that:

- The service and manufacturing industries differ in terms of the characteristics of quality,
- Different criteria must be used for measuring these industries, and
- The focus of quality management is rather different than similar.

The final manufacturing products can be measured objectively, while the quality can be managed by output control. Meanwhile, the deliverables of services are frequently intangible, which is difficult to measure objectively. In addition to the simultaneously delivery and consumption of services, the quality certainly cannot be managed by either output control or process control. Brophy and Coulling indicated that with the broad applications in the service sector, the sector has come to the recognition that some aspects of quality management must be approached somewhat differently in the service industry.

The most distinguishing characteristic between service and manufacturing industries is that in the former, there is usually a direct interaction between the customer and the service. Libraries and information services have intensive direct interaction and also indirect contact with the customers. Because of the immediacy of the interface, libraries must develop their own framework when integrating quality management approaches into libraries.

MANAGEMENT OF DIGITAL LIBRARY EDUCATION

The concept of digital library has several differing interpretations, derived from different communities involved in digital library research, practice, organization, and commerce. Educational offerings followed these activities.

The major aim of the paper is to present results from a survey on the current state of digital library education in academic institutions. But we also examine the rationale and orientation for digital library education. We suggest several models that have emerged in the teaching of digital libraries and in incorporation of relevant topics into various curricula.

Digital library is a term and concept that serves as an umbrella for a great many of diverse activities. Virtual library, electronic library, library without walls and a few other terms have also been used to carry a similar connotation, but the term 'digital library' seems to be here to stay.

But what does this concept cover? A number of differing interpretations exist, as formulated by sharply different and divided communities that have something to do with digital libraries.

In this paper we are concerned with education for digital libraries. Clearly, the differing interpretations of what is meant by digital library, as well as what topics or activities are covered provide necessary educational context(s) and perspective for choices and orientation from curricula to courses to topics.

The classic educational questions, asked about teaching in all educational areas, are being asked in great many institutions in relation to digital libraries:

- Why teach digital libraries?
- What to teach about digital libraries?
- How to teach about digital libraries?

The first question relates to specification of a rationale to incorporate teaching of digital libraries in a given educational perspective, framework, curriculum, or even course there is much more to a rationale than pragmatically saying: "It is there, thus we teach."

The second question deals with selection of content from a myriad of topics from general to specific that are directly connected with digital libraries and are based on the chosen rationale. The third question gets to choices not necessarily only of pedagogy, but more importantly, of ways and means to incorporate and organize the chosen topics into given curricula, courses, and offerings.

In this paper we explore the three questions in an analytical way and with the 'real world' as a primary source. Our goal is not to be prescriptive. For the question on rationale, we briefly explore the nature and growth of different activities related to digital libraries. Their existence is forcing educational choices.

For the second question, we explore the different conceptions of digital libraries as perceived in different communities. The third question constitutes the bulk of the paper: we provide results of a survey on digital library education from a number of academic institutions, mostly, but not all, from the U.S. Based on results we discuss differing models that have emerged in the teaching of digital libraries.

This is a work in progress. We plan to continue and expand this work with further analyses, covering more institutions, disciplines, and efforts, both nationally and internationally, and present the results in comprehensive reports.

A similar survey was conducted in 1998. This report could be considered as a continuation of that effort.

This is also an outgrowth of interest in teaching and research in digital libraries at our institution, the School of Communication, Information and Library Studies, Rutgers University.

A course Digital Libraries was first offered in the Fall 1998 and continues to be offered. Along with the course, we established D-Lib Edu: Resources for Education in Digital Libraries, a web-based, collaboratively constructed compendium of sources useful for education and study in this area.

Multidisciplinary research in digital libraries at Rutgers University is covered by the Rutgers Distributed Laboratory for Digital Libraries (RDLDL), involving participants from several university departments and schools, as well as others holding seminars on digital libraries covering a wide array of research topics. All of these have contributed to our thinking and work reported here.

Digital library as a concept and a reality

Digital library as a concept and a reality is defined in a number of ways; at times it is even treated as a primitive, undefined concept. In other words, there is no agreed upon definition of digital libraries. We will reflect more about this in the review of definitions in the next section.

In order to develop a rationale for teaching, we interpret digital libraries and all the associated activities in a broad sense as to encompass great many variations on two general themes of:

(i) Organizing and accessing human knowledge records in

(ii) Digital and networked environments.

More often than not, this understanding is an implicit rather than an explicit assumption in the majority of works claiming to deal with digital libraries. The first of the two underlying themes is not new, of course.

Collecting, organizing, preserving, and accessing human knowledge records were themes of many efforts from the dawn of civilizations, across time, cultures, geographic boundaries, and societies.

It is a permanent theme, because the evolution and functioning of any advanced society is connected with creation and use of a societal memory through records. And the first theme was always connected with the second one, reflecting the technology of the time, and thus, the types of implementations over time.

The permanence of these themes and the connection to the new technology is subtly reflected and summarized in the title of a recent book about digital libraries: "From Gutenberg to the Global Information Infrastructure: Access to information in the networked world.".

The assumption is that the new digital technology and networks will affect and even revolutionize the handling of human knowledge records, and through it, the society as a whole, as much, if not more, than the technological invention symbolized under Gutenberg's name. Although it is too early to tell, this seems indeed to be the case.

Given that understanding and the advances in capabilities of digital and network technologies, it is not surprising that digital libraries draw a lot of interest. The history of digital library is short and explosive. A number of early visionaries, such as Licklider, had a notion of libraries in the future being highly innovative and different in structure, processing, and access through heavy applications of technology.

But, besides visionary and futuristic discussions and highly scattered research and developmental experimentation, nothing much happened in the next two decades. By the end of the 1980s, digital libraries (under various names) were barely a part of the landscape of librarianship, information science, or computer science. But just a decade later, by the start of 2000s, research, practical developments, and general interest in digital libraries has exploded globally. What a decade for digital libraries!

Several trends affected this digital library explosion.

- *First,* advanced societies in the Western world kept evolving into a new form variously referred to as information-, knowledge-, or post-industrial society. Managing knowledge records became an ever more important part AND problem of that evolving society, especially since the phenomenon of information explosion, the unabated growth of knowledge records of all kinds, kept accelerating.
- *Second,* the digital and networked technology reached a certain level of maturity and spread rapidly, which provided for more involved, varied, and broader opportunities and problems at the same time.
- *Third,* in most, if not all fields, the nature of scholarly communication changed drastically, creating problems and fueling exploration for new approaches for supporting and sustaining it.

- *Fourth,* substantive funding became available for research and for practical developments and explorations on a variety of solutions to these problems. Digital libraries have been embraced as one (but not the only one) of the more advanced and more encompassing conceptual and practical solutions.

The impetus for explosive growth of activities associated with digital libraries came from two sides: a wide recognition of the enumerated social and technical trends and associated problems, and more importantly, availability of substantial funding to address the problems.

The amount of funding for digital libraries in the last decade is hard to establish, however, it is in the range of several $100 millions internationally. Here are some examples as to highly diverse funding sources, illustrating at the same time a variety of efforts and approaches:

- Funding for research on digital libraries came from a variety of governmental organizations. In the U.S., digital library research is guided and even defined through the projects supported by Digital Library Initiatives (DLI). The Initiatives are funded by a consortium of government agencies under the leadership of the National Science Foundation (NSF). DLI-1 (1994-1998, ~$23 million), funded by three agencies, involved six large projects. DLI-2 (1999-2003, ~$55 million), funded by eight agencies, involves some 60 large and small projects.
- Funding for practical developments from government and organizational sources. A major leader in the U.S. is the Library of Congress through a number of projects, such as the American Memory Project, funded by public and private funds. Many such projects are reflected in the efforts of Digital Library Federation. In the U.K. purpose of funding for the eLib projects is "to stimulate and enable the cost effective exploitation of information systems and to provide a high quality national network infrastructure for the UK higher education and research communities." A number of other European initiatives, most with practical aims, are surveyed by Raitt.
- Funding for operations from academic and public institutions. An example is our own institution, Rutgers University Libraries, which has a long range plan (as do many other universities) for academic digital libraries. Other notable examples are University of California, Berkeley Digital Library SunSITE and Oxford University, U.K. Bodley Library.
- Funding for new implementations in their realm from professional and scientific societies and subject-specific institutes. A society-based example is the Digital Library of the Association for Computing Machinery. A subject-based example is the Perseus Digital Library at Tufts University.

- Funding from publishers to enter the new age of digital publications and access. An example is Elsevier Science which developed an array of resources for digital libraries and funded also exploration of various economic models.
- Funding for putting their treasures in the digital domain from historical societies, archives, and museums. An example is a collaborative effort The Museum Educational Site Licensing project (MESL) at Cornell University (now completed).
- Funding from collaborative contributions to provide for common good in the new Internet tradition of 'free' information. An example is the Virtual Library, (Switzerland, US, UK and other countries)

Clearly, much more funds and efforts have been spent on digital libraries in great many countries and world regions, way above the few examples provided above. The Library of Congress on its web pages provides an impressive set of links to various digital libraries internationally, and so does the journal D-Lib Magazine.

These efforts produced a large number of practical developments, a considerable amount of professional experiences, a number of new practices, a score of new methodologies, many new technology-based applications, considerable research on a number of complex problems, and an evolving body of (as yet widely scattered) scholarly knowledge. All these exist and they provide choices for establishing a rationale for education in digital libraries. But the array of choices is wide.

Unfortunately, education has had little direct or organized connection with any of these rapid and substantive developments. There was little or no funding for education in digital libraries, as related to any of the multitude of the diverse activities. True, a number of research leaders in digital libraries have also been connected with some or other course in digital libraries, but the whole connection is sporadic rather than organized and systematic.

Overall, education is not a leader by any stretch of imagination, but a follower in digital libraries. Mostly, the existing rationale for digital library education, if offered at all, is reactive, meaning that education reacts with a time lag to both research and practical developments in digital libraries.

TEACH ABOUT DIGITAL LIBRARIES

The answer depends, to a large extent, on having a relatively clear idea about what are digital libraries. As mentioned, no agreed upon definition exists, which is fine, because the same constructs can be viewed from a number of viewpoints or perspectives. Let us explore some of these perspectives through definitions offered. Of course, a choice of a given perspective dictates the choice of the content.

Different perspectives about digital libraries, together with competing visions and associated definitions, come from several communities that are involved in digital library work. We are concentrating here on two communities: research and practice.

While they work and proceed independently of each other, they can be considered on two ends of a spectrum, which as yet have not met in the middle. To use another metaphor: the research and practice communities are in the same planetary system, but one is on Mars, the other on Venus.

The research community grounded mostly in computer science, on one end of the spectrum, asks research questions directed towards future vision or visions of digital libraries, or rather of their various technology oriented aspects and components, unrestricted by practice.

On the other end of the spectrum, the practice community, grounded mostly in librarianship and information science, asks developmental, operational, and use questions in real-life economic and institutional contexts, restrictions, and possibilities, concentrating on applications on the use end of the spectrum.

In research, DLIs did not define 'digital library.' In order to incorporate a wide range of possible approaches and domains, the concept is treated broadly and vaguely. Thus, the projects, particularly in DLI-2, cover a wide range of topics, stretching the possible meaning of digital library to and even beyond the limit of what can be considered as being digital and at the same time recognizable as any kind of a library or a part thereof.

This is perfectly acceptable for research frontiers need to be stretched. But at the same time, it makes choices for educational content diffuse and difficult.

The closest to the definition applicable to the approaches taken by the research community is the one given by Lesk in the first textbook on the topic:

- "Digital libraries are *organized collections* of digital information. They combine the *structure and gathering of information*, which libraries and archives have always done, with the *digital representation* that computers have made possible." (Emphasis in this and following definitions is added to illustrate possible choices for educational content).

Arms in a newer text on digital libraries, also from a research community and technology applications perspective, provides what he calls an "informal definition:"

- "A digital library is a *managed collection* of inform-ation, with associated *services*, where the information is *stored in digital formats* and *accessible* over a *network*."

The practice community, whose majority is residing in operational libraries, concentrates on building operational digital libraries, their maintenance and operations, and providing services to users. The approach is developmental, operational, and eminently practical, with relatively little or no research involved.

As a result, hundreds, if not thousands of digital libraries have emerged worldwide, with more becoming operational every day. The efforts are diverse. Many approaches are being used. Many types of collections and media are included and processed in many different ways. Many are located in libraries, creating a hybrid library (combination of a traditional and digital library); others are not bound to brick and mortar libraries at all.

In the US, the Digital Libraries Federation (DLF) (formed in 1995) is an organization of research libraries and various national institutions. The stated goal of DLF is "to establish the conditions necessary for the creation, maintenance, expansion, and preservation of a distributed collection of digital materials accessible to scholars and the wider public." The organization represents libraries and practitioners.

After considerable deliberation, DFL agreed on a "working definition of digital library," representing the definition of the practice community:

- Digital libraries are organizations that provide the resources, including the specialized staff, to select, structure, offer intellectual access to, interpret, distribute, preserve the integrity of, and ensure the persistence over time of collections of digital works so that they are readily and economically available for use by a defined community or set of communities.

Borgman provides a more complex definition (including an extensive discussion) of digital libraries, a definition that may be considered as a bridge between the research community definition and practical community definitions:

- Digital libraries are a set of electronic resources and associated technical capabilities for creating, searching, and using information. They are an extension and enhancement of information storage and retrieval systems that manipulate digital data in any medium The content of digital libraries includes data, [and] metadata Digital libraries are constructed, collected, and organized, by (and for) a community of users, and their functional capabilities support the information needs and uses of that community.

Following these perspectives, the content choices fall into categories that are based on: systems, networks, and technology; collection and resources in various media; representation, organization, and operability; storage and searching; functionality, access and use; institutions and services; and user communities and related applications.

The educational choices are among technology, resources, organization, access, institutions, and use, or a mix thereof. A balanced and at the same time a comprehensive mix is difficult, if not impossible, to achieve.

SURVEY OF APPLICATIONS

In order to go beyond generalities and into observation of existing educational practices we conducted a survey. The survey consisted of two parts:

a *Web survey* of curriculum and course information as posted on the sites of a number of schools and an *Email survey* of answers to invited questions posted on several listserves. We report the results of each survey separately.

Each of the survey methods has strengths and definite limitations. Deriving conclusions about the content of education of given institutions through an examination of information provided on their own Web sites is fraught with peril. It is similar to the well-known peril of examination of catalogs.

However, Web listings are more current and inclusive; they provide, by and large, much more information than catalog listings, up to inclusion of syllabi; and they are updated more often. As a rule, general e-mail surveys have a small rate of self-selected returns.

But the answers tend to be specific to the questions. Both surveys complement each other. The methodology was considered appropriate for a general (rather than detailed) assessment of the emerging approaches to what is taught and how these approaches are positioned in the existing teaching practice.

Web Survey

Method

In the first part we examined the Web sites of 56 accredited programs listed in the directory of the Association of Library and Information Science Education (ALISE) as found on their web site.

The schools housing these programs are generally known as schools of library and information science (LIS), but in reality a good number of them have changed from this designation to several classes of different names. For brevity, we will use the LIS label for the programs.

The accreditation is by the American Library Association (ALA) and covers the professional degree programme on the master's level. It does *not* cover doctoral or undergraduate education, offered by a number of these schools. Geographically, it covers schools in North America the U.S. and Canada. Thus in this part no other countries were included.

We looked at course titles, course descriptions and syllabi when available. In line with the broad definition of digital libraries (or lack of definition) as discussed above, we cast the net widely. We concentrated on courses where *digital libraries* or *digital librarianship* were mentioned as a term, but we also included courses that used synonymous concepts, exemplified by terms such as *electronic library*, or *library of the future*; we also included *virtual museums*, as having a strong connection with digital libraries.

On a broader level, we included courses that mention processes that are closely related to digital libraries, such as management and preservation of electronic records, electronic text design, metadata for digital collections, production of network multimedia, designing accessible web based materials, and electronic text.

Finally, on the broadest level we included courses that are oriented towards *information technology* and address the technological bases of digital libraries, such as *network architecture, managing networks, digital tool kits, Internet applications*, and the like. We used these gradations and distinctions as tools for classification as incorporated in tables below.

Inclusion

Of the 56 LIS programs, 47 (89 per cent) include digital library in some form or another or to some degree in their curriculum; for 5 (9 per cent) programs, this cannot be determined and 4 (7 per cent) programs show no presence of digital library education.

This analysis shows that digital library education is included in the curriculum of most LIS programs. However, the degree of inclusion varies widely.

When considered closely, the inclusion ranges from a full course or courses on digital libraries to metadata standards being covered in organization of information courses to cases in which digital library focus is relegated to continuing education. Participation of the students in a local digital library project is another way of including the digital library topics within LIS education.

Integration

To what degree are digital library courses offered as independent or full-blown courses? To what degree are digital library topics integrated in other courses? Table addresses these questions.

Table. Course Integration in Digital Library Education in ALA-accredited Library and Information Science Programs. (N=47 Programs that Include Digital Library Educationfrom 56 Accredited Programs).

Digital library content in relation to the curriculum	No. of LIS programs
1. Independent DL courses	15 (32%)
2. Combination of independent DL course and DL content integrated in other courses	8 (17%)
3. DL content integrated in other courses (without independent DL courses)	23 (49%)
4. Other (DL content integrated with continuing education)	1 (2%)

Note: Two major types of courses are

- Tndependent digital library courses (typically titled "Digital Libraries" or a similar version), and
- Digital library content integrated in other courses.

As shown in Table, half of the schools have significant digital library content in the curriculum. They include schools with specialized digital library courses on the books; we call these independent courses, although we cannot tell to what degree these are also segregated courses, with little or no connection to the rest of the curriculum.

Such an independent course is either an elective or special topics course offered either as the only course with digital library content in the school's programme or a course offered in addition to other digital library topics that appears elsewhere in the curriculum.

The other half of the schools have some level of digital library content integrated in their programme, but no course specifically focusing on digital libraries. The programs that integrate digital library topics in their courses vary in the level of inclusion and strategies for inclusion.

LIS programs

LIS programs at the masters level are *professional* programs; this defines the context for digital library education in such schools. An examination of digital library course descriptions from Web sites reflects that education for digital librarianship in many cases does not reflect a systematic view or programme of education. Presumably, digital library content is simply an acknowledgment of an emerging field of practice and institutional realities. Even schools with a full course devoted to the problem area of digital libraries show variation in their approaches.

The courses offered under the umbrella term 'digital libraries' range from theoretical and survey courses to project-focused courses. Some are broader and some narrow in focus. A combination of theory (highlighting multiple facets of digital library research) and application (giving an overview of existing practices and providing hands-on experience) seem not to be practiced in such courses.

Weighing one against the other, theory against hands-on experience, it seems that theoretical and survey courses provide a more flexible framework to be expanded with an on-the-job training and apprenticeship in the changing digital library practical environment. An ideal would be the integration of practice-based with survey and theory-based approach to digital library education.

As mentioned, we have been inclusive rather than exclusive in defining what constitutes integrated content. We have considered courses in networking, topics in telecommunications, metadata standards, courses integrating topics on the preservation of electronic-born information as integrating digital library content and digital libraries as developmental form in the history of knowledge records and therefore contributing to digital library education.

In many cases, from brief course descriptions and sparse online syllabi, the degree to which digital library problems were truly addressed is not always clear. In our conservative estimate, in more than half of the schools.

The degree of inclusion cannot be determined with certainty with the methodology used here. The question is whether information technology course addressing the *'library of the future,'* a course dealing with social roles of information organization that includes traditional and digital libraries, archives, network architecture, or the concern with 'structures, processes, dynamics and applications that determine the effective use of motion imagery in multimedia, on-line, and other digital media,' all relate to the problem area of digital libraries.

Together, the approaches represent a pandemonium typical of the general uncertainty towards digital library education. The choices result from an undisciplined mix of the pressures of the libraries as market for graduates, ten years of research and development in the area of digital libraries, and varying degrees of faculty expertise and perceptions of what constitutes a meaningful approach. Multiple and often overlapping approaches in different schools are symptomatic of that general uncertainty.

Because the schedule and frequency of offering is a determinant of impact of specific courses or a mix of courses on digital library education in specific LIS programs, clearly one cannot make sweeping statements. Several schools that integrate digital library content into other courses, or offer courses that do not have digital libraries in their title but focus on the creation of distributed electronic repositories of information, are taking an integrated rather than independent approach.

The "independent" (segregated) vs. "integrated" approach and the "combined independent with integrated" approaches reveal an underlying philosophy of digital library education. Integration is the ideal, but it may suffer from superficiality. Segregation is also fraught with peril of a different sort of offering a view of compartmentalized technology.

A smaller fraction offers a combination of independent and integrated approach to digital library education (17 per cent). There may be a number of reasons for this, one of which may be a reflection of competing perspectives within a given programme. We did not detect that any school has a organized course of study in digital libraries, such as a specialization or track.

E-mail Survey

We also invited e-mail answers to a list of questions posted on several listserves oriented towards audiences as individuals (rather then institutions) in different areas.

They included: listserve JESSE in library science, the member list of the American Society for Information Science and Technology (ASIST), listserve of the Special Interest Group on Information Retrieval, Association for Computing Machinery (ACM SIGIR), listserve of the Humanist Discussion Group, and ETEXT-L.

We sought answers to the following questions:

- Does your institution offer course(s), seminars or institutes in digital libraries and/or related areas? If so, please provide as much information as possible, particularly including URLs.
- Does your institution teach digital library topics within (or as a part of) other courses, seminars, or institutes? If so, please provide as much information as possible, particularly including URLs.
- In what department or school are the digital library course(s) offered?
- On what level undergraduate, graduate, doctoral, professional development?

While the listserves reach great many recipients, we received only a total of 27 responses, of these 20 were relevant. The small number of responses was very disappointing, but then responses to general surveys are always low. We know that in reality there are many more programs and courses related to digital libraries, and that this is but a very small sample. We cannot tell how representative it is. Still it is worthwhile to analyse this sample.

Given the nature of the sample and the size of the returns, about all that could safely be concluded is that there is an interesting and broadening array of disciplines other than LIS in which digital library courses are being taught and such courses are at a variety of levels, undergraduate and graduate.

Digital Libraries Taught

To answer the question on how were digital libraries taught we did not look at pedagogy. Instead, we have looked at broader issues: How did various programs address the basic and connecting areas for digital library education?

What models have emerged? This illuminates the contexts of digital library education within the programs; more specifically it shows area clusters where digital library education has gravitated.

Method

Here we deal only with 47 ALA accredited LIS programs that have presence in digital library education to some degree or other. We undertook a detailed examination of presented curricula, course descriptions, syllabi, and other information as provided.

The level of available information differs greatly from programme to programme, thus our conclusions are only as good as the information available on the programs' Web sites. The analysis is qualitative, with all the strengths and weaknesses of such methods.

In a grounded theory approach, we derived classes from data, and then grouped the data in these classes. Subjective? Of course. But the derivative approach also enables to show clusters in the greater body of data, which are otherwise not visible. To provide consistency, we applied the same analysis criteria to all programs.

Results

We identified several dimensions or models of digital library education emerging in the programs examined. Various approaches that LIS programs are taking in conceptualizing the digital library education, with regard to areas of application. Of the 47 LIS programs that were identified as including digital library education in their programs, six have digital library content contained within a single course, one programme shows digital library content to be integrated across the curriculum; and for six programs we could not determine the area of application.

The derived classification is divided in two classes. The first or general class identifies four broad areas of application, *i.e.,* the general domain of emphasis and orientation for digital library education that could be identified as predominant in a given programme.

These are:

- T-tools (technologies and technology based processes);
- Environments (the context in which digital libraries operate),
- Objects (representation, structure and life cycle of documents in various formats), and
- Combined (several areas of applications present without any one being distinctive).

The second, or specific class, identifies perspectives within the broad areas. It shows a more detailed or specific orientation of programs.

In the perspectives the'basic' and'advanced' tools refer to the level of technological sophistication. The'compartm-entalized' approach is one in which digital library is conceived as a contained phenomenon.

These models show how digital library education is conceptualized and focused within a particular programme. The approaches are not exclusive and many schools combine several of these approaches. We presume that this is either as a result of competing discourses within the schools themselves or because of the uncertainty that the notion of digital library entails.

EXAMPLES

The following schools have been identified as representing the various emerging approaches to digital library education:

University of British Columbia

School of Library, Archival, and Information Studies (Vancouver, British Columbia) combines an approach through digital continuity with tools (multimedia authoring) approach. Although there is no identification of digital library as such, a number of courses deal with metadata standards and include courses which address the status of digitally-born information and the role of digital libraries in managing cultural heritage.

University of California, Los Angeles

Department of Library and Information Science reveals a combination of approaches focusing on tools, administration, standards, and preservation.

Florida State University

School of Information Studies (Tallahassee, FL) reveals (within a compartmentalized approach) an interesting multidisciplinary perspective on digital library design.

University of Illinois

Graduate School of Library and Information Science (Champaign, IL) introduces a combination of museum informatics and more traditional approaches to digital library education, including courses in electronic text creation. Some focus is on content within a museum informatics course and project-oriented coursework.

The information technology is introduced at the undergraduate level, and electronic text design on the graduate level. The focus is on project-based learning and application, accessibility, and electronic publishing. The content and structured text approach is combined with an advanced tools approach.

Kent State University

School of Library and Information Science (Kent, OH) presents an interesting case in that the graduate school offerings and continuing education offering reveal a completely opposite approach.

While the first is a traditional programme, various continuing education topics introducing metadata for digital collections with courses on XML and content management. This is a tools-approach that is segregated into continuing education programme.

University of Michigan

School of Information (Ann Arbor, MI) is by far the most developed programme of study for digital librarianship. It combines practical and skill-based programme with a focus on advanced tools, content, format migration, digital continuity, the digital library as community building agency, and even an emerging theoretical approach that identifies the general laws of infrastructure development with attention to differing national cultural styles of structuring of knowledge. One of the strengths of this programme is that it does not single out one route, such as found in other instances, when it is combined with tools approach. The education for digital libraries combines proficiencies with critical analysis of digital library as cultural form.

The technological proficiency courses are included in the Digital Tool Kit module; advanced proficiencies are included in graduate coursework. In addition, a number of digital library courses explore specialized areas related to digital libraries.

This school is defining the emerging area of digital libraries through its curriculum. An important component of teaching is related to research and development. It may be useful to ask what is not included in this developed programme? The archival aspects are present but not overwhelmingly.

While usability is included in the information infrastructures general course, use and user studies focus is not obvious.

There is no evidence of representational (metadata) aspects of digital libraries but this may be due to the limitation of web site analysis as data collection tool.

The traditional library organizational aspects and issues of access are weak in conceptualizing digital library education at Michigan, in spite of its bursting innovative energy with focus on social informatics.

Université de Montréal (Ude M)

École de bibliothéconomie et des Sciences de l'Information (Montréal, Québec, Canada) is one of the programs that addresses important theoretical aspects in which digital library education is conceptualized through a focus on structured documents which, for example, is lacking in the otherwise strong Michigan approach.

This school includes technological proficiency courses (tools-approach) to continuing education and probably computer science. The strength in document representation, usability of systems for document presentation, and organization of information in general as well as information retrieval is a definite strength in this programme that could serve as a model for development of other programs.

University of North Texas

School of Library and Information Sciences (Denton, TX) is unique in building the concept of digital library from the context of networked environment. One may identify this as syntetico-analytic approach, which does not start with the digital library as an isolated phenomenon but focuses on indirect effects of that phenomenon.

It is invoked as a process of cultural transformation in the social environment of information work which is dependent on technology.

University of Pittsburgh,

School of Information Sciences (Pittsburgh, PA) combines an integrated approach with focus on document structure, digital preservation, and digitizing library and archival research collections for access, as well as introduction to SGML/XML standards, usability studies of digital libraries, and other topics.

University of Rhode Island

Graduate School of Library and Information Studies (Kingston, RI) reveals an interesting attempt to integrate digital library technology through an understanding of media perception and interpreting the emerging environments of the digital libraries in terms of development of new visual media.

This programme presents a departure from tools approach often practiced as a response to market pressures. All programs might not have resources to offer special courses in digital libraries or those that are developing a specialization track (such as Pittsburgh with the focus on the archival aspects) or a full-blown programme like Michigan's.

The approach taken by this school may be narrow in focus, but it also reveals an interesting aspect often neglected in other approaches to digital library education, focusing on visual information.

Rutgers University

Department of Library and Information Science (New Brunswick, NJ) provides access to digital library education through a master's level courses including a regular offering of digital libraries course as one of the central courses within the information systems theme, with specialization courses including organization of information and multimedia production.

Rutgers Distributed Laboratory for Digital Libraries (RDLDL) enables doctoral student participation in university-wide interdisciplinary programme of research. The new undergraduate programme in Information Technology and Informatics will provide a new context for digital library education.

University of California, Berkeley

School of Information Management and Systems provides a model for digital library education closely tied to research and development, especially through its Digital Library seminar series. The LIS programs focus primarily on the interpretation of research and development coming out of the computer science community to fit the LIS discourse.

In many cases, this means repositioning the digital library within established social purposes of LIS programs. Berkeley, while it symbolically repositioned itself outside of these approaches by not seeking ALA accreditation, expands the problems related to digital environments beyond but not excluding the library settings.

In this model, the functioning of a system is a dominant component of the curriculum. The content component is hidden and so are the human agents and digital library as social and cultural agency.

At this point, we may agree with David Levy's statement from his keynote address to the ACM Digital Libraries'99 conference in which he pointed that "the current digital library agenda has largely been set by computer science community and clearly bears the imprint of this community's interests and vision."

In our survey, the focus on tools and information technology that underlies the tools approach identified as the prevailing one among the LIS programs in their approach to integrating digital library content in education shows the traces of this agenda.

Levy identifies the omissions from the agenda of the first decade of digital library research and development in the area of attention to preservation. Related to this is our finding that although an emerging model as seen in Michigan, the University of British Columbia, and Pittsburgh, focuses on various aspects of preservation, there is a relative absence of attention to content.

In LIS programs, the current educational approach for digital library education places it within information technology context. This is not surprising because digital library is easily interpreted to epitomize the promises of technology and progress, an acceptable ideological position in LIS programs.

Integration of digital library education in the context of foundations, knowledge representation, and archives is not surprising either. It is driven by the concerns of research and practice communities. The schools with least developed programs of digital library education (as indicated by the number of courses offered) typically contain this education within information technology or foundations context.

However, there are alternative homes for digital library education with no connection whatsoever with LIS programs. Our e-mail survey provided a glimpse only. They reside in: departments of computer science, medical informatics (Oregon); and at the University of Virginia, in the new Master's Degree in Digital Humanities.

In particular, computer science departments provide a strong educational component through research in digital libraries. Our survey did not reach that area. However the degree of involvement of the computer science community with digital libraries is huge.

We can see that from even a cursory examination of the programs of the First ACM/IEEE-CS Joint Conference on Digital Libraries and the predecessor conferences on Digital Libraries organized separately by the two societies. In hundreds of presentations given at these conferences, overwhelming numbers were from computer science faculty. This must be reflected in educational offerings, formal or informal at their institutions.

Digital library education in the two areas, library and information science on the one hand and computer science on the other, do not have any relation that we can see.

This exactly follows the practice of development and operation of digital libraries in library institutions on the one hand, and the research in digital libraries as funded by programs identified in the section on rationale, on the other hand. While they are in the same planetary system, one is from Venus and the other from Mars.

Now to the'big' picture: The problem of purpose of digital libraries, seen in the communications' circuit of creation, organization, distribution, preservation and use of knowledge records and knowledge itself, needs to be considered in digital library education. This includs an attention to the societal purposes of digitally available information.

If we are to have:

- Collections with "associated services", persistent collections of digital works "readily and economically available for use by a defined community or set of communities"(cf. definition of Digital Libraries Federation (DLF)), or collections "constructed, collected and organized, by (and for) a community of users,"and functional capabilities of digital libraries to "support the information needs and uses of that community", then digital library education needs to spend more time on understanding the collections, usability of current digital libraries, and their social and cultural purposes.

As yet, library education does not really deal with the questions such as:

- What is the digital library made for?
- What is the meaning of collection in a digital library context?
- What issues are faced in access? How are digital libraries used?
- Should and could be used?
- How are they evaluated?
- What are the effects on the communities of users and their tasks?

Or "Digital Rights Management:

- What Does This Mean For Libraries?

"(This is the title of the keynote address at the Digital Libraries conference by Pamela Samuelson, Professor of Information Management and of Law, UC Berkeley). These issues are above and beyond the technology and they need to be included in education in some detail. We suggest that digital library education does require integrated and comprehensive programs and attention of its own.

If we accept Levy's assessment, research and development community and those involved in the education for digital libraries suffer from the same lack of purpose. Moreover, it might be expected that as the field develops, that there will be less compartmentalization and more integration of all approaches with what we have identified here as tools approach. The educational needs differ significantly from education for library and information science proper or computer science proper.

Education for digital libraries is a complex proposition, in part because it involves so many layers of technology and at the same time so much that is new in creation, content, representation, organization, access, and use, and in social, legal, and cultural issues. The importance of paying attention to digital library education lies in this: as all other areas, the quality of education will eventually determine the quality of the whole enterprise.

MANAGING LIBRARY TECHNOLOGY: PLANNING FOR THE FUTURE

Whether public, private, or corporate, libraries are experiencing rapid changes as technology increasingly permeates their methodology and functionality. These technological changes affect all levels of librarianship, and management of new library resources and new expectations of staff must adapt accordingly.

As suggested, discuss management of resources and staff in today's fluctuating technological environment. In the first part, as suggested, use a systems development model to organize the discussion of resource management. In the second part, as suggested, turn our attention to issues that arise in the intersection between staff and technology by focusing on barriers to learning, online learning alternatives, and changes in staff development practices.

MANAGING RESOURCES

Librarians may be called upon to manage public and staff hardware, software, networks, digital products such as commercially owned databases and other online services, and output such as web sites and social networking. In short, managing library technology may initially feel like herding cats.

Fortunately, several frameworks exist for organizing technology management. The work system life cycle, suggested by S. Alter is an example of such a framework. However, it should be noted that there are many other methodologies used by systems analysts, developers, and project managers that are equally adaptable to library technology purposes.

Alter's model is cyclical – it begins with initiation, followed by development, implementation, and operation and maintenance. During the operation and maintenance phase, if a given resource no longer adequately meets the needs of the institution, the cycle moves back into initiation, and the process begins again.

PHASE I: INITIATION - MAKING A PLAN

Alter describes initiation as an evaluation of goals, scope, and resources. For libraries, initiation begins with the drafting of a technology plan. Rachel Gordon writes, "since technology is now so tightly interwoven with all library functions, planning for the future of technology means planning for the future of the library itself". A good technology plan includes the following: a vision statement, background, goals and objectives, funding, training, and evaluation. Technology advances rapidly, and the key to crafting a good technology plan lies in forming objectives and goals that will not only withstand the onslaught of new products and services, but will also allow librarians to make decisions based on the library's needs rather than the perceived popularity of new services.

At this stage, in addition to clearly defined institutional goals, it is necessary to evaluate existing resources, both technological and financial. Evans, Ward, and Rugaas observed that the life span of technology is growing increasingly short, while library budgets are not accommodating the necessary expenditures needed to keep pace. They suggest a rolling budget to accommodate necessary upgrades, migration, support and training. M. Breeding mentions trends towards open source software and shared resources within library consortia as possible means of working with limited budgets.

PHASE II: DEVELOPMENT - FINDING/CREATING THE RIGHT RESOURCES

In Alter's model, development encompasses purchasing, licensing, and design of systems, as well as the research necessary to carry out each process. Librarians must make wise purchasing decisions regarding hardware, and must take into consideration the hidden costs lurking in maintenance, support, and staff training. Furthermore, most software and many digital services are provided not through purchasing, but instead through licensing. A license to use a product must be understood and negotiated by the librarian in order to ensure that the product fulfills the library's goals. In addition to cost, librarians must pay careful attention to patron privacy considerations when negotiating contracts with vendors. Librarians designing web sites or social services, such as Facebook profiles and Twitter feeds, must follow a similar evaluation process, as they must design these services for patron usability. Particularly with library web site design, standards compliance, privacy, and security must also be considered.

PHASE III: IMPLEMENTATION - PUTTING TECHNOLOGY TO WORK

During the implementation stage, librarians work to ensure that all goes smoothly through adequate testing and consistent deployment, whether they are rolling out a new web site, a new ILS, new software, or new hardware. Librarians will need to be prepared for the headaches caused by data migration, resistance from both staff and users to new interfaces, and lengthy time commitments. The importance of adequate testing and familiarization with a new technology cannot be stressed enough.

PHASE IV: OPERATION AND MAINTENANCE - KEEPING OUR HEADS ABOVE THE WATER

Operation and maintenance is a critical stage of technology management; if this area is neglected, previous planning, research, and testing is worthless.

Critical issues in this phase include security, upkeep, support, and evaluation.

Culp writes, "eternal vigilance is the price of security". Virus scans, testing, and continuing attention to developments in the nefarious world of security attacks is necessary to maintain a safe technological environment for both patrons and staff. This extends to public and staff machines, as well as stored patron and staff records. In addition to security, routine maintenance can greatly extend technology's lifespan. Basic tasks such as cleaning keyboards, defragmenting hard drives, changing printer cartridges, and downloading software updates should be performed by library staff, if at all possible.

When maintenance issues go beyond the reach of a librarian, the institution must have a tech support plan in place. Libraries rely on a variety of tech support systems. Bertot identifies seven broad categories of tech support: no tech support, internal library support without technology staff, internal library support with technology staff, library consortia, technology partners, city county or other agency IT support, and state library support. Regardless of a library's tech support plan, it is vital that all staff understand the procedures for troubleshooting and reporting problems.

Of course, during the operation and maintenance phase, it is important to constantly evaluate each piece of library technology in terms of its adherence to the library's goals. If it should fail that evaluation, then the librarian must move into the initiation phase and start again by planning upgrades or even entirely new systems.

MANAGING STAFF DEVELOPMENT

There can be no doubt that the need for professional development, continuing education, or workplace learning in regard to technology is vital for today's libraries. Never before have the profession's tools undergone such extreme and rapid transformations, and these transformations are not about to cease, as illustrated in the various thesis compiled in Core *Technology Competencies for Librarians and Library Staff*. It is, therefore, incumbent upon library administration to develop, implement, encourage, and support policies on staff competency and development. It is, also, necessary for both professional librarians and paraprofessionals to—at the very least— be proficient in the current trends of technology, if not embracing the changes by keeping pace with them. In short, with a little innovative leadership, learning options are endless, as well as accessible, user-friendly, and exciting.

BARRIERS TO LEARNING

The "graying" of today's library is perhaps the most cited obstacle for staff development in technology. Long and Applegate, for instance, provide statistical data that reveals the willingness to learn of library staff according to their generation. Many professional librarians who received their degrees prior to 1995, or before the study of computers in Library Science programmes in the

United States, understand the importance of keeping up with technology, yet a surprisingly large percentage of support staff is unwilling to adapt to the technical changes or to explore the possibilities that new technology brings.

Time constraints are another barrier to staff development. Workers who are given the time to develop skills are more apt to do so. However, many employees say there is little time to complete their usual tasks, much less learn new skills, regardless of whether employers allow the time for it. One thing is clear and that is that management needs to understand their employee's learning needs, as a number of investigations note the lack of managerial support in staff development. In fact, even professionals must often be self-motivated and seek out learning opportunities on their own.

E-LEARNING, WEBINARS, AND LEARNING 2.0

E-Learning, or learning delivered through electronic tools, is clearly the most popular form of staff development today. Both professionals and paraprofessionals may choose from a myriad of sources for such learning. Among the many options are webinars from WebJunction, OCLC, EbscoHost, and Gale Cengage Learning, to name a few. However, Learning 2.0 has not only gained considerable attention, but it has also been implemented, studied, and documented, thereby, raising its stature and effectiveness.

Developed by Helen Blowers and based on Web 2.0 technology, Learning 2.0 is an incentive-based model programme for training library staff in new technologies. Students, who are self-directed, are asked to complete "23 Things," or online interactive projects on, for example, RSS feeds, flickr, wikis, podcasts, and LibraryThing.

Kingsley and Jensen's paper on Learning 2.0's implementation at the University of Alaska Fairbanks Rasmuson Library stands as the most comprehensive study to date of the freely shared model, illustrating the programmes success rate and offering some concluding recommendations, such as making staff development mandatory.

ADMINISTRATION AND STAFF DEVELOPMENT

Not only are the tools with which library staff work changing, but so, too, are the philosophies and practices of management, especially in regard to staff competency and development. Mosley and Kaspar describe the challenges of hiring and retaining competent employees that can meet the ever-changing demands of library service. They suggest that management needs to look to the future by reconsidering job descriptions and job postings by avoiding the use of traditional library wording.

Management also must consider incentives when encouraging staff development. Incentives, such as the MP3s, PDAs, and laptops offered by Blower's pilot Learning 2.0 programme at the Public Library of Charlotte and

Mecklenburg County, are not always possible, especially in the current economy. However, there are other methods of motivation. For instance, the University of Arizona Library restructured their monetary compensation, or wage, plans, which were based upon a traditional hierarchical scale. Their innovative and team-based "pay-for-skill" programme rewards employees for developing advanced capabilities, along with the willingness to learn and take on more responsibility.

7

Management in Library Information Service

While forecasting the next must-have library information service can be difficult, it is likely that the service will be available in the cloud. Library IT vendors more frequently offer hosting options along software and are developing new systems that leverage cloud architecture to share data and make adoption and management easier for libraries. In addition, open source projects such as DuraCloud and Omeka are using cloud computing to facilitate adoption and generate income. This means that libraries have new choices to make when selecting information services but also means that they must evaluate IT platforms as well as information services. This stage explores some of the criteria that libraries can use to make these decisions and examines the long term implications of the cloud-computing trend.

WHERE SHOULD LIBRARIES FOCUS THEIR IT RESOURCES

With an understanding of these four factors (cost, expertise/capacity, service quality and policy/legal) libraries can make better informed decions about their IT environments. Libraries operate in a complex information environment comprised of multiple information systems and guided by professional ethics including an interest in ensuring free, open and ethical use of information.

Cloud computing provides both an opportunity and a challenge for libraries seeking to hold onto these principles as they adopt new information systems. It is increasingly common to find software vendors and open source software developers that offer systems on hosted platforms. DuraCloud, Equinox and Omeka are just a few examples of open source software offered by non-profit and commercial hosting organisations that also engage in software development. Many commercial developers offer some form of hosted or cloud-based service as well.

This approach has been successful in growing the market for co-operative library services in the US. For example, the Georgia Pines Library system that led the creation of Evergreen not only succeeded in migrating its branch libraries to a new single-ILS platform, it also led the way for other states seeking the opportunities for data sharing and economies of scale. This is good news for open source projects seeking to find long term viability. A recent Ithaka research report discussed the difficulties associated with finding ongoing support for open source projects including new projects, shifting priorities and lagging community involvement. By leveraging cloud-computing hosting, some open source projects are both expanding their community of adopters and benefiting from a revenue stream to enable ongoing development.

My research on cloud computing adoption in libraries showed that it was more common for libraries who had turned to cloud computing to have turned to a SaaS as opposed to PaaS or IaaS platforms. SaaS solutions also pose a long-term challenge for libraries by eliminating local capacity and expertise and ultimately impacting the ability to migrate to new systems. In contrast, PaaS and IaaS solutions provide libraries with tools that level the playing field by preserving local expertise and expanding capacity. Unfortunately, it can be rather difficult, if not impossible, to implement many current commercial and open source systems in a PaaS or IaaS environment.

Many open source and commercial products operate on very specific IT stacks. Although PaaS providers, including Heroku, Cloud Foundry and Google Apps Engine are expanding support for different programming languages and database platforms, library applications have not been developed using these frameworks or deployment techniques. This means that the redundancy, replication and backup features that come with PaaS platforms is out of reach of libraries who either must rely on a vendor-provided SaaS approach or turn to local or IaaS solutions.

Further complicating the situation is the difficulty inherent in migrating to new platforms for libraries using SaaS or IaaS solutions. While PaaS providers may not always support easy migration, by focusing on building applications using industry standard frameworks, vendors and open source communities could make migration more realistic. Unfortunately, few if any commercial or open source library systems operate in these environments. This limits the range of IT solutions available to libraries and can push libraries towards either largely localised or outsourced options.

While cloud computing offers new opportunities for large and small libraries, it also raises the stakes on information service selection. Libraries are increasingly moving towards network-based data and more complex information services. At the same time they are grappling with constrained resources and a new range of IT platforms. In selecting an information system and IT platform, it is important that libraries choose solutions that improve service while also ensuring that their choices are good for the long-term.

FACTORS THAT INFLUENCE IT ADOPTION

The choice to adopt a particular IT service depends on a number of organisational, technical, and community factors. Differences in funding sources,

IT staff expertise, information service needs and policy and legal issues means that there is no one right solution for libraries exploring whether or not to adopt cloud-based IT services. Before we consider the longer-term implications of cloud computing adoption we will consider each of these factors.

COST

Ongoing service cost and requirements of funding sources can be a major barrier to cloud adoption. Many IT organisations are focused on a capital or one-time investment model for technology assets. On the other hand, libraries have a background with subscription-based financial models and may feel more comfortable with lower capital but higher ongoing costs than their IT department counterparts. A way to understand the differences in cost is to complete a high-level return on investment (ROI) analysis comparing the differences between cloud and local IT services.

Reese provides an overview of how to compare ROI on cloud and local IT services including start-up vs ongoing costs, staffing/support costs and direct service vs required infrastructure costs. He suggests comparing cloud and local approaches based on your organisation's capital depreciation schedule to better understand the long term costs. While this enables an apples-to-apples comparison it also masks some of the advantages that cloud platforms offers in service flexibility and scalability.

EXPERTISE

Having a strong understanding of local IT staff expertise and capacity is particularly important when selecting an IT infrastructure. Capacity can be defined as the ability of an IT department to provide technology and staffing resources to ensure quality service. In contrast, expertise can be defined as the technical ability of staff to support a service. While these two factors are often directly correlated (*e.g.* an increase in expertise results in an increase in capacity) this is not necessarily the case. In my own research many libraries cited expertise as either a motivating factor (*e.g.* lack of local organisational IT capacity motivated the library to seek external support) or an inhibiting factor (*e.g.* lack of internal IT expertise limited which cloud solutions were explored).

Expertise and capacity in your organisation can be difficult to quantify but tools such as a time-allocation analysis or skill survey may be useful. If your IT staff's skills typically do not include server or datacentre management skills, then infrastructure as a service (IaaS) based cloud solutions are not likely to be successful. If, in contrast, your IT staff has considerable expertise in software development and tweaking, then platform as a service (PaaS) will provide them tools that may expand their service support capacity.

Defining capacity and current workload can be difficult, but at the least should include understanding your staff's recurring tasks and ongoing workload.

Scholars explore capacity planning from a staffing perspective in depth in their chapter on Organisational Structures and discuss tasks including service deployment, ongoing management, end-user support and service decommissioning.

SERVICE QUALITY

Service quality is often where libraries begin their exploration of a new application. Service improvements may include new discovery features, better mobile accessibility, or wider research resources. In deciding whether or not an IT service will be of higher quality in a local or cloud-based platform depends in part on how the data being provided in the service can be managed locally over time.

For example some information services depend on rapidly changing data that can only be managed via an outsourced subscription (*e.g.* OpenURL resolvers and journal subscription services).

Because many library services feature large data repositories there are a number of services including journal databases, resource linking applications and 24/7 research support services that are often only available as a cloud-based or at least externally supported service.

In these cases, the ability of the vendor to update the database is an important consideration that may sway libraries towards a SaaS versus a locally implemented approach. Other systems, such as digital library applications, integrated library systems, research support and web site services, however, may be influenced more by other factors including expected uptime and reliability, speed and interoperability. Understanding these issues and how they relate to capacity and skill issues can help libraries understand the essential elements of what will make a service successful.

POLICY AND LEGAL FACTORS

Organisational policy and legal factors should be one of the first areas to explore when considering cloud-based services. Understanding the implications of privacy and accessibility laws on information services and having an appreciation of organisational policy can save time by eliminating solutions that are a poor fit. In addition to speaking with organisation experts about service regulations it is important to evaluate Service Level Agreements (SLAs) of cloud providers to ensure that their services are in compliance. When exploring SaaS providers it is also important to understand which cloud platforms these providers are using to provide their services.

While it is important to be aware of these issues, it is equally important to not get bogged down in them when exploring potential IT solutions. Low risk or low sensitivity services may be entirely appropriate for cloud platforms that do not provide bulletproof SLA agreements while services that have private data or management requirements are best in locally managed environments.

RESOURCES FOR WEB BASED LIBRARY SERVICES

Today, users may have access a variety of textual information resources. There are different kinds of webbased reference resources and services for accessing information from libraries such as OPAC, Gateways, Portals, Subject Portals, Electronic Journals, Online Databases, Subject Directories and Search Engines. These resources overlap considerably in the type of information they cover, and sometimes it is difficult to distinguish between some of them. A library should have a good collection of these resources like selected Web links, subscription resources, and library materials in well-organised pages for serving better services to their users.

Many libraries and organisations are providing digital reference service through collaborative services. Existing library consortia are adding digital reference to current shared services, and networks of libraries. Some regional library consortia are offering member libraries the opportunity to share reference questions with each other using the Internet and other technologies.

OPAC

OPAS's - On Line Public Access Catalogues, form an important part of many digital library's collections. It allows users to search for the bibliographic records contained within a library's collections. Now days, some OPAC also provide access to electronic resources and databases, in addition to the traditional bibliographic records.

GATEWAYS

A gateway is defined as a facility that allows easier access to network based resources in a given subject area. Gateways provide a simple search facility and a much-enhanced service through a resource database and indexes, which can be searched through a web based interface. Information provided by gateways is catalogued by hand. Gateways cover a wide range of subjects, through some areas, such as music and religious studies, currently lack subject gateways. Some well-known gateways are as follows:

- Internet Public Library (IPL),
- Bulletin Board for Libraries (BUBL),
- National Information Services and Systems (NISS),

PORTALS

In the library community, portals may be defined as an amalgamation of services to the users where the amalgamation is achieved through seamless integration of existing services by using binding agents such as customisation and authentication services, search protocols such as Z39.50, loan protocols such as ISO10161, and e-commerce.

The result is a personalised service which allows the individual to access the rich content of both print-based and electronic systems. Portals are either commercial or free web facilities that offer information services to a specific audience. The facilities include web search to communication to e-mail to news ,etc.There are three kinds of portals; Consumer (or horizontal), Vertical and Enterprise.

- Consumer portals are aimed at consumer audiences and offer free e-mail, games, chat ,etc., Examples are Yahoo!, MSN and AOL.
- Vertical portals, target a specified audience, such as a particular industry, and offer many of the consumer portal features. Example includes VerticalNet.
- Enterprise portals on the other hand are similar to consumer portals, but they are offered only to corporations or similar organisations. Examples include Epicentric and Corporate Yahoo! These portals can be best understood as electronic pathfinders for users, pulling together in one place in a web site selected links to subjects or interest-oriented resources located on the WWW.

SUBJECT PORTALS

Web Search Engines had been developed initially by computer scientists, by borrowing techniques from information retrieval search such as best match searching and relevance ranking. Information professional are increasing bringing their skills to help organise the growing wealth of Internet resources.

A good example of their influence is the development of subject-specific web search engines known as subject portals, where evaluation of material covered is a major concern. Two prime UK subject portals are SOSIG Social Science Information Gateway, covering social science resources and OMNI Organising medical networked information covering medical resources. Subject portal sites can be very helpful, but they should be used with care. Users should bear the following points in their mind:

- The aim of the subject portal is to list and review the most important sites on the web relevant to that subject. The sites are usually constantly peer-reviewed to ensure that the site is relevant and up to date.
- New sites are appearing all the time. Relying on a subject portal site to find everything users require may mean that they miss an important site that has recently appeared and has not yet been reviewed by the producers of the particular subject portal.
- A subject portal is a one stop shop for information on the topic it covers. Users don't have to carry out extensive Internet searches in order to find the information require. They can simply go to the required subject portal site.

- Subject portals save users having to have long lists of bookmarks (saved addresses of web pages), which are often, cumbersome and time consuming to arrange and keep up to date. However, if users do prefer to use bookmarks they can arrange them in an order to suit the way they work and not have an order forced on them by the subject portal.
- A subject portal site is only as good as the reviewers who peer-review the site listed. The reviewers need to have a policy of keeping the portal sites up to date and of constantly reviewing the sites they list, to make sure that they are still relevant and still contain good, timely information.
- A subject portal may be available to everyone who needs to use it to only certain groups of users. A good portal should be publicly available to anyone who needs it.

ELECTRONIC JOURNALS

Electronic journals form a large part of the collection of a library for providing web based services. Today many journals are available electronically - some are full text and some contain only bibliographic information with abstract. Major advantage of electronic journals is that they are constantly updated and easy to access but disadvantage is that breaching of copyright law is very easy.

They are available as bitmaps, PostScript, PDF, ASCII, SGML and HTML. Library services may be delivering to users on CDRom, through e-mail or through web. Some international societies and associations have developed their own digital libraries through which users can get access to all their publications. Services are available to the members of society or associations through subscription.

ONLINE DATABASES

These are large collections of machine-readable data that are maintained by commercial agencies and are accessed through communication lines. Many libraries subscribe to them for easy access and use of current information. The disadvantage is that only bibliographic data is presented and not full text. The information cannot be accessed when the system is down for any reason. Examples Ei Compendex, SciFinder Scholar, Web of Science, Current Contents ,etc.

SEARCH ENGINES

Search Engines are huge databases of web page files that have been assembled automatically by machines where as the subject directories are human-compiled and maintained. Search engine indexes every page of a Web site and subject directories linked only homepages.

Search Engine is the popular term for an information retrieval (IR) system. A search engine is computer software that searches a collection of electronic materials to retrieve citations, documents, or information that matches or answers a user's query. The retrieved materials may be text documents, facts that have been extracted from text, images, or sounds. A query is a question phrased so that it can be interpreted properly by search engine. Depending on the type of software, it may be a collection of commands, a statement in either full or partial sentences, one or more keywords, or in the case of Non-text searching, an image or sequence of sounds to be matched.

SUBJECT DIRECTORIES

Subject directories differ from search engines in that search engines are populated by robots that finds and index sites whereas humans making editorial decisions that populate subject directories. Subject directories are basically index home pages of sites and can be classified as general, academic, commercial or portal. Among the well known subject directories are the Argus Clearinghouse and Yahoo. Strengths include relevance, effectiveness and relative high quality of content. Weaknesses are that they lack depth in their coverage of the subjects.

LIBRARY SERVICES: CHALLENGES AND OPPORTUNITIES

The provision of appropriate and meaningful reference and instructional services to e-learners is fraught with both challenges and opportunities.

E-learners require more than access to e-resources. Traditionally, a reference librarian acts as an additional resource, someone who can be counted upon to provide expertise in making sense of library systems and research tools, and to offer a helping hand along that often slippery path known as the research process.

Virtual library users face additional challenges in mining relevant information out of a computer system that "obstinately" returns zero hits in response to a query that does not match the character strings in its database files.

The most common means of providing electronic reference services to remote users has been e-mail, the advantages and disadvantages of which have been well documented in the literature. The around-the-clock and around-the-world accessibility of e-mail enables e-learners to connect with librarians beyond the walls of library buildings and outside the usual hours of operation.

E-mail provides a written record of requests and responses, permits the electronic transmission of search results, and allows librarians time to reflect on requests. One of the most serious concerns about e-mail reference services is their impact on traditional face-to-face reference interviews, particularly the absence of verbal and non-verbal cues, which typically assist a librarian in effectively responding to a question.

A well designed reference web form, such as that provided on the Athabasca University Library's "Ask about a Research Topic" web page, encourages e-learners to include full identifying and course information.

This web page encourages users to clearly describe their research problem and search terminology, and to state the parameters of their assignment. The feature also clarifies requests for librarians and reduces the need for e-mail. Automated e-mail replies sent out in response to the receipt of a message reassure e-learners that their messages have been received and lets them know what to expect in terms of service.

E-mail reference service can be enhanced and supplemented with additional technologies that raise the level of interaction via real-time communication. Chat technology allows e-learners and librarians to send text messages back and forth instantly, using a form of communication that is familiar to most Internet users.

A number of issues surround the use of chat in the provision of reference services to remote users. Choosing the appropriate programme for the library's specific needs and resources is essential if the virtual reference initiative is to be successful.

Available programs range from vendor-based systems that offer features such as "co-browsing, patron queuing, sharing files, and the ability to keep more extensive statistics", to instant messaging programs, which are freely available. Some chat programs require downloads on the part of users, which can be problematic and may also discourage e-learners from using the service.

In an effort to reach more e-learners, some libraries have begun using instant messaging programs such as AOL's *AIM* product, MSN's *Messenger*, and *Yahoo! Messenger*, primarily because many e-learners are already using these systems.

More recently, libraries have begun experimenting with programs such as *Trillian* and *Pidgin,* which log into a number of instant messaging accounts simultaneously and allow librarians the flexibility to respond to instant messaging questions coming into the library, no matter which system the e-learner is using.

This reduces the need to monitor several different instant messaging programs at the same time. Virtual reference consortia have the potential to expand the library's abilities to serve its community of users effectively.

Libraries in the consortia answer questions from e-learners in other parts of the consortium service area. Traditionally, chat reference services are only available during specified hours, so virtual reference consortia are beneficial for e-learners in different time zones than their home institution, because they increase the likelihood of a librarian being available to answer questions immediately.

Even if the initial reference transaction is received through chat, however, it may ultimately prove difficult to provide a complete answer using this method. If a user requires assistance in learning how to use a particular library resource, it may be possible to provide a complete response via chat.

However, if the user is requesting assistance to find information on a complex topic, the librarian may need time to determine appropriate search strategies before responding. In these cases, the follow-up response is often done by e-mail. Providing e-learners with a toll-free telephone number remains an effective and convenient reference services strategy, particularly for intricate inquiries. The telephone reference interview works best when both librarian and e-learner are working in front of computers connected to the Internet.

Instruction

E-learners are frequently silent and invisible as they search and explore a library's online resources, and they do not have the same access that oncampus learners have to formal library instruction sessions.

With the array of digital resources available to them, the many different interfaces and search tools, and the need for evaluation and critical thinking when using the Internet for research, information literacy skills are essential. Information literacy has been defined in relation to competencies, with information sources in a variety of formats. According to the Association of College and Research Libraries, an information-literate student

- Determines the nature and extent of the information needed.
- Accesses needed information effectively and efficiently.
- Evaluates information and its sources critically and incorporates selected information into his or her knowledge base and value system.
- Individually, or as a member of a group, uses information effectively to accomplish a specific purpose.
- Understands many of the economic, legal, and social issues surrounding the use of information, and accesses and uses information ethically and legally. Supporting the integration of information literacy skills training into the core curriculum has become an important issue for libraries.

A discussion is also emerging around the need to promote critical reflection in relation to information and knowledge, to conceptualize a *critical information literacy* that goes beyond a focus on competencies.

Critical information literacy draws on scholarship in critical theory and critical education to provide librarians with a theoretical framework that acknowledges their responsibility to help students see that knowledge is not neutral but socially constructed and contested.

Teaching the value of incorporating peer-reviewed journals in research papers, for example, need not preclude a discussion about how alternative voices may be silenced by the peer-review process and how to find alternative literature.

As an extension of their traditional role in providing library instruction sessions and developing instructional materials, librarians design online tutorials and courses that promote information literacy and encourage active learning. Particularly fine examples are the University of Texas System Digital Library's TILT – Texas Information Literacy Tutorial; and Utah Academic Library Consortium's Internet Navigator, a multi-institutional online course developed by a team of librarians and web developers.

The Open University Library created SAFARI, a freely available interactive tutorial, as well as an information literacy course called Making Sense of Information in the Connected Age or, more commonly, MOSAIC. Athabasca University offers the undergraduate course, Information Systems 200: Accessing Information. Many libraries provide instruction to e-learners by making information available on their web pages, including research guides and "how-to" pages. for example, Athabasca University Library's Help Centre.

An awareness of the importance of context-specific help has grown and it is quite common to find links to tutorials at the point of need. Software packages for developing animated tutorials, such as ViewletBuilder, Camtasia, and Captivate enable librarians to demonstrate effective database searching techniques asynchronously.

Brief tutorials that incorporate voice-over and demo-nstrate database features within the context of real searches are particularly effective. Joining an existing, collaborative initiative reduces workload and removes the need to "reinvent the wheel." The Council of Prairie and Pacific University Libraries (COPPUL), a consortium of twenty university libraries located in Manitoba, Saskatchewan, Alberta, and British Columbia, is responsible for the *Animated Tutorial Sharing Project* (*ANTS*).

Participating libraries, including libraries outside of COPPUL, access a wiki where they can adapt databases for tutorial development, upload tutorials, and download tutorials developed by other libraries. Online tutorials usually operate on a model in which the e-learner interacts in isolation with a computer.

Their effectiveness can be enhanced by the addition of more interactive forms of instruction. The librarians at the Florida Distance Learning Reference and Referral Centre, for example, have experimented with chat software to simulate a virtual classroom and open a "live" group instruction to e-learners. Librarians can be incorporated through the learning management system, participating in online courses as teaching assistants, co-instructors, or co-designers.

This 'embedded librarian' approach increases learner awareness of the value of the library in research and scholarship, and improves access to the expertise of librarians within the context of course needs and assignments. In addition, podcasting and video clips have become a popular choice in the delivery of instructional materials to remote users, as libraries recognize the popularity of mobile devices such as the *iPod.*

According to a Pew Internet and American Life survey, "more than 22 million American adults own iPods or MP3 players, and 29 per cent of them have downloaded podcasts". These methods allow e-learners to access the materials "anytime, anywhere," while still providing them with the type of instruction that their on-campus counterparts may receive.

Tutorials range from a simple orientation to the library and its services to more in-depth tutorials on the research process or searching specific databases. For example, Mount Allison University Library makes audio *libcasts* available. These libcasts can be downloaded or subscribed to and listened to, using *iTunes* or a similar product.

THE SUCCESSFUL VIRTUAL LIBRARY

PARTNERSHIP AND COLLABORATION

In reviewing definitions of the virtual library, Sloan identifies an emphasis on the technological and informational building blocks, and a neglect of the human components, such as the service tradition and human interaction.

The continuing changes in technology have been truly astonishing, and the scope for building new information services and new ways of representing content seem unlimited. Although technology is the key infrastructure of the virtual library a tool used to support library goals human factors are the most important determinant of the success of the virtual library.

As noted by Colgate, Buchanan Oliver, and Elmsly, technology could cause problems in building relationships because of the difficulty in developing a successful rapport between people via remote contact.

One of the major challenges that virtual libraries face is the lack of opportunity for face-to-face reference service and communication. Combine this with a lack of awareness of library services and the end result is poor communication between library staff and e-learners.

The digital library serves mainly as a facilitator in organizing and providing knowledge and resources to its users. Sharing knowledge and information among library staff, researchers, faculty, students, and other departments within the institution encourages them to work together, develop their skills, and form strong and trusting relationships.

One method which can be effective in the development of strong relationships with faculty is the librarian-liaison role, where a librarian liaises with specific departments regarding resources, library services, and the provision of instructional support for students in those departments. When the liaison focuses on building effective channels of communication and understands the effects of technology on communication, it becomes easier to share knowledge and information among institutional stakeholders.

In addition, the focus on collaboration between the library and the faculty promotes a responsive approach to course design and supports teaching and learning objectives, particularly when this collaboration incorporates student contributions and feedback.

This approach considers the library as an active partner of the learning community, helping e-learners to become "information literates" by integrating information literacy skills into the curriculum.

The library can help e-learners to think critically about information, offer reference and instructional support, mentor their work by offering one-to-one communication and interaction, and work collaboratively with them to achieve a deeper level of understanding of what e-learners need.

A number of models can be involved in creating an environment that is responsive to the scholarly information needs of a diverse group of e-learners. Librarians select, describe, and ensure access to quality digital resources, providing e-learners with content from a wide range of resources and publications, including peer-reviewed journals.

Within this framework, the library works with faculty, researchers, scholarly societies, and publishers to develop and manage a collection of enriched online scholarly resources. Such a partnership enables researchers to interact with others, exchange experiences, and publish their works online.

The library role is thus transformed from simply providing library resources to meeting the ongoing support needs of the parties involved. The library also fosters research skills by encouraging e-learners to search, investigate, discover, and take advantage of these valuable online resources.

Further, senior management support and involvement is as much a key to success in developing the virtual library as in any other project.

They need to work closely with the library staff to understand the nature of services, values, and support the library should be offering, and to adopt successful communication and interaction strategies.

An institution providing distance and online education has an ethical obligation to ensure that its learners have access to appropriate library support. The Canadian Library Association *Guidelines* categorize responsibilities in terms of funding, administration, personnel, facilities, resources, services, publicity, and professional development of librarians.

The *Guidelines* note as essential advance planning by the library in consultation with faculty, programme administrators, and other appropriate campus personnel, and with librarians at unaffiliated libraries. The *Guidelines* also advocate that leadership should come from all levels of the institutional administration, but particularly from the library. All staff involved in providing library support to e-learners must be included in the partnership. Technological changes have been the dominant force reshaping library services.

Instilling a culture of sharing, motivation, equity, and active partnering encourages library staff to respond positively to the changing roles, responsibilities, and skills that the integration and use of technology requires.

A well-designed, ongoing training programme enables library staff to upgrade their skills to their new assignments, and helps them to understand and control fear of change. The home institution has primary responsibility for library support, but can benefit from external partnerships, collaborative efforts, and consortia in supporting e-learners.

Within Canada, university libraries extend in-person borrowing privileges to students, faculty, and staff from across the country, through the *Canadian University Reciprocal Borrowing Agreement.*

There are also initiatives to share virtual reference desks, such as the Library and Archives Canada's Virtual Reference Canada, through which e-learners benefit from the range of information resources and staff expertise available at a variety of participating institutions. Consortia approaches to database subscriptions enable libraries to expand the scope of the electronic resources they are able to offer their e-learners in a time of shrinking budgets and escalating journal costs.

The Lois Hole Campus Alberta Digital Library (LHCADL) initiative, through funding provided by the Government of Alberta, provides participating post-secondary institutions in Alberta with digital information resources for teaching, learning, and research.

LHCADL includes an information literacy and awareness component dedicated to sharing expertise and training resources with participating libraries.

In summary, library services are an essential component of a quality online learning experience. As access to online courses grows, an increasing number of e-learners are dispersed around the globe, often in parts of the world where physical access to the collections of large academic and research libraries is impossible or severely limited.

These learners are largely dependent on the quality and academic usefulness of services that the library can offer electronically.

The strength of virtual libraries and digital collections depends on the relationships libraries develop and maintain with the creators, publishers, and aggregators of e-resources, as well as with those who use, learn from, and evaluate these resources. Providing ongoing technical, reference, and instructional support to e-learners requires that libraries redefine their values and services, collaborate with their users and other partners, and approach their tasks creatively.

SAVING LIBRARIES WITH TECHNOLOGY

There has never been a harder time for libraries: unprecedented public funding cuts, required to cope with a deep economic downturn; the challenge of keeping abreast of rapid change in the technologies of content and search and discovery; and the quiet but insistent questioning of what role there is for public libraries in the modern world. Responses have been varied but predictable. In one camp are those people who cling to the values which led to the development of the modern library service – books, education, self-advancement and personal development – and in the other those bureaucrats who argue that if money has to be saved libraries must be sacrificed in order to divert funds to more pressing social problems. Of course not everyone takes such extreme views, and many feel there is a middle way to be found which protects the best of the library tradition, exploits the existing network of buildings, and doesn't put pressure on rapidly dwindling funds.

Book Industry Communication (BIC) is firmly of this view. BIC is partially a creature of the library sector, having been set up in 1991 by the British Library, the – then – Library Association, the Booksellers Association and the Publishers Association to develop and promote standards for electronic communication in what we now call the supply chain. Its first chairman was Tony Hall, managing director of what is now Capita Software Services but was then BLCMP and subsequently Talis. Its original focus was to bring EDI (electronic data interchange) to the wider book world, but it quickly broadened its outlook to include bar code technology, product metadata, identification standards and subject classification. Much of the book trade – and a significant part of the library supply chain – runs on standards that BIC has developed over the past twenty years.

We believe that, unlike the book trade, the library sector has never been able to leverage available technology sufficiently to gain real cost savings from its deployment. The savings are there to be had, but only a comparatively small number of libraries have taken advantage of the opportunities. There are various reasons for this. One is the lack of the commercial drivers which galvanise interest from the book trade. Another is the lack of technical expertise in libraries themselves. Another is the huge diversity that comes from multiple library authorities making independent investment decisions on the basis of their own needs.

Perhaps the most telling, though, is the fact that the companies which exist to serve the library sector – LMS providers, RFID suppliers, stock suppliers and others – have made too good a living from the non-standard environment which these other factors have allowed to develop. Stock suppliers have made their money from servicing books to the specific needs of their customers rather than from the books themselves; LMS and RFID suppliers have been only too glad to tailor systems to individual needs rather than sell a standard product. These are the costs which BIC believes can be saved; and we are encouraged in this by the growing realisation by the companies involved that better delivery of standard products is in the end a more realistic and appropriate policy to adopt.

BIC's remit is about standards, collaboration and consensus. We believe there are huge wins to be made from eliminating waste in the library supply chain, by using technology and standards in a judicious way to cut away at the cost structures that have been allowed to exist in the public library sector because of its fragmented structure.

WHAT ARE THE KEY COMPONENTS OF THIS STRATEGY

EDI is one. Though the BIC standards are widely adopted by libraries and their suppliers, only a minority of libraries has implemented the full cycle of EDI messages – quotes, orders, delivery notes, invoices – and reaped the benefits of error avoidance, once-only keying and paperless transactions. Fewer still have been able or willing to create electronic links between library and corporate finance offices, so that invoices can flow electronically between approval and payment. EDI may be a little complicated to set up, but all the major library suppliers have invested heavily in standards-based electronic communication, and transaction costs are a fraction of any alternative and repay the investment many times over when it is in place.

RFID is another. This technology is hardly new, having been widely adopted by libraries, primarily as a more sophisticated alternative to bar codes for self-service applications, and where it has been implemented it has been universally acclaimed as a way to enable the more productive deployment of staff, facilitate longer opening hours, and provide a more welcoming environment for users. Now, with the help of the BIC/CILIP RFID in Libraries Group and its support for the new ISO 28560 standard, RFID is expanding its potential beyond self-service to stock management and other functions in the library, reducing workloads and providing ongoing cost reductions.

What is more, the standard enables libraries to invest in the technology, confident that they are not locked in to any specific vendor's software or hardware. BIC has published a UK profile for the standard, which has the acceptance and support of all the major RFID suppliers.

The work BIC has done on RFID has spawned other things too. For many years the required communication between self-service devices and LMSs has been handled by 3M's SIP2 protocol. In response to growing dissatisfaction from LMS providers, BIC has commissioned an entirely new communication framework which both extends the functionality of SIP2 but also defines web services as a mechanism for the transfer of information.

METADATA AT DIGITAL-INFORMATIVE ERA

Collection of Items are called Data. The additional Information's about the objects stored within our collections may be Traditional or e-format is represented in the form of Metadata, which is nothing but data about data. In General, metadata is machine understandable information. In Library environment, metadata is commonly used for any formal scheme of resource description, applying to any type of object, digital or non-digital. From Computing Point of View, the content management system contains digital objects. Thus, Metadata is also one of the components of Digital Library. Both Digital objects and Metadata are components of Digital Library. Digital objects are described, structured, summarized, managed and otherwise manipulated in surrogate form through the use of "metadata", which literally means data about data. Metadata is usually produced through a process called "cataloging" that is often carried out by trained librarians. Collections of such information are commonly stored in "catalogs". In computerized environments, metadata may be automatically or semi-automatically extracted or derived from the original content or the "full text" may simply be indexed and searched.

WHAT IS METADATA

Metadata is "DATA ABOUT DATA" or "INFORMATION ABOUT INFORMATION" Metadata is structured Information that describes retrieval for managing Information Resource. Which states that most data is waste without Metadata. Metadata describes data elements and their attributes such as name, size, data type and also Data Structures like length, field, columns, etc. It also has information about the location of data, how it is associated ownership, etc. Also, metadata describes specific characteristics about spatial data, which provides guidelines with a Standard Format. The Information may includes Name, Ownership, Description, Currency, Status, Access, Quality, Contact Details, etc., It helps us to know where exactly Information locates, Information requirement, relevant Information where exactly locates, even with in another part of your Organization, etc., are the special features of Metadata. Metadata can be encoded in MARC in "keyword=value" pairs or in any other definable syntax. Many current meta data schemes use SGML or XML. XML is an extended form of HTML which allows for locally defined tag sets and the easy exchange of structured information. SGML is a superset of both HTML and XML and allows for the richest mark-up of a document.

PURPOSE OF METADATA

The purpose of metadata according to Haynes the Purpose may be expressed as information retrieval, management of information services, documenting ownership and authenticity, interoperability.

- Information retrieval is a dynamic process which involves the user, the system and the librarian. The system indicates the usage of the computers, but can also be the manual catalogue. To obtain proper retrieval of relevant documents, the metadata representation is most important and should satisfy the users.

- Metadata also helps in management of various information services like OPAC, SDI, etc.
- It is a vehicle for documenting ownership and authenticity of the information.
- It also focuses importance towards the interoperability of information across continents.

Also, the Purpose extends to:

- Resource Description
- Administration and Management of Resources
- Record of Intellectual Property Rights
- Documenting Software and Hardware Environments
- Resource Discovery
- Preservation Management of Digital Resources
- Providing Information on context and Authenticity.

TYPES OF METADATA

Metadata is divided into different types:

- Descriptive Metadata
- Administrative Metadata
- Structural Metadata and
- Subject Metadata

Descriptive Metadata

Descriptive Metadata are used in the Discovery, Indexing and Identification of Digital Resources by semanting means. It is visible to the User of a system. Descriptive Metadata refers to the author, title content, etc. Preservation information refers to the best way of preserving documents like air conditioning or preserving books in the form of files at Systems, which requires meta fields to maintain with.

Administrative Metadata

To maintain Collections, this Administrative Metadata is used. Administrative Metadata is Managing metadata. Rights management metadata is a form of administrative metadata dealing with intellectual property rights. This Administrative metadata pertains to acquisition, vendor, location, etc., Also, it encompass a variety of data related to viewing, interpretation; use and management of digital objects over time. It includes technical data on creation and quality control, which has rights management, access control and user requirements.

- Management Information: Managing Information according to User requirements and reflects the output.
- Technical Information: Technical Information expresses the Technical

details such as Name of the file, its Type, Hardware, Software, Resolution of the Images scanned, Colour space, Pixel dimensions, File relationships, Compressions, etc., Using related Information provides User Tracing Information.

- Structural Metadata: Structural Metadata is nothing but interface which complies individual digital object into more meaningful units for the users. Structural metadata indicates how compound objects are put together. Structural Metadata is used for representing Physical Entity through Navigation, Information Display and Display. Searching Contents among them or with in them. Structural metadata has information about Physical forms of the resources.
- Subject Metadata: To have effective Searching this Subject Metadata is used. For Browsing structure this Subject Metadata is used, with Keywords, Classification Codes, Classification System, Terms from Thesauri and Subject Heading.

HOW METADATA IS USED IN TRADITIONAL LIBRARY CATALOGUING

Traditional Library Cataloging is a form of metadata, and MARC 21 and the rules sets in AACR2 are metadata standards. Other metadata schemes have been developed to describe various types of textual and non-textual objects such as archival materials, visual materials, geographic information, and science and social science datasets.

In mid 1990's Schwartz mentions the term metadata, which is used with database management, began to appear in the LIS literature. However, within a short period the topic became very popular in the area of research concentration, giving rise to several hundred publications, including an ARIST chapter in 1998.

Lange and Winkler traced the history of the term metadata back to the 1960s, but noted that it began to appear more frequently in the DBMS literature in the 1980s. Vellucci notes that the term metadata transcends boundaries among various stakeholders in the development of the internet and provides a common vocabulary to describe a variety of data structures.

XML (EXTENSIBLE MARKUP LANGUAGE)

XML is a Markup Language in the world of Web Designing and Programming. The markup text is a methodology for encoding data with information about it itself. Examples of markup are universal in the real world. The systematic arrangement of data elements for machine processing contains metadata multiple applications. The *Resource Description Framework* (RDF) is developed under *World Wide Web Consortium* (W3C), which enables encoding exchange and reuse of structured Metadata. RDF is a language for representing information about resources of World Wide Web, which is particularly representing Metadata with Web Resources.

RDF utilizes XML as a common syntax for processing of Metadata. XML is a simple and very flexible Markup Language with a great technology also runs in any platform with any Environment. The XML syntax is a subset of the International text processing *Standard Generalized Markup Language* (SGML) which is meant for Web. The XML syntax provides vendor independence, flexible framework, instant push technologies with *Channel Definition Format* (CDF), Electronic Commerce uses the *Open Trading Protocol* (OTP) and *Mathematical Markup Language* (MML), Pre-defined Tags, User Extensibility, Validation, Human Readability, etc., to indicate complex structures. By exploiting the features of XML, RDF focuses the structure of expression of semantics with machine processing standard Metadata.

WHAT DOES METADATA DO

An important reason for creating descriptive metadata is to facilitate discovery of relevant information. In addition to resource discovery, metadata can help organize electronic resources, facilitate interoperability and legacy resource integration, support digital identification and support archiving and preservation.

HOW TO CREATE METADATA

To encode Information the Data should be expressed in proper way. Create a Single disk file for each metadata record, that is, one disk file describes one data set. Then use some tool to enter Information into this disk file so that the metadata confirm to the standard. The procedure is,

- Assemble Information about the data set.
- Create a Digital file containing the metadata, properly arranged.
- Check the Syntactical Structure of the file. Modify the arrangement of Information and repeat until the syntactical structure is correct.
- Review the content of the metadata, verifying that the information describes the subject data completely and correctly.

DIGITAL IDENTIFICATION

Most metadata schemes include elements such as standard numbers to uniquely identify the work or object to which the metadata refers. The location of a digital object may also be given using a file name, URL, or some more persistent identifier such as a Persistent URL (PURL) or the Digital Object Identified (DOI). Persistent identifiers are preferred because file locations change frequently, making the URL invalid. In addition to the actual elements that point to the object, the metadata can be combined to act as a set of identifying data, differentiating one object from another for validation purposes.

ARCHIVING AND PRESERVATION

Recently created resources are the current metadata. However, there is a growing concern that digital resources will not survive in usable form into the future. Digital information is fragile; it can be corrupted or altered according to the requirement. It may become unusable as storage media and hardware and software technologies change. Format migration and perhaps emulation of current hardware and software behaviour in future hardware and software platforms are strategies for overcoming these challenges. Metadata is key to ensuring that resources will survive and continue to be accessible into the future. Archiving and preservation require special elements to track the lineage of a digital object to details its physical characteristics and to document its behaviour in order to emulate it on future technologies.

RESOURCE DISCOVERY

Metadata serves same functions in resource discovery as good cataloguing does by

- allowing resources to be found by relevant criteria
- identifying resources
- bringing similar resources together
- distinguishing dissimilar resources and
- giving location information

ROLE OF METADATA IN INFORMATION MANAGEMENT SYSTEM (IMS)

The role of Metadata in Content Management is something Interesting and worth interrogating. Metadata is used in variety of Situations and applications with widespread web applications. For "Searching" techniques, the metadata role is very very important. If the user started searching in the name of " Isolation and Purification" one can get number of references for the above said Topic. The associated keywords are analyzed and the related topics may also appear to satisfy the user needs. The terms can be grouped into associative and hierarchically subordinate or super-ordinate terms. This can be represented with the concept of Isolation and Purification. According to Dr. Ranganathan classification, the Personality, Energy, Matter may be defined.

The subordinate terms can be incorporated into the classification schedule and used in assigning subject headings or keywords. This will serve the purpose of the user and the classificationist. However, change of keyword into subject heading is a different procedure. These are all metadata contents. Also, it serves as a good example for Information Retrieval. Finally, the most important fact is that there should be facility in the software for upgradation of the metadata when required. The elements holds related detailed border schema for description, which is enumerated from narrower schema, to increase both recall and precision. This type of Principle is applicable to any type of Information Management System.

NEW INFORMATION TECHNOLOGY IN SPECIAL LIBRARIES

Planning for library automation has been defined as planning for "integrated Library management systems" that computerize an array of traditional library functions using a common database. As physical, spatial and temporal barriers to acquiring information continue to crumble, libraries must plan for a broader and more comprehensive approach to providing automated services. Currently, libraries find themselves confronted with a second computerization wave. The first wave took place during the seventies and turned manual back-room activities, such as acquiring, distribution and cataloguing, into computer-controlled activities. Essential in the computerization wave of the 90s is the deployment of computer networks: campus-wide networks at universities as well as national and international networks.

These networks provide access to remote electronic information by means of library information systems. Furthermore, available electronic information is no longer limited to socalled secondary information. Also primary information has now become electronically available. Presently, we can refer to the electronic full-text versions of scientific journals. Electronic textbooks and readers enable us to consult information outside the library, *i.e.*, at the professional and private work site of the library's traditional customer. We must realize that all traditional library activities are being affected by this innovation: the character of all library tasks is about to change as a consequence of technological developments. Within this context, we can observe a number of trends. One very important trend is the fact that the physical collection is becoming less important.

Of course, in the humanities books will keep playing an important role in the next decades, but the number of electronic sources will gradually increase. The library is shifting its focus from concentrating on supply towards centering on what is asked for by its customers. In correspondence with this trend, information reference is becoming more and more significant. The library acquires a gateway function, referring to information, irrespective of the location where it has been physically stored. Growing emphasis will be put on navigation. By and large, users will prefer to find their own way across the large amount of available information. To an increasing extent, service will be provided from a distance: the users will choose to consult their sources sitting at their own desk, at their own computer. This, in turn, implies that the library needs to increase the accessible electronic collection, which is accomplished by disclosing sources elsewhere, but also by electronically providing material that has already been available on paper. Of course, this development entails new problems related to the storage of electronic information.

IMPORTANCE OF LIBRARY FOR ORGANIZATION/R AND D CENTERS IN IT ERA

Special library have been in existence from the beginning of this centuries, whereas information centre engaged from the fifties and have now developed into major group of information institutions. Although special libraries and information centers has over lapping functional characteristics. Special libraries disseminate information and matter acquired by them answers, research questions, and direct users needs details on research information to appropriate some and handle towards periodicals to keep their user informed current development in this field. Parent organization special libraries after serves a widely distributed group of users who only link being the common subject interest. The concepts of special libraries have been change in all aspects and librarians are known as cyberians.

NEED OF LIBRARY AUTOMATION IN SPECIAL LIBRARIES

In the changing scenario of information storage and retrieval, we have no option but to automate our information and library systems due to various reasons. Consequently, there is urgent need to reply following questions before/ and after automation planning. Questions you might ask are basic but important:

- What are the information needs of the organization ?
- Who will access the database?
- What will the content be?
- What is our computing environment or can it be changed?
- Who will maintain the data?
- Who will determine the process and procedural controls and standards?

We have to discuss the said questions with library staff, library committee and with users for better planning for library automation and use of new information technology in library.

STEPS FOR PERFECT LIBRARY AUTOMATION

Redefining and Planning for Library Automation

Library automation is a very complete process and needs exhaustive planning looking to the present and future needs of the users. This includes hardware, software, *moony manpower, materials and mechanics* (4M's), obsoleteness, updating, adoptability and very fast changing IT environment.

Selection of hardware and others required equipment

- System Purchase: Purchase of the System if not available latest configuration of hardware and software, as well as the cost of preparing a site for the computer system. As having following latest configuration as follow:
  - Processor: Intel Pentium 4 processors up to 530J with Hyper threading
  - Operating system: Windows XP Professional
  - Memory speed: DDR2 PC2-4200 SDRAM
  - Memory expansion: Four DIMM slots for expansion to 3GB memory
  - Graphics: Integrated Intel Graphics Media Accelerator 900

Hard Disk Drive: Up to 200GB 7200rpm Serial ATA]

- Networking of Computers (LAN) in library: Think and complete the library networking if not already available, etc., as Telecommunications dedicate at least one standard phone line that the vendor can use to dial up to your system. Internet accessibility is become more common for vendor troubleshooting, but you may still need that extra phone line.
- Retrospective data conversion costs are those associated with the creation of machine-readable bibliographic and, for circulation systems, patron records.
- Site Preparation—updating power supply, updating electrical wiring, cable for networking, furniture, remodeling that may need to be done, adequate HVAC system
- Conversion Costs—This includes the costs of converting the catalogue and patron records. However, also consider the cost of staff time dedicated to the project. Bar-coding costs also fall into this category.

Operating Costs—This category is often forgotten in automating a library. Typical costs in this category include on-going utility and telecommunications costs, software license renewals, software updates, system maintenance fees, and miscellaneous supplies

Selection of Library Software and others Required Software

Following criteria might help the librarians to select the right software for other housekeeping operations:

- Who are the developers, whether an institution, or reputed company or few individuals. The preference is for institution and second preference is for the reputed company. One has to be skeptical about the software developed by individuals as there will be no continuity
- How many times the software has been revised since the time of its first launch.

- How many parameters are available for each module? More the parameters better will be the flexibility and needs no or minimum customization.
- Whether the software has facility to import bibliographic data available in MARC 21 format and similarly export of data in this format
- Training and guidance after installation
- Whether available on major operating systems.
- Whether it is web interfaceble
- Whether it can be interfaced with the e-mail system of the campus network.
- How many installations it has got in the country, since when and major clients.
- Whether it can offer OPAC and different rights to different logins
- Database architecture, Database migration, maintenance, database security, etc,

The Following are Latest Trends to be Considered Library Automation Software

- Integrated library Management system: An automation system in which the various applications share one bibliographic database. Each system comes with a set of core modules as well as additional modules, which can be added on, if necessary. The system should not only
- Core modules as: Circulation, cataloguing and online public access catalogue are necessary minimums. Additional modules often cost extra and are therefore not always used by as many of the system's clients which can lead to less responsive development. Additional modules include acquisitions, community information, course reserves, imaging, *inter-library loan* (ILL), materials booking and serials. Acquisitions and serials are sometimes part of the same module and are often part of the core package, content management, e-learning, etc.
- Client-server architecture: Turnkey systems are quickly becoming a thing of the past. A client/server system is identified by a more powerful server machine that handles database manipulation and retrieval while leaving the user interface to the desktop client software. This shares the computational load between the client and server machines and gives the user a better experience through a faster interface.
- Z39.50: This is a protocol for computer-to-computer information retrieval. It allows users to access dissimilar library catalogues from the host institution's catalogue while using a familiar interface. Both a Z39.50 client and server are needed if you want to visit others and

have others visit your catalogue. A Z39.50 client allows access to others' catalogues. A Z39.50 server allows others to access your catalogue. Ideally access works both ways.

- GUI interface for all modules: Graphical and menu-driven interfaces have or are replacing commanddriven interfaces in systems.
- MARC 21 and non-MARC compliance: First, library systems developed to use MARC records. Now systems must allow for cataloguing formats, such as Internet resources, for which no MARC formats yet exist alongside MARC records.
- Web-based patron catalogue: Patron access is greatly increased when catalogues can be accessed remotely via the World Wide Web. Better systems contain password-protection to allow patrons to access portions of their own records remotely.
- UNICODE: This protocol expands the character set allowed and is essential for collections with materials in non-Roman languages. UNICODE encodes 65,000 different characters compared to the extended ASCII character set of 256 characters. Not all vendors have fully implemented this yet, but most are working on it.
- RFID (Radio Frequency Identification Technology): RFID is the latest technology to be used in library theft detection systems. Unlike *Electro-Mechanical* (EM) and *Radio Frequency* (RF) systems, which have been used in libraries for decades, RFID-based systems move beyond security to become tracking systems that combine security with more efficient tracking of materials throughout the library, including easier and faster charge and discharge, inventorying, and materials handling? Following are the advantages of RFID systems, *i.e.*, Rapid charging/discharging, Simplified patron self-charging/ discharging, high reliability, High-speed inventorying, automated materials handling, long tag life, etc.

Accordingly, today's integrated system must not only provide access to the traditional cataloging, circulation, public catalogue (OPAC) and acquisitions modules, but must be capable of connecting through the local system into the systems of other vendors, remote bibliographic databases, CD-ROM drives on a local area network (LAN), and the Internet. Users are expecting that their library systems be capable of, among other things:

- providing seamless integration between online gateway and OPAC modules;
- providing access for external users on the Internet to the library's OPAC;
- Monitoring the usage of remote databases that have been accessed through the gateway; and,
- accessing the Internet using a variety of online database

Essentially, what this means is that libraries must plan to use a library automation management system as a gateway for achieving access to resources outside campus. Stimulated by the Internet, which has created universal connectivity to information resources heretofore public/society/respected community and by Z39.50 interoperability standards and "gateways," users of individual are expecting to access the resources of other systems— anywhere and anytime. Moreover, the traditional definition of "publishing" has been stretched by the creation and CDROMS, E-books, online databases, informational home pages and Web sites worldwide.

Finance Matter

Finance is an important aspect of any planning and automation is no exception to it, these are: Hardware, Software, Training, Staff, Networking (LAN, WAN, MAN and Internet). Speaking of funding, planners need to be aware that there are certain cost elements involved in the installation and operation of any automated system. These may be summarized as follows: Planning and consulting costs include direct, out-of pocket costs and indirect costs associated with getting started, etc.

Developing a Library "Profile"

One of the most important planning tools involves collecting basic statistical information on the library collection, library in-house activities, user services, users' education, etc. The following are examples of commonly needed data of:

- Number of titles and volumes in the collection, current and projected;
- Number of borrowers, current and projected;
- Number of materials circulated current and projected;
- Number of new materials acquired current and projected;
- Interlibrary loans lent to and borrowed from other libraries;
- Description of any cooperative arrangements involving the library; and,
- Library in-house activities and hours of operation.

In addition, it is important to take stock of any existing automation in the library by compiling the following data:

- Percentage of collection that has catalogue records in machine-readable form;
- Description of collection without machine-readable records, by category;
- Description of currently-automated library functions;
- Estimates of the location and number of workstations; and,
- Specifications for any existing equipment to be re-used with any future system.

At the same time that this data is being assembled, it is important to assess user needs and set service priorities. This can be accomplished by undertaking a focused, strategic planning process designed to involve the library's "stakeholders."

Developing a Strategic Plan

A library planning to automate should undertake a process by which representative staff and users can identify service needs and objectives. The purpose of such an effort is to allow participants to articulate their interests and concerns share perspectives and learn about possibilities in a collaborative setting. Group interaction is an important contributing factor in the success of the goal, which is to develop and sustain library automation in the years ahead. Here are the basic steps involved in this process:

- Ask participants to identify strengths, weaknesses, opportunities and threats in the library's environment
- Group these factors into critical issue areas that are likely to have an impact on the libraries' future in developing and sustaining automation.
- Ask participants to explore their ideas and perceptions in relation to the question: "How do you see the library providing user-friendly, cost-effective automated services as *Current Awareness Services* (CAS), *Selective Dissemination of Information* (SDI), online database, online journals, etc.
- Through a method of your own devising, ask participants to prioritize all of the ideas that come out of the above two "brainstorming" exercises.
- Ask participants to shape these priorities into the draft of a strategic "vision" for automation development consisting of a statement of purpose, goals and objectives for the library.

Setting Service Priorities

Your strategic vision must now provide the framework or context for the next step in the automation process, which is to determine which library functions should be automated and in what order of priority. For example, processes that are repetitive, occupy large amounts of staff time, require retrieving information from large, unwieldy files, or are high-profile functions of the library are prime candidates for automation.

Developing a Formal Specifications Document

It is very difficult to compare systems sensibly and pragmatically solely by randomly looking at systems, talking to sales representatives, reading literature or comparing broad cost quotations. For this reason, libraries use a formal document — often known as a "Request for Proposal," or RFP — that organizes and standardizes the information provided to and requested from the various system vendors. Utilizing an RFP to solicit written responses from vendors makes it possible for you to systematically compare functionality, cost, maintenance, support, and all the other issues that are involved in system procurements. The process can save you money and will result in a wiser decision.

An "Request For Proposal" Document

The following points should include these essential elements, among others:

- Library Background Information
- Libraries Service Plan, Mission Statement, Technology Plan, other supporting information
- Technical Inventory-Inventory of your existing hardware/software, and infrastructure:
- Size of your collection
- Number of terminals
- Number of patrons
- Network operating system
- Number of servers
- Type of wiring
- Existing database that may need to be migrated into the new system—People soft, access database, etc.
- Specifications-Detailed listing of requirements the system should provide.
- Module Requirements: Circulation, Bibliographic Maintenance, Acquisitions, Serials, General System, and Report Generator, etc.
- System Technical Requirements
- Network, System Design, Database Management System, Data conversion requirements, Hardware requirements
- System Performance and Testing Requirements

Be ready for the Following Upon the Receipt of Vender Proposals against our Floated RFP

- A description of how the proposals should be arranged and submitted;
- Instructions on receiving vendor business and financial information;
- Criteria the library will use to evaluate vendor proposals;
- Questions regarding vendor training and documentation;
- Your functional and technical specifications;
- Also, vendors should be asked to describe:
- How they will create bibliographic, item and borrower databases;
- Their system maintenance programmes and services;
- Their site preparation requirements;

- Their delivery and installation methodologies;
- Their system performance guarantees; and
- Their pricing and cost strategies.

Criteria for Vendor (for Hardware and Software) Selection

Upon the receipt of vendor proposals, it will be time to begin the process of system evaluation and selection. This process involves a number of key steps:

- If possible, form a project team of persons to assist with the evaluations and the selection who have some knowledge of automation or who work in the area(s) being automated. People involved in the strategic planning process would be a good choice.
- Try to weed out proposals that are "fatally flawed," *e.g.*, where the vendor fails to reply to any of the functional specifications or the system is missing a module for a high-priority function.
- Begin in-depth reading of the "surviving" proposals, carefully noting both deviations from the requirements as defined by the RFP and any aspect that is handled unusually well. Make a list of any parts of the response that are not clear and require further clarification.
- Schedule system demonstrations. They are an important component of the evaluation process. Allow the vendors to show off the vendor's system in the most attractive light; however, be prepared with a list of what you want to see along with questions you would like answered. Use the same list with each vendor. This permits more effective cross-comparisons.
- Consider using computerized spreadsheet software in order to compare and evaluate vendor cost proposals. Costs may not be what they seem at first glance.
- Contact some of each vendor's current clients— sites of the same library type, and of similar size, where the hardware and software modules that have been proposed to you are currently in use.
- Assign point values to the criteria listed in the RFP and assign scores to the different proposals. The system with the highest score becomes the number one finalist, the system with the second highest score number two and so on. To maintain a negotiating edge, it is better to cut to two vendors rather than one. If that is impossible, maintain the illusion anyway. Remember: The selection process is not over until the contract is signed. Until that point, never let any vendors know that they have been eliminated, including those with fatal flaws.
- Compare studies: Do compare study of all received proposal from venders with theirs features, etc.

Putting your System into Place

After the system selection process is complete, there are several important steps which must occur. You and your vendor will have to negotiate and sign a contract. You will want to test the system and make sure it suits your needs. You will want to make provisions for system maintenance. Finally, you will want to train both your staff and your users as much as possible to prepare them for when the system is up and running. With regard to training, the following must be considered: In thinking of automation planning, there is often a tendency to focus on the hardware and software aspects of planning, and to ignore the human aspects of automation— training and public relations. Without these, however, even the most carefully designed system may not be accepted by library staff or library users.

To assure the success of your hard planning work, training and public relations plan should be part of any automation project. Fortunately, training can begin long before the system is installed. By involving staff at all levels in the analysis of operations, the identification of needs, the setting of priorities, the development of specifications, and the evaluation of systems, staff will gain much of the knowledge they need as the planning progresses. User acceptance and enthusiasm for your new automated system is certainly an important ingredient in a successful planning effort. If you are implementing a public access catalogue, it is probably the most important measure of success. Public relations can allow you to accomplish three things:

- Make users aware of your new system and services;
- Motivate them to use the system; and,
- Train them in using the new system and services effectively.

About the Database

In the rush to acquire hardware and software, librarians often forget that their most valuable product is the library's database. The creation of a high-quality machine-readable database provides the cornerstone upon which all present and future automation efforts rest. Vendors will come and go, hardware will become obsolete, software will be replaced, but a well-constructed, well-maintained database, with its accompanying local holdings, will be the library's transportable and viable link from system to system. Moreover, as library users begin to access not only their local system but systems in other libraries as well, the quality of respective databases will influence both the outcome of search strategies and the availability of materials. Database readiness has several important facets:

- Catalogue records must be carefully converted from manual to machine-readable formats;
- Collections must be prepared for conversion through effective and ongoing weeding and inventory programmes;
- Once converted, collections must be properly maintained as titles are added, withdrawn, transferred and re cataloged; and,

- Standards — for bibliographic, item and patron records as well — must be adhered to. In particular, adherence to well-established and accepted standards of description for bibliographic information in a machine-readable database is critical because
- Without standards, files cannot easily be transferred from one automated system to another, and,
- It is essential for libraries wishing to participate in resource sharing arrangements with other libraries, which will require such adherence as a condition of participation.

Results of your Good Planning

- Confidence that you have selected the best possible system available, give technological and financial constraints;
- Confidence that you have addressed the priority needs of your library;
- Confidence that you have established a firm basis of understanding and a methodology for future planning;
- Confidence that automation activities are being implemented as part of a clearly articulated, overall plan for the development of library services; and,
- Confidence that you have the ability to respond quickly and effectively to unexpected opportunities and challenges, with a clear understanding of how these unexpected developments may be used to support the library's long range goals.

Feasibility Study of your Plan

Immediately after the analysis and design for the system has been completed, a feasibility study must be conducted. The aim of a feasibility study is to determine if the project is achievable, if the benefits outweigh the disadvantages and to examine alternative solutions. It is designed to answer these questions: Is the proposed system realistic? Is it necessary? What other options is available? Is it affordable? The final output of a feasibility study is a report to be presented to the management.

8

Role of Information Technology in Managing Organisation

Researcher provide a comprehensive remark of the role of IT in managing organisational change and interdependence. He commented that the world is observing a strong trend of convergence of the technologies of computing and telecommunications. Changing technology economics, merging of formerly disparate technologies with different managerial traditions, and the problems of managing each of the phases of IT assimilation in different ways calls for a major reappraisal of the organisational structures designed for yesteryears. IT is becoming all pervasive and is having impact on all business—in service as well as in manufacturing. It is affecting workers at all levels of organisations—from the executives to assembly hands and clerks. IT is increasingly becoming an integral component of all types of technologies—craft, engineering, routine and non- routine.

THE EVOLUTION OF INFORMATION TECHNOLOGY

Researcher provide a comprehensive remarks of the evolution of IT where he claimed that during the 1950s, computer systems were used mainly for scientific applications, with scientists the primary users and custodians of these systems. Business use of computers for mainly functional applications, such as accounting, began in the 1960s. The era of the 60s is known for the birth of *Data Processing (DP)* or *Electronic Data Processing (EDP),* which created a whole new profession.

During this period:

- The computer was perceived as a number crunching tool.
- Attention was focused on the power of these modem tools to compute, with much less emphasis placed on the overall value of information as a resource.

In the 1970s, more organisations moved towards the use of computers to provide management with information. This concept soon became known as *Management Information Systems (MIS).* Although MIS concepts were considered to be a major breakthrough in the use of computer systems to process information, organisations still emphasised the computer itself rather than focusing on the data and information as major components of the systems.

Many other concepts evolved during this period, examples:

- Database Management Systems (DBMS).
- Decision Support Systems (DSS).

The domination of mainframe computer systems gave way to the introduction of *minicomputers.* This new generation of computers became instrumental in the development of *Distributed Systems (DS).* The introduction of personal computers or microcomputers was another landmark development of this period. The technological advancements of the 1970s paved the way for a new era in the 1980s, which became known as the *Information Age.*

The significant phenomena of this era include the greater recognition of information as a major organisational asset and its importance in a competitive world economy. Another important characteristic of this era is the emphasis on the management of information and related resources utilised to maintain information resources. Furthermore, greater participation by users of information services became a major fact of this age.

The new generation of end users are more knowledgeable than their counterparts of a few decades earlier, and they created many networks of information systems sharing the vast powers of computers, data, information, and knowledge. In addition, technological advancements in telecommuni-cations allowed information users to exchange information more freely than ever. The old dream of developing computer systems that could think intelligently, learn, and make recommendations to decision makers carne closer to reality through many new applications of *Artificial Intelligent (AI)* and its component Expert Systems (ES).

New Information Technology Resources

There are several developments which have lead to a new perception and assessment of the use and management of information technology resources.

These include:

- Recognition of information as a major organisational resource.
- Greater emphasis on utilisation of information as a major driving force in achieving effective strategies.
- New integration of telecommunications and information processing systems.
- A vast array of components comprising information technology resources.

Today, information technology resources consists of all types of information, representing various *functional entities* of organisations. Organisational information now can appear in all forms, which are processed by a conglomeration of computer machinery, examples:

- Mainframe,
- Minicomputers,
- Microcomputers,
- Reprographics, and
- Video discs.

It is communicated through the use of communication systems. The information is generated through the use of many information processing and management systems in diverse organisational structures. In addition to mechanical, procedural, and technical components of information technology resources, one must also consider the human elements.

These human elements can be divided into three categories:

1. Those individuals who are involved in different activities of generating information.
2. Those who are the primary users of information.
3. The management team responsible for the overall management planning functions of information technology resources.

One can argue that the role of the information technology resources management team has become more important to the overall success and growth of many organisations. In addition, the task of managing these resources is far more complex and sophisticated in the information age. Information technology resources are no longer viewed by many organisations as number crunching 'black boxes,' but rather as vital resources for identifying new opportunities and developing strategies.

Information Management in the 1990s

The cost of computing has dropped drastically in the past two decades. There is considerably more advanced information and communication devices available. AB a result, organisations of all sizes and types have been employing this technology to increase their competitive advantages. With the rapid evolution in information technology, the effectiveness of the traditional management techniques to the management of this technology has been the subject of much speculation by both researchers and practicing managers.

Clearly, this changing technology is in need of an evolution in its management as well:

- A management approach that is as dynamic as the technology itself,
- Keeping pace in its methods and strategies as the technology matures,
- Making drastic shifts in direction when necessary, and
- Always providing new opportunities for growth, is the essential ingredient for strategic management of information technology resources.

As information technology resources become more important to the overall success of the organisation, its management may not only be limited by technical planning and execution as was true in the past. With the current number of end users and their demands for information technology services, successful organisations will utilise the expertise of their information technology personnel to provide needed support for the end user in order to obtain the necessary competitive edge.

COMPONENTS OF INFORMATION TECHNOLOGY RESOURCES

Processing Hardware:
- Mainframe-based Systems.
- Mini-based Systems.
- Micro-based Systems.
- Word Processing.
- Micrographics.
- Reprographics.
- Video Disks Processor.
- Desktop Publishing Systems.

Telecommunications:
- Private Branch Exchange (PBX).
- Broadcasting Systems.
- Local Area Networks.
- Telecommunication Access.
- Systems.
- Facsimile Systems.
- Satellite Communications.
- On-Line Processing Systems.

Information:
- Marketing.
- Production.
- Personnel.
- Financial.
- Strategic.
- Intelligent.
- Accounting.
- Legal.
- Economy.
- Government.
- Trade.
- Publication.
- Public.

Office Automation:
- Text Management Systems.
- Electronic Mail.

- Teleconferencing.
- Computer Conferencing.
- Video Conferencing.
- Intelligent Copies.
- Intelligent Printers.
- Dictating Systems.

Systems Professionals:

- Chief Information Officer (ClO).
- Systems Managers.
- Systems Security.
- Administrators.
- System Analysts.
- Database Designers.
- Programmers.
- Computer Operators.
- Data Entry Personnel.
- User Support Personnel.

Processing Software:

- Operating Systems.
- Database Management Systems.
- Procedural Programming Languages.
- Fourth Generation Languages.
- Word Processing Software.
- Electronic Spreadsheet Software.
- Communications Software.
- Graphics and Desktop Publishing Systems.
- Project Management Software.
- Miscellaneous Software.

Management Structures:

- Centralised vs. Decentralised Structures.
- Departmental Computing Structure.
- Information Center Structure.
- End-User Computing Structure.
- Chargeback Processing Structure.

Information Systems:

- Data Processing Systems.
- Management Information Systems.
- Decision Support Systems.
- Transaction Processing Systems.
- Expert and Knowledge-Based Systems.
- Database Processing Systems.
- Executive Information Systems.
- Distributed Processing Systems.

End Users:

- Strategic Planners.
- Financial Managers.
- Marketing Managers.
- Inventory Managers.
- Production Managers.
- Personnel Managers.
- General Managers.
- Accountants.
- Legal Advisors.
- Economics.
- Publication Personnel.
- Training Personnel.
- Public Relations Personnel.
- Clerical Staff.
- Technical Specialists.

NEW INFORMATION TECHNOLOGY (IT) PRODUCTS

MOST IMPORTANT PRODUCTS OF THE '90S

The 1990s was a decade of rapid technological advances. Client-server architecture evolved into a viable alternative to mainframe computing. Enterprise applications such as groupware, inventory control, supply chain, and systems management emerged as platforms for the evolution of business systems. The PC became a Ubiquitous and increasingly powerful desktop tool. And the Internet was embraced as a communication medium, consumer platform, and business conduit. Here are 10 of the most important and influential products introduced in this decade.

1. *Sun Microsystems' Java:* The brave little embedded operating system started out as a platform for write-once-run-anywhere computing and ended up as the Web's favourite tool.
2. *Nets Cape Navigator:* There's probably no greater development in the history of IT than the emergence of the Internet and World Wide Web. By the time Marc Andreessen and Jim Clark launched their graphical Web browser, Navigator 1.0, in 1994, there were more than 1 million Internet hosts. While Mosaic was the first widely distributed browser, Navigator set the standard in terms of look and functionality. And in the process, it shook Microsoft to its core—no small feat.
3. *Lotus Notes:* Lotus Development Corp. licensed Notes, the product most commonly associated with the term groupware, from Iris Associates in 1989. By the time IBM bought Lotus in 1995 for $3.5 billion—primarily to acquire the groupware technology—Notes had an installed

base of almost 2 million seats. Lotus made a successful effort to integrate Notes with the Internet when it introduced Domino in 1996.

4. *Microsoft Office:* Microsoft didn't come up with the idea to bundle a spreadsheet, word processor, and graphics package into a productivity suite, but it made the most of the concept-and created a business computing standard. Microsoft has continued to enhance the bundle, including links to the Internet.
5. *Oracle's Relational Database:* The original work on relational database technology was done by Edgar Codd when he was at IBM in the early 1970s. However, Oracle took the relational model and established it as a database standard, through both rapid technological advance and aggressive marketing. In the 1990s, Oracle continued to enhance the basic architecture to incorporate symmetric multiprocessing and object extensions.
6. *Sun Microsystems' Enterprise 10000 Server:* Sun made believers out of many of those who had been skeptical about the scalability of symmetric multiprocessing servers when it shipped the 64-node E-I0000 in May 1997.
7. *SAP Rl3:* The third version of SAP's suite of enterprise applications, introduced in 1992, integrated and automated back-office systems and convinced many companies to re-engineer their business processes to accommodate the software.
8. *Computer Associates' Unicenter:* Introduced in 1993, CA's systems management software unified a disparate set of products and processes, and provided a comprehensive view of IT systems. CA continued to strengthen the product with the introduction of the graphical, object-oriented TNG version in 1997 and the three dimensional TND version in 1998.
9. *Intel's X86 Architecture:* Intel led the PC industry on a price/ performance curve that mirrored Moore's Law-and then some. When Intel launched the 66-MHz Pentium processor in 1993, it set the stage for a quantum leap in desktop processing, making possible powerful personal productivity applications and eventually online commerce.
10. *Microsoft Windows:* In the spring of 1990, Microsoft CEO Bill Gates introduced the latest iteration of the company's graphical front end, Windows 3.1 and it was an instant hit with the public. Since then, billions of copies of the operating system have been sold, and, along with its siblings, Windows NT and Windows CE, Windows has proved to be one of the highest-impact products in IT.

WELCOME TO THE INFORMATION SUPERDORM

Malone regard that "we are now at the threshold of a new era, driven this time not by the technologies of production and transportation, but by the technologies of information, communication and coordination." An extraordinary array of information technologies is providing not only powerful new tools for dealing with these changes, but also a promising framework for creating entirely new opportunities. Advances in computers, software, telecommunications, networking, and electronic media are vastly increasing the quantity, quality, and accessibility of all forms of information.

Internet

Internet as a "bunch of communications protocols that enables millions of computers to talk with each other. It is already replacing overnight mail and faxes as a way to communicate quickly and over long distances.

Begun as a research project of the US Defence Department in the 1970s, it has become the:

- Technological trend in academic libraries of the '90s with dial up databases such as CompuServe, small corporate and university databases that are interconnected via the Internet.
- Thousands of companies have started to promote and sell products over the Net and at the same time, businesses are discovering that they can streamline operations and increased productivity by connecting their in-house networks to the Internet.

Almost overnight, the net grows from an academic resource into an ocean of capitalist dream.

World Wide Web

Subscribing to the Internet opens the door to many different types of information and communication possibilities. The World Wide Web, a *subset* of the Internet and one of the Internet's most popular and employs simpler computer applications, such as Windows, and more transparent commands then the internet.

By using browser software and fast modems, a subscriber can easily:

- View individuals' and organisations' home pages.
- Graphical tables of contents to more-detailed files contained within.
- Best of all, a user need not be a computer pro or a rocket scientist to surf the Net.

With the attributes such as multimedia, hyper linked, dispersed, dynamic, versatile and multi platform, the reason for Web popularity is the ability it affords to send and receive graphics, photographs, movies, and sound along with text. Several factors have contributed to this rapid growth, "most notably, technological advances in software, hardware, and communications that have made connections more economical".

Electronic Mail (E-Mail)

A way for computer users to exchange messages in completely different offices, locations, organisations, cities, countries, even continents using the e-mail programme available through the *Internet Service Provider* (ISP) to create, read, and manage the e-mail messages. Educationally, e-mail has continue to grow more important.

It has also become easier to exchange not only textual messages but a variety of files, including graphics, software programmes, spreadsheets, and databases. Ingram believe that e-mail will become part of a total distance-education system that might include elements of videoconferencing, interactive multimedia, and other learning tools.

Lotus Notes

A complete 'environment' or 'platform' for several computer applications and can be used:

- to send electronic mail,
- As an electronic calendaring system,
- As a scheduling system.
- As a bulletin board.
- As a publishing system for the web,
- As an automated workflow system and
- As a group ware system.

Intranets

James view Intranet as a network that lets people within an organisation share the kind of information one's can experience—and create—with Netscape Communicator Professional such as:

- Pages full of text, graphics, sound, and video;
- Fill-out form;
- e-mail with pictures;
- Specialised newsgroup and interactive conferences;
- Directories full of files one's can download; and
- A broad range of custom-tailored resources for research, education, or business.

Thus by using a standardised methods, or protocols for moving information from one computer to another, an entire office, or even a corporation with many physically remote sites, can communicate without worrying about specific hardware or software.

Multimedia

Multimedia tools enable us to express ideas that are more difficult to describe with words than they are to demonstrate in some way. For those who are aural or tactile learners, for example, multimedia provides a fresh new means of comprehending something.

Videoconferencing

Ingram claim that videoconferencing is increasingly used for individual and group meetings as well as to deliver education and training at a distance. Brown University Computing and Information Services view videoconferencing as an interactive audio/visual meeting channel to sites worldwide via high speed telephone lines.

Thus, videoconferencing combines the benefits of face-to-face interaction with the power of telecommunications.

As claimed by Littman, the videoconferencing rationales are as follows:

- Enhance the quality and intensity of communications.
- Engender a sense of responsibility and involvement among individuals who could not otherwise meet with each other.
- Lead to the articulation of policy, goals, and objectives through consensual decision making.
- Enable academic librarians to hold interactive sessions regardless of location on such topics as Internet access and use, intellectual freedom and copyright.
- High school students can be introduced to resources in an academic library, thus saving field trip and liability insurance costs.

Virtual Reality

Virtual reality has captured most organisations. It benefits an organisation, by gathering information on customers/users, competitors, and potential markets.

Cavanaugh describes the creation of 'virtual offices' that has enable:

- Communications between employees and vendors.
- Advertise products and services globally.
- Deliver new products or packages of services.

CD-ROMs

Rogers view that the advent of CD-ROMs in libraries was the introduction to the world of high-tech ware for many librarians. CD-ROMs are found in every library today and are loaded on most business networks but are often simply presented to end users, from car mechanics to astronauts. This technology is revolutionising the way students and professionals can assemble and access information.

Being fixed systems:

- The *content* on CD-ROMs is finite, although the amount of information on a disc is still impressive.
- The *functionality* of CD-ROMs and the number of tricks they can perform is finite.

Amendments to the software, indexing, and content are done at the will of the developer and information provider. A number of business databases available on CD-ROMs has increased steadily over the past few years. At the same time, most major public libraries, colleges, and *university libraries* have made available at no cost numerous CD-ROM databases for user and customer use.

CD-ROMs Into the Future

Beiser stresses that the emergence of a high-density CD (HiCD) technology opens exciting new possibilities for all sectors of our society—not the least of which are *libraries.* CD-ROMs was a distribution and publishing medium, and not a competitor to hard disk drives.

Meanwhile, HiCD can deliver text, graphics and multimedia content as well or better than a high-speed link. It is the stuff of memory cells, the repository of incredible amounts of otherwise evanescent data, a resource without which libraries will be unable to perform their designated role in an information intensive universe.

Online Databases

It offers full texts of journal and magazine articles. Tenopir claimed that academic librarians are actively looking for alternatives to print journal collections:

- As serials budgets stagnate,
- Print journals take up as much space.
- Patrons want to locate and access everything from a single workstation.

Some examples of online databases are EBSCO Elite Periodical Database, FirstSearch Online Databases, INFOTRAC Periodical and Newspaper Databases, etc.

Electronic Journals

Researcher claimed that electronic journals are mushrooming online, on the Web and in CD-ROM format. This phenomenon is due to the rapid advancement of information technologies including the Internet and digitising techniques.

The quantity of e-journals is growing larger although no exact number is available. In recent years, many more journals have been earmarked for digitising, a necessary process for turning a paper journal into an electronic one.

In addition, a considerable number of journals are now published only electronically, which significantly enlarges the size of the e-journal pool. Among all the users of e-journals, academic libraries especially, are the major subscribers of e-journals.

IT'S ROLE IN MANAGING ORGANISATIONAL CHANGE

IT AND ENVIRONMENT - GOALS-STRUCTURE

Researcher defined environment as those factors which not only are outside the system's control but which determine in part how the system performs.

Uncertainty is the difference between the amount of information required to perform the task and the amount of information already possessed by the organisation:

- *Proposition* 1: Turbulent environment drives organisations to use IT for monitoring the preferences of the environment. System theorists have recognised the importance of 'feedback' for the survival of the system and for maintaining a 'steady state' or 'homeostasis'. Organisations are purposive systems that learn of the impending threats by scanning. Scanning is the process by which the organisation acquires information for decision making. The modes of scanning are primarily determined by the external environmental stimuli and are determined by the magnitude and by the direction of the discrepancy between the goal and its realisation. While surveillance is useful for information-gathering process, search is oriented towards finding a satisfactory solution to a specific problem. Complex systems require complex controllers. IT will provide the 'complex controller" to the increasingly complex organisation. The information systems of an organisation need to evolve to remain consistent with the changing organisational structure. Referring to the obscurity of causal laws of turbulence, Aldrich argued that scanning could provide the firm with the desired 'competitive edge.'
- *Proposition* 2: Turbulent environment drives organisations to use IT for translating the information on environmental preferences into goals. Continuously changing environment requires organisations to continuously reassess their goals. Effective structuring requires a consistency among the design parameters and contingency factors have demonstrated that organisations' goals can be generated by external forces, such as other groups seeking to use the organisation to further their own ends.
- *Proposition* 3: Turbulent environment drives organisations to use IT to align their structure with environmental preferences. The very efforts of the organisation to maintain a constant external environment produce changes in organisational structure. Scott argued that organisational structure and goals are driven by the preferences in the environment. The structure is determined by the information-processing capacity requirements of the organisation which in turn are governed by the IT being used. Aldrich, Perrow, Walker and

Woodward have attributed structural differences to the organisation's technology. Mintzberg had suggested that the organisation's environment and technology are the independent variables that determine the structural variables of the organisation. Fowles, in his narrative on the history of organisational communications technologies contends that the phenomenal expansion of organisations can be largely attributed to advances in the technologies of organisational communication. Yates argued that in absence of technological communication organisations could have evolved differently. Preliminary econometric analyses of the overall U.S., economy for the period 1975-1985 further confirms that the increased use of IT is correlated with decreases in firm size and vertical integration.

IT and Organic Structure

- *Proposition* 4: Turbulent environment drives organisations to make more use of IT for increasing their 'organic' characteristics. 'Organic' firms are better equipped to sustain themselves in turbulent environment. A dynamic environment will drive the structure to an organic state despite other forces; the more complex the environment, the more decentralised the structure. Introduction of IT at the 'operating core' level transforms a bureaucratic administrative structure into an organic one. Effectively, automation of routine tasks eliminates the source of many of the social conflicts throughout the organisation. Law of requisite variety implies that the rate of change of organisational systems must correspond to the rate of change of environmental systems, *i.e.*, organisations with complex environmental interactions would develop complex structures like adhocracies or networks. Adhocracy is suitable for a dynamic and complex environment, when the firm has sophisticated technical systems and the focus is upon consistently offering differentiated products for retaining the customers. Future organisations would be 'networks' characterised by adhocracies with flexible systems of projects and teams brought together quickly to accomplish specific tasks. Some existing organisations have already 'farmed out' their operations by establishing them as separate organisations or contracting them out to other organisations.
- *Proposition 4a:* Turbulent environment drives organisations to use IT for empowering workers at all levels. Growing availability of telecommunications has offered technologies like distributed systems and client-server architecture that facilitate the process of empowerment of the lower levels. In the 'informated' organisation, workers would be 'empowered' by virtue of access to necessary information to perform higher-level tasks. Ramstrom has argued that

tactical decisions relating to 'soft' information would be delegated to the 'grass-roots' where there is easy access to relevant information concerning the immediate environment, at the same time providing these levels with the information generated within the system by means of 'cheap' internal information systems.

- *Proposition 4b:* Turbulent environment drives organisations to use IT for increasing the spans of control. Information technologies, by facilitating the standardisation of coordination would facilitate larger spans of control or work units which would be characterised by extensive lateral communication and self- contained authority structures.
- *Proposition 4c:* Turbulent environment drives organisations to use IT for increasing lateral communications. Selective use of lateral decision processes for situations involving task uncertainty increase the information processing capacity of the organisation. Bringing the points of decision down to the points of action reduces the information overload on the managers. Since specification of 'procedures' in complex situations creates inefficiencies, organisations in turbulent environments would use more IT resource for delegating the decision-making to workers. Increased use of groupware for lateral coordination will spell the demise of middle management.

IT and Differentiation - Integration

- *Proposition* 5: Turbulent environment drives organisations to reduce their 'dimensions' by focusing on core competencies by leveraging their use of IT.
- *Proposition 5a:* Turbulent environment drives organisations to use IT to reduce differentiation and integration to focus on increased specialisation. Organisations structure themselves to minimize coordination costs and group together similar activities to achieve the benefits of process specialisation. Environmental uncertainty or 'task predictability' is the basic independent variable influencing the design of the organisation. Faced with increased uncertainty, organisations can reduce the need for information processing by decreasing the 'diversity of outputs'. Reduced differentiation and integration of activities would decrease the coordination effort involved thus reducing the information processing requirements. Reduced coordination costs with IT would result in the substitution of IT for human coordination. Greater specialisation would be achieved by focusing on few core competencies.

IT's Role in Managing Organisational Interdependencies

- *Proposition* 6: Turbulent environment drives organisations to actively seek Inter-organisational relations to leverage their core competencies.

Cooperation, especially in the international context, will be necessary to gain a competitive advantage in the future. To survive in an increasingly competitive environment, firms would form alliances that would bring together their core competencies to create the 'best of all" products.

- *Proposition 6a:* Turbulent environment drives organisations to reduce environmental complexity and uncertainty by seeking interdependencies with other organisations in the environment.
- *Proposition 6b:* Turbulent environment drives organisations to use more IT - effort to establish coordinating mechanisms with other firms.

To survive in the fast-changing environment the 'adaptive organisation" would be more like a shifting 'constellation' that has 'linkages' with independent and semi- autonomous organisations. Use of inter organisational linkages such as EDI would enable new forms of organisations and reduce the coordination costs of increasingly market-driven organisations. Increasingly, electronic linkages are becoming the necessary condition of doing businesses with larger firms. Using an analogy to the study of community chests conducted by Litwak and Hylton, we observe that in the increasingly global competition, the firms are competing for the common customers' 'fund' and the increase in one firm's revenue would come at the expense of other firm's loss. Coordination, being a function of interdependency, should grow in periods of increased competition for 'funds.'

The IT Paradox

- *Proposition* 7: Increasingly turbulent environment would feed the need for further advancements in IT which would further increase turbulence.

Business needs are incessantly driving the demands for increased capabilities of IT. In turn, increasingly advanced IT is being utilised in more and more sophisticated ways by the businesses to outdo competition. IT, which is being deployed as a solution to the increased complexity and uncertainty of the environment, has paradoxically contributed to the situation by 'compressing time and distance.' In absence of the present day advances in IT, would we be talking of globalisation or time based competition? Perhaps, not.

The pace of complexity is increasing fast. Hopefully, the advances in technology would be able to keep up with the environmental changes. Turbulence refers not to chaos in the environment, but to an increasing causal interconnection that renders environments obscure to local observers. Thus how can IT help organisations in responding to the challenges of an increasingly complex and uncertain environment? How can IT help the organisations achieve the 'flexible' organisation structure? We provide academic libraries as a living educational example that has been impacted by the strong trend of convergence of the technological advancements.

IMPACT OF INFORMATION AND COMMUNICATIONS TECHNOLOGY

Information and Communications Technology (ICT) have transformed Library and Information services globally. The Internet has provided universal access to information. Technological innovation has dramatically increased the rate of conversion of knowledge, information and data into electronic format. Developments in the software arena has generated powerful knowledge management software which has transformed the way knowledge is organised, stored, accessed and retrieved.

The digital revolution driven by ICT innovation has transformed academic libraries fundamentally. It has impacted on every sphere of academic library activity, *e.g.,* the form of the library, collection development strategies, library buildings and consortia. Information and communications technology have changed the academic library in a profound way. Computers and networked electronic resources had become an integral part of the academic library the past decade. This has been underscored by the phenomenon of knowledge or information commons in academic libraries, which refer to a specific environment in the library where a designated number of PC workstations, networked to databases and other e-resources, are made available to students. Every sphere of the academic library is being affected by ICT quite radically.

No longer is the library the untouchable custodian of information. It is being shaken to its very foundation, in fact its existence is being threatened. The academic libraries' traditional role of information custodian had been reduced to that of being one of many information providers. Of all the information and communication technologies the Internet and particularly the World Wide Web with its graphical user interface, has had the greatest impact on the information revolution. The number of electronic resources available on the Internet is growing at a phenomenal rate.

One of the major search engines Alta Vista has reported in 1996 that it has indexed 30 million Web pages. By 1998 the number of Web pages indexed by this search engine has leaped to 90 million. According to Farrow wide spread publicity has lead to assumptions that the Internet will meet all user information needs and that there will be no need for professional librarian intervention in future between user and information resources. Moyo states that student expectations that all their research needs will be met online are on the increase. Not only do students expect to find the information they need online, they also expect it to be available in full text. According to Tam and Robertson these assumptions have lead to a reluctance to use the physical library materials and to a decrease of visits to the library.

This phenomenon has fuelled fears of potential future job losses amongst librarians. Cheng explores the impact of information technology from an information ecological perspective. In information ecology the focus is not on information technology but on the human activities that are served. Cheng cites Nardi and O'day who draw a parallel between the explosive growth of information technology and the consequential Information explosion and a volcanic eruption. This eruption is impacting on everyone existing with the information ecosystem. Cheng emphasise the importance that we as academic librarians are clear about the challenges posed by this situation and also the opportunities offered.

Cheng highlights some of the changes that took place within the information ecology:

- The way we gather information, organise it, disseminate and use information has changed.
- The evolution of the Web has lead to availability of masses of information, electronic journals and databases.
- The way information is being published is evolving rapidly, *e.g.,* it is threatening current practices.
- New problems have come to the fore, *e.g.,* the issue of intellectual property rights of e-resources.
- User expectations have changed. Users expect full text delivery to the desktop.

Researchers are of the opinion that the changes that library and information services face are of an unknown and unpredictable nature. He states that it is impossible for library managers to predict future trends accurately. He feels traditional change management techniques are inadequate to deal with the changing environment that libraries are facing. For him it is a scenario where one has to brace oneself for whatever occurs. Under these conditions it is crucial that libraries make optimal use of the entire workforce.

It is of fundamental importance that customer service be given top priority. It is also essential that flexible organisational structures be created where workloads and responsibilities are shared and trust and responsibility are the norm rather than control. For library and information services in academic libraries to prevail under these conditions real leadership and real changes in management styles and organisational structures are necessary.

CONCEPTS DEFINED

Change

Robbins and Coulter defines change as any alterations in people, structure or technology. Change involves moving from the current state of things, the status quo, to a new state of things. It is therefore a process of moving from what is known to the unknown.

Information and Communications Technology (ICT)

Adeyoyin cites Bayode who defines ICT as "the acquisition, processing, storage, and dissemination of information by means of computers and other telecommuni-cation equipment." The Wikipedia free Internet encyclopaedia defines "information technology (IT) or information and communication(s) technology (ICT)" as the "technology required for information processing. In particular the use of electronic computers and computer software to convert, store, protect, process, transmit, and retrieve information".

From the definitions it is clear that the terms IT and ICT are used interchangeably and has the same meaning. According to Jimba information technology is rooted in three sectors namely information technology, telecommunications and the media and these sectors are converging on one another.

TYPES OF CHANGE

Researcher define change along a continuum ranging from low-scope to high-scope change.

Evolutionary Change

Evolutionary change is incremental by nature. Incremental change is smooth and happens gradually in an organised and predictable way. Incremental change tends to be small changes that lead to improvement but does not alter the operational structure of the academic library.

Strategic Change

Strategic, revolutionary or transformational change leads to radical transformation and often changes the general organisational structure. Transformational change tends to be very traumatic by nature. It can be generated as a response to a major crisis or a complete change in organisational strategy or purpose. The outcome of this type of change can lead to organisational transformation to the effect that the organisation might look completely different from what it used to be.

Discontinuous Change

The academic library is confronted with change that is unlike anything it has been exposed to before. Management theorists use the term discontinuous change. Pugh notes that discontinuous change is different from revolutionary change that is change undertaken to generate rapid results. Discontinuous change is unique in the sense that established management practices are inadequate to deal with it, in fact there is no model, paradigm or pool of experience that managers can fall back onto.

Researcher describes discontinuous change as turbulent, complex, traumatic, uncertain and of a revolutionary nature which requires different management skills to survive, supported by highly trained, motivated, flexible and multi-skilled staff that can be redeployed quickly and effectively if necessary. There is a stark contrast between the clearly defined boundaries of businesses in the 1960's and 1970's and the postindustrial era that is characterised by volatility, complexity and uncertainty. "This type of random, discontinuous change—which, by definition, is fast, traumatic, and revolutionary – requires very different management and leadership skills if the challenges it presents are to be handled innovatively and opportunistically." What organisations need in order to survive is highly committed, skilled, informed and trained staff which is willing to give their all.

Until 15 years ago change was incremental. One could build on lessons learned before. Since then change had become discontinuous. In this climate old management behaviours are inadequate. New ways of doing things are imperative which questions the practices that worked in the past. Information services in the academic library are driven by ICT with all its uncertainties and instability. Change is occurring at a greater dimension than ever before. The volume, pace and complexity of change is increasing at an unprecedented rate. A comparison between 1970 and to-day reveals that in 1970 only 5 per cent of change within organisations was of a continuous nature. Currently 75 per cent of all organisational change is of a continuous nature.

IMPACT OF ICT DEVELOPMENTS ON STAFF

Managers often introduce drastic change without considering its impact on people. People respond to change in a myriad of ways. Any significant change will impact on people's self-esteem, their motivation to do well, their status or the stress they experience be it positive or negative. It is of vital importance that managers do not overlook people when dealing with an ever-changing environment.

According to Morgan research suggests that 90 per cent of change initiatives fail because people are not taken into consideration. Change is good for academic libraries but its adoption requires tremendous input of physical, mental and emotional energy. After having to make intense inputs to accomplish change people expect to reach a plateau, a period for review and restoration of energy. The problem is that in the academic library this plateau had become non-existent because one peak follows after the other.

Phases People go through when Exposed to Radical Change

Elizabeth Kubler-Ross has identified 5 stages that patients experience when confronted with personal loss or death. These stages are denial, anger, bargaining, depression and acceptance.

Conner has used Kubler-Ross's 5 stages as a basis and extended it to 8 stages:

1. *Stability:* This is the phase just prior to change where everything is still normal.
2. *Immobilised:* When confronted with radical change people initially experience shock, confusion and become disoriented. During this phase people are out of touch with reality.

3. *Denial:* Conner defines denial as a refusal to accept reality. According to Fossum denial is a psychological defence mechanism that kicks in when individuals are confronted with radical change. It is a refusal to accept reality while the person's internal resources are being mobilised to eventually face a situation. To help staff to deal with this phase managers should use techniques designed to promote awareness that change has occurred or is in the process of occurring. The denial phase is a critical stage in the change process and people experience it differently. While some people are still dazed and out of touch with reality others may be ready to move on. Spending time on an individual bases with people struggling with this phase can be very useful.
4. *Anger:* During this phase people experience anger and outrage. They become emotional, irritated, frustrated and hurt and may often lash out at those supporting them.
5. *Bargaining:* This is a negotiation phase with a view to avoid the negative aspects of change. A typical example would be negotiating an extension of a deadline one is facing. This phase indicates the person is reaching a position where he or she can no longer avoid reality. This phase also demarcates the beginning of acceptance.
6. *Depression:* It is normal for people to become depressed when confronted with major change that affects them negatively. This is a very unpleasant phase but is an indication that the individual has come to complete realisation of the negative change being faced. It is an unpleasant phase but indicates another step towards acceptance.
7. *Testing:* At this point a sense of control is regained. A person might explore how to set new goals.
8. *Acceptance:* At this point people accept change. To go with an employee through the negative response model can be a costly exercise because people need support at every step of the way. However the cost of an employee failing to go through the process can be more costly to an organisation.

Resistance

Managing change within the academic library is essentially about managing people since it is people that effect change. People who are such a critical factor in change implementation can also be a stumbling block to the change process by resisting change. Change initiatives are often shipwrecked because of resistance. Resistance leading to escalation in costs often delays change processes.

Resistance is such a central element in change management that it deserves serious attention in the change implementation process. Researcher states that one must neither fear resistance nor make efforts to avoid it. The inertia of systems which have relied on doing things as they have always been done and achieving objectives through well-tried methods is not to be underestimated. It is part of the organisational instinct for survival and as well as comfort and complacency and it breeds resistance.

The successful implementation of change in the academic library is by and large dependent on the attitudes of people to the change process. People respond in different ways to change. Whereas some people will experience change as an exiting and stimulating event others may find it frightening and intimidating and consequently resist change.

Causes of Resistance

Pendlebury identified the following causes of resistance:

- Lack of realisation of a problem.
- Not grasping the implementation of a solution.
- Outright rejection of a solution as it is seen as the incorrect option.
- Fear of the outcome of change.
- Lack of interest.

This kind of behaviour is often the result of a vision not clearly communicated or staff's unwillingness to face up to the demands of change.

Researcher identifies the following additional reasons why people resist change:

- *Security:* Fear of potential job losses.
- *Financial:* Fear of loss of income.
- *Pride and satisfaction:* Technological innovation might make jobs and skills redundant.
- *Freedom:* Structural changes might impact on freedom of decision-making.
- *Authority, responsibility and status:* Restructuring might lead to a loss of authority and respon-sibilities.

Resistance tends to manifest itself in many different ways. Conner distinguishes between overt and covert resistance. Overt resistance is open and can be constructive. Covert resistance is submerged and can gain momentum unobtrusively and ruin a project. Fossum describes covert resistance as a passive-aggressive form of resistance. It is difficult to manage because on the surface a person appears to do nothing but is often busy sabotaging a project through negative statements. In major change there will always be resistance.

Creating an environment where people can openly express their fears will go a long way to minimize resistance. Managers need to be aware that resistance often manifests itself in an increase in absenteeism, reductions in quality, decreased productivity, strikes or slowdowns and increase in grievances.

STRATEGIES TO FACILITATE CHANGE WITHIN THE ACADEMIC LIBRARY

The prevailing organisational culture will determine how easy or complex it will be to communicate the need for change, share the vision and get people's opinions and participation. In an open culture communication is easiest. The leadership style, the trust people have in top management and the extent to which people are able to openly express themselves is of cardinal importance. Managers who have successfully implemented change understand that resistance is a natural reaction and would encourage it rather than suppress it. They would even reward people for open resistance in a constructive manner.

Fossum states that clear and open communication about pending change is crucial. Managers must not allow people to hear via rumours or the grapevine or the media about pending change. They should be open and upfront about pending change. Hearing from a third party will undermine trust and credibility. When communicating change it is important to send out positive and optimistic messages. Conner is of the opinion that effective leaders can change people's mindsets to a realisation that meaningful change is not only essential but also possible.

Morgan argues that buy-in is crucial in change management. If staff can take ownership of change, it will bolster commitment and assist in overcoming any obstacles. It is also crucial to involve staff in the decision making process. Participation will break the management versus staff syndrome. Instead of letting management do the problem solving it is useful to involve staff at all levels in this process. Managers must be careful not to make assumptions about the acceptance of change. It is better to get accurate feedback through interviews or surveys.

Techniques to Make Change Positive

Change creates conflict but the negative energy generated can be turned in constructive energy. Managers should realise that conflict in itself is not necessarily negative. It creates an opportunity to do creative problem solving with the staff. Conflict must never be taken personally. If people disagree managers should see it as an opportunity to find a more elegant solution that more staff members will find acceptable. People should be encouraged to be honest about how they feel and support one another. Managers should maintain their sense of humor. It is essential to cultivate an atmosphere that will transform negative issues of conflict into positive constructive energy.

Celebrate Success

It is important to sign-off change to ensure closure and enable people to move on. It need not be a celebration in the real sense. It could be a scenario where the team is thanked for their contribution. In that way they will see smaller change events as temporary unpleasant things to deal with and move on. If change events are seen as individual unrelated events it can lead to resistance.

AUTHORITATIVE AND VALIDATED INFORMATION

The growing demand from users for authoritative and validated information to be delivered in any format—print, e-mail or on disk at any agreed time and price. Users are overwhelmed with the vast array of information because of job pressure, and need to be able to contact the most reliable information services and resources.

COLLECTION DEVELOPMENT

There are significant increases in the quantity, range, and variety of globally published resources available for acquisition. Especially in the academic, research, and scholarly arena, tremendous and explosive growth in the volume and kind of material produced challenges the collection development objectives and resources of the university's library. This growth is fueled both by the drive towards specialisation creating sub disciplines, inter disciplines, and cross or multi disciplines or 'twig subjects'—and by technology's ability to create greater volumes of research data.

PUBLISHER/LIBRARIES

Researcher comment that in the Gutenberg era, publishers supply libraries with journals and other information products. Based on license agreements, libraries distribute these materials to their users. But now in the Post Gutenberg Galaxy, publishers distribute their products in digital forms. Therefore, a special issue has been raised by license agreement on digital information. The libraries should be aware and care about the future role of publishers. Will they still continue to distribute those materials via the library? or will they provide this service to the user directly? If the libraries continue providing these services, do the publisher allow them to store the materials on the library site? It is obvious that license agreements on digital materials with publishers are necessary in order to deliver these materials to the users to make print-outs and to download them. Publishers will not accept that libraries store digital archives at least at beginning of the publication because they worry about the control access. However, the long-term digital archiving will remain the task of the libraries.

To this end, profound expertise and qualified infrastructure are necessary to ensure the usability and preservation of this digital archive in the far future. Furthermore, a major issue is whether institutions could publish their own materials over the network instead of employing official publishers. There are some libraries and other institutions which collect in-house published materials and make them accessible via the Web.

DEALINGS WITH COPYRIGHT ASPECTS

Copyright protects 'literacy and artistic' works, such as scientific papers, stories, movies, music, software, etc. In libraries, very large part of the information is available in digital form and will be accessible to remote users. This lead to problems with the copyright owners regarding the exploitation of the work. The digital era has changed the content of the normal work exploitation.

So, on the one hand agreements between libraries and publishers should be negotiated, and on the other hand copyright regulations should be adapted to the new challenges. Current copyright legislation with regard to photocopies is very ambiguous and different from one country to another. On the other hand, it is quite clear that electronic copying is strictly forbidden without the explicit agreement of the copyright holders. It requires the understanding of what users actually want to do with information: 'how it will be used, by whom, for how long?" It is for this reason that many working groups and commissions are discussing what the legislation on electronic delivery should be.

COST AND MAINTENANCE

Financial pressure is driving much of the change taken place in academic library. Rapidly increasingly costs of IT materials, human resources, and facilities maintenance resulting in a gradual shift in library expenditure patterns. Expenditures required on IT for academic libraries will approximately increase.

VISION AND BUREAUCRACY

Problems of 'vision' and people not understanding the direction in which the top management of the libraries intend to take the organisation. Bureaucratic issues and culture are barriers to a more effective in delivering the best services to library patrons. The need to address quality issues/targets/standard as we move into a global arena.

FEE FOR SERVICE

Charging for educational and intellectual reasons are also confronted with the issues of pricing. Charging direct fees to patrons for printed documents is an economic, practical, and managerial necessity if librarians are to provide users/patrons with the fullest possible range of service options. Librarians must choose to impose charges to users of specific services or be forced to eliminate and reduce services altogether.

THE LIBRARIANS' IMAGE

As in other countries, librarians for example in Southeast Asia have been facing the same crisis of low image. This problem consists of several factors including low salaries, lack of excitement, passive role as information resource custodians in providing services. Their work and capabilities have not been highly recognised by the society at large. And now with the future evolution in the world of the digital and virtual libraries, librarians fear that their profession as intermediary for the users will disappear when there are no longer any printed documents, but only computer terminals. Do digital libraries need librarians for future service and operations?

IMPACT OF INFORMATION TECHNOLOGY ON INFORMATION PROFESSIONALS

As quoted by Matson, new technology is, of course, very powerful and brings in 'an imperialistic thrust' not only into librarianship, but into everyday life. Not surprisingly, the new roles created by the changing technology have commanded attention and have made up a large part of recent literature about librarians. He added the resulting proliferation of online catalogs, librarian have been spurred by technological developments to become more efficient organisers and planners. They have, in short, brought their traditional skills to the service of the new technologies. As claimed by Hyams, the role of the New Information Professionals (NIP) in the learning environments is likely to be much more global. It is a call for librarians to rethink their job functions and the future of the academic library as center of technology. The change that's happening isn't at all like the automation change the librarian went through. It is a fundamental kind of change: 'To Who We Are and What We Do."

NEW ROLES, NEW SKILLS AND NEW PEOPLE

Researcher argue that library jobs and jobs for information professionals are changing at the same—or even greater as experienced in other parts of our economy and society. Are librarians, new and old, keeping pace with these changes? Are they stuck in a traditional mind-set about their jobs and the settings for those jobs? What are some of the new horizons available to librarians willing to 'think outside the box" as far as their careers are concerned? What prepares the librarian for these emerging jobs? The struggle of librarians in academic libraries to cope with the dynamic changes brought by technology is real. The new roles and skills include:

As Library Webmaster

The single most significant factor in the changing information jobs has been the Internet. It has changed everyone's job, some people's job descriptions', and the job market itself, example as Webmaster.

Definition of Webmaster

The essential assignment of the Webmaster as defined by Richmond is:

- "... a person who manages a Web; a mediator between Web authors and system administrator—ensures that applicable standards such as

HTML validity and link liveliness are met; optimises the Web architecture for navigability; takes editorial responsibility for the content, quality and styles of the site; finds, creates and installs tools to create Web content and check consistency; develops and enforces the house style; liaises with graphic artist; provides first level user support..."

From this definition, it is clear that Webmasters must be responsible for several roles in their day to day activities.

Task Analysis of the Webmaster

Van der Walt strongly believe that Webmasters were originally depicted as members of an organisation who were early adopters of Internet and Web technologies and who saw the need to educate the rest of the library users in using those technologies. His statement is strongly supported by the researchers who claimed that an area where early Web expertise could be found was the *academic,* and specifically *university,* environment.

Vander Walt listed several responsibilities of the Webmaster such as:

- Administration and daily management of a Web site such as home page design, Web-based online searching, searching Web sites, Intranets and Internal database publishing
- Understand the broad purpose and potential of a Web site—that is, what the site can accomplish and what it may be able to do in future
- Possess a thorough understanding of the organisation and have a background in marketing, familiarity with the Internet
- A solid understanding of programming languages and technology
- Keep up with and also recognise the significance of emerging technologies and business models, and be able to inform and educate the rest of the organisation
- Experiment with unproven technology to develop WWW sites and the Webmaster is a solo space explorer, often looking at way-out-in-front technology'
- A person with the necessary technical talent in user interfaces and a good knowledge of operating systems, as well as creative skills in graphic design, marketing, advertising, copy writing and event planning

The Growing Importance of the Webmaster

These basic responsibilities are slowly being enhanced. Today the Webmaster has become an integral part of an education venture vital to the entire strategic planning of the library. As a newcomer in the information retrieval field, the Webmaster forms an essential part of the online presence of any organisation, as it is he or she who leads the Web site development team in managing an effective and efficient Web site.

The value of librarians as webmasters in the university as claimed by Stover is for a number of reasons:

- First, to support the scholarly communication process because disseminating information is a function that traditionally been associated with librarians
- Second, librarians have a certain measure of expertise in the area of organising and providing access to information. What better way to share their skills with the academic community than by turning Web documents into one-stop-shopping malls that offer the end user subject access to a document along with the full-text of the document itself?
- Third, Web publishing gives us a higher profile on campus, which is an important asset these days because of the changing nature of higher education and changing role of librarians
- Fourth, the Web provides unique access to scholarly information because of its serendipitous nature, its immediacy, its hypertext structure, and its universal appeal. Why wouldn't librarians want to be involved with this exciting technology at the publishing level?
- Fifth, it provides our parent institutions a positive reputation in the national and international academic communities. This is more important ever given the current climate of declining enrollments that many colleges and universities face today.
- Sixth, Web publishing allows us to bypass the profit-based system of print publishing that has tormented librarians for years by gouging out huge chunks of money from their budget.

As claimed by Van der Walt, many Web sites are now becoming mission critical in the sense that they are seen as a marketing tool for the university and also as a support tool for the end-user or library customers. The Internet and World Wide Web are both essential elements in the IT infrastructure of any organisation. Thus the Webmaster can play an important role in managing the library assets according to the information center's strategic planning.

As Systems Librarian

Shearer describes the term Systems librarians as:

- "Individuals who are responsible of designing, supporting and developing systems to enhance access to and management of the library's collection. Ensuring that the computer-based systems are essential to the library's work at all times."

Responsibilities

- Evaluation, planning, implementation and maintenance of library automation and Internet access, network maintenance as well as web page design and maintenance.

- Evaluation and selection of databases and software and staff training.
- Maintains computer security and hardware.

Skills

- Knowledge of networking, Internet and software applications.
- Ability to master new computer hardware and software.
- Ability to diagnose and solve hardware, software and networking problems.
- Ability to communicate technology to the uninitiated.
- Ability to work in a dynamic and changing environment.

Electronic Access to What and by Whom

Selecting academic information resources requires a broader view. For any library, the determination of which databases to provide and who will access them has become an ever more complex due to the number of databases that are now available has grown by leaps and bounds over the past few years. Today's systems librarian is often involved in the decision of which database service to supply to end-user desktops. There are myriad choices of general topic and specialty products available online, on the Intranet, on CD-ROM, and via the Web, at all price points. In today's academic setting, the librarian not only has to take into account the resource for the library's own collection but has to weigh offering the database to a wider user base against what end users within the university are already accessing by way of their own desktops.

Thus the systems librarian must weigh the type of access to provide against questions of:

- Timeliness,
- System capabilities, and
- Client expectations of good service.

Access Policies

Schuhnan quote that once the library decides which databases to select, it must determine how to deploy them and who will have access to them. As electronic access to external databases becomes more prevalent throughout all academic areas, the systems librarian's budget and equipment come under greater pressure. Whenever contemplating the addition of a new database resource it's also a good opportunity to review internal corporate access policies. As quickly as events dictate change in resource selections, policy revisions will naturally be carefully thought about more frequently. Decisions such as supplying access to information for those with a 'need to know' are undergoing modification.

Increasingly, those with a 'need to know' occupy expanding outward circles within organisations. Schulman added, smart organisations are extending information resources access to more employees as competitors become more aggressive and move more quickly. They are finding that providing more employees with timely access to competitive information allows an organisation to respond to competitive threats more quickly.

As the system librarian continuously evaluate databases and the provision of access to them, here is a series of questions to ask each time considering a new source:

- Is this source unique or does it duplicate an existing resource.
- If it's a close duplicate, is it less expensive, easier to use, or unique in another beneficial way.
- How does this database fit in with the corporate mission.
- Who within the university will benefit from this database—all users, faculty members and university community.
- What is the cost-benefit ratio.
- What critical element does this database supply that overcomes a poor cost-benefit ratio.
- Does this resource fit within our existing budget.
- Does another resource have to be eliminated to bring on this resource, and, if so, what impact will that have to the budget and to those who depend on the resource under consideration for elimination.
- Will this resource improve service to our clients/customers? How?
- In what format will we purchase the database.
- How will this database be integrated into our other resources.
- What changes have to be made to the hardware/software configuration to accept this new database and how will this impact our budget? How will it impact access to other resources?
- How will we provide access to this resource?
- Who in which departments and at which levels within the university will have access to this resource? Directly? Indirectly.
- Will end-user training have to be provided?
- Will additional staff be required?
- What other departments should be involved in this decision?
- How much time and effort is involved in implementing access to this resource?
- When will the corporation see a return on investment?

Thus by using this list as a guideline and foundation for decision making should help the system librarian to revise the questions as the mission, budget, environmental influences changes and stay ahead of the game.

As In-House Content Providers

The meaning of In-house Content Provider refers to:

- "one who was interested in exploring the balance between making its content freely available on the Internet while protecting its print-based revenue stream."

Funke provide a comprehensive comment on the new role of the Information Professionals as an In-House Content Providers. He claimed that along with the new technologies comes interacting with different groups within an organisation such as the MIS people, an information professional must have the ability to effectively 'bring content to the table" and work effectively with MIS as a team to make this content readily available. In order for information professionals to effectively do this, they must keep up with the latest technologies related to text retrieval, content organisation, search technologies, and knowledge management.

Bringing Content to the Table

Making MIS people understand the importance and expertise of people who know content and how clients will use it can be a constant uphill battle. Many programmers in this situation view another 'player' either as a threat or someone who doesn't have their background. Unfortunately, the onus lies on the information professional to make programmers understand what we can contribute, the value we can provide.

For starters, before you can integrate content into a Web site, you must understand:

- The overall requirements of the current Web site, including servers,
- Their ability to handle various indexes; search engine capability; and
- How the parser is set up to integrate content.

The Information Professional can provide expertise on how to organise content on a site; how users might search for the content; and the search requirements needed to access the content.

Metadata

Many information professionals have taken courses such as cataloging and indexing. These courses can serve as a foundation for the resource-organising activities on the Internet involving metadata.

Metadata provides document information on and from Web sites, producing an index or directory to the resource.

With the tremendous growth of content on the Web, there is a need to standardise the organisation of the information.

As metadata standards are further defined and organisations embrace these new standards, many questions will need answering such as:

- What will be worth cataloging?
- How detailed should the descriptions of various resources be?

Information Professionals can play a major role in helping answer these questions.

Search Engines

Researcher added, the evaluation and use of search engines is a 'product' that Information Professionals should manage within their organisations because they:

- Understand and know how to use Boolean logic.
- Can evaluate search engines from the user perspective?
- Know how to implement effective user searching of content.

Some of the major Intranet search engines available these days include Fulcrum Surfboard, Verity, Microsoft Index Server, and Excalibur. Thus, when implementing the Boolean logic features of these search engines, most programmers, will say that users cannot grasp Boolean logic or that such control is unnecessary as long as the search engines do relevancy rankings of documents retrieved. Users can go beyond basic Boolean operators such as AND, OR, NOT, which programmers usually dictate for them, and take advantage of proximity operators such as NEAR and NEARIN.

From experience, when one explains the differences in search results to users, *e.g.,* the effect of using the Boolean operators and NEAR, end-user searchers understand and respond positively right away. Programmers may support their positions by doing a query to see how many searches were performed using each Boolean operator. Information Professionals should try search queries for this type of data, too. Request the tools to perform this kind of query. What some programmers find difficult to understand is that you just can't implement a feature without some user education. Information Professionals can play an important role by providing this guidance within their organisations.

Information Retrieval Agents

Making sense of the overwhelming amount of indexed information constitutes one of the biggest challenges of the Web. To help, we see a rising use of Web robots, called information retrieval agents. These agents know where to look for relevant information based on user direction, advanced search algorithms, and learned behaviour. Major players in this area include NewsBot, Agent ware, and Wise Wire. As organisations move towards managing knowledge, intelligent information retrieval agent software tools will playa major role and will require people with the ability to manage and evaluate these tools. Search agents work when a user sets up search queries to 'train the documents,' whereby the agents learn from human behaviour and use pattern recognition to find relevant information to automate the retrieval process.

Information Professionals with expertise in searching and content analysis can help manage and evaluate these tools. Note that several of the traditional electronic publishers have already begun exploring this technology, *e.g.,* LEXIS-NEXIS and UMI with WiseWire Professional, an agent technology that evaluates user's viewing habits. Like it or not, new technologies are changing the information professional's role and the opportunities to enhance one's role have become boundless. To take advantage of the opportunities, Information Professionals must keep up with the emerging technologies, recognise the opportunities to utilise our skill sets, and work with MIS to effectively implement change. At times it can be frustrating and overwhelming, but the opportunities to grow and learn outweigh any negatives.

AS KNOWLEDGE MANAGER

Peter Drucker has predicted that the most important profession in the next century will be knowledge worker, and knowledge workers are not the same as computer systems specialists. He claimed that the most competent ones are likely to be reference librarians using sophisticated hardware and software, tools which the end user does not know how to use. Certainly, those who have exploited the almost unlimited opportunity to provide more information have taken advantage of this development.

Still, Drucker assumed that this deluge of knowledge would drown us and force us to seek people to manage that knowledge. Knowledge workers would assess knowledge on behalf of those who had neither the time nor the inclination to do so. The concept of knowledge management embraces the need to organise large data files, and to link and integrate different but related files and databases to one another so that users can move between and among related resources efficiently.

Thus, Church believe the transformation from librarian to knowledge manager is clearly underway; however, a deeper look at the direction that the Internet is taking business reveals the possibility of more far-reaching changes. As many library services processes move to the Internet, the use of information will become integrated with these processes. In this environment, information as a distinct function or resource may no longer exist.

Changing Roles and Responsibilities

The information transfer cycle is directly affected by Internet use. They should "embrace the entire new information transfer cycle, from the creation, restructuring and representation of information to its dissemination and use." They have an important and valuable role to tell users what users ought to see and read. It is to protect library clients from drowning in the information overflow and help them work smarter.

How their role as knowledge managers would evolve within the next few years, Church outline five key functions:

1. *Consultant:* Their role would involve less 'doing' and more consultation. This role would require remote support to endusers within the organisation. In effect, 'foot traffic' would be replaced by remote consultation for complex search strategies.
2. *Analyst:* Some information professional felt that their role would

require increased value-added in the form of analysing and interpreting information that is presented to end-users.

3. *Intranet content manager:* With the integration of external data into corporate Intranets, a key function of the information services professional will be to source and manage the content which is accessible through the system.
4. *Product planner and marketer:* Data integration also forces information professionals to become product developers and planners, with responsibility for packaging information and marketing products, services and delivery strategies to internal audiences.
5. *Corporate knowledge manager:* Increased recognition of knowledge as a valuable strategic resource could heighten the importance of the information professional. It foresee a merger of all information functions into a single department or function. Being the Knowledge Manager just means that they create value to my organisation by facilitating access to high quality information and by networking people and their ideas together using the technological infrastructure.

These new responsibilities imply a totally different skill set. The emphasis will shift from:

- Technical skills in the library to communication,
- Facilitation, training and management skills.
- Interact with IT staff and managers beyond Knowledge Management (KM).

To adjust to these more far-reaching changes, information professionals must search beyond current bounds and think in terms of benefits to their organisations. Right now, information can be used to enhance competitiveness and productivity. These same benefits will remain in the future, no matter what the role involves.

If information is to be seamlessly integrated with transaction processes, then someone must scope out work-related behaviours to ensure that it is done in the most efficient and effective manner. And, if equal information and technology is available to everyone, then competition rests on the ability to interpret and apply these tools. Clearly the impending shift to knowledge management represents an exciting change for academic librarians. However, it's an opportunity that requires a great deal of preparation, and a new way of thinking.

AS COLLABORATORS/PARTNERSHIPS

All organisations are in the period of transformation including academic libraries and librarians should use this period of change to establish, refocus and strengthen partnerships with other professionals groups within their institutions.

There are two significant groups with which library professionals should establish strong collaborative relationships:

1. Faculty and
2. Technologists.

Creth suggest in order for a real partnership to succeed, librarians need to see themselves as part of the teaching and research endeavor, and participate as an active and integral member of the education team. He added, for some librarians this idea of a partnership with faculty may require incorporating a different concept of their importance in relation to the faculty and developing new expectations and different behaviour. In the most general sense, librarians need to be certain that their commitment to service does not display itself through behaviour that is like of a servant.

Library professionals also need to reshape and strengthen their relationships with the computer specialists in the university with reasons such as:

- To eliminate much of the waste that occurs in most organisations where computer and information technology remains untapped or barely utilised because the learning curve is too steep for so many people and because the design of the equipment and software is so often far from intuitive.
- The New Information Professionals can provide constant feedback to designers and programmers about what works, what does not work, what new functions are needed.
- They can become the voice of the inexpert user, the typical person who is not technically inclined but strongly needs the service that the technology promises to deliver.
- They are both dealing with changing and chaotic times, and their activities are centered around information technology, so they should naturally consider themselves partners in addressing the many challenges that exist.
- They need to be willing, to share the act of discovery, to be able to identify shared goals, and to work together as peers.

If, librarians are to be prepared to absorb and even help shape the magnitude of predicted change into this 21st century, then it will be important for librarians to realign their relationships within the university so that strong partnerships exist to provide us with necessary support as well as knowledge for meeting the challenges ahead.

AS EDUCATOR

Anderson emphasised that librarians have always played a key role in education. They have formed relationships with subject specialists to build library collections to support instruction in the classroom and provided instruction in the form of classes on library skills and have conducted library instructional orientations sessions to assist students doing research in their classes. Today, in the digital age, librarians can no longer be simply information providers or the 'keepers of knowledge'.

The changes in technology using electronically stored and retrieved information has changed the way patrons and students are able to access, retrieve and use information. The instantaneous access of information through the Internet has made vast amounts of information and data available to anyone with a computer, a modem and a provider. Digital information is changing the role of librarians from "a person who students ask for assistance in finding information to someone who needs to provide services and instruction regardless of place, time or format." But how do we make important and valid information available to our faculty and students that may appear on the Web tomorrow?

Big Six Information Skills

As educators, Eisenberg have suggested that librarians must acquire these skills; the ability to:

- Define the task,
- Information seeking strategies,
- Location and access,
- Use of information,
- Synthesis,
- Evaluation.

The librarian's role too has:

- Expanded with a much broader instructional and participatory role in the instructional process. This role can be one of actively participating in the building of on-line courses by providing assistance in finding current and valid information for instructors delivering instruction on the Internet.
- Extend into the area of providing instruction and librarians must be involved in creating independent thinkers.
- Enhanced their roles to knowledge navigators and instructors teaching the discipline called information literacy.
- Be one of teaching critical thinking and resource-based learning.

New vocabulary in education such as: living curriculum, critical literacy, information power, information literacy, and information problem solving mandate that we re-examine our roles as professional information providers and educators. Students need to acquire the skills of evaluating information. This new vocabulary is bringing new challenges in library instruction. Changes in education such as the infusion of instructional technology and the use the Internet to deliver instruction has also changed how libraries and librarians can provide and assist instructors in teaching in the digital age.

New Trends in Instruction—Web Based Course Delivery

The trend in education towards distance learning and web-based courses is providing new challenges for information professionals as service providers as well as instructors. We are required to provide access to quality and valid information to support on-line instruction as well as provide on-line instruction both indirectly in the form of guides and on-line tutorials as well as directly in the form on courses to teach information literacy. Universities are recognising the necessity of requiring an information literacy course as part of the curriculum in the digital age.

As educators, the librarians are using a variety of tools and teaching techniques to assist students such as:

- *Provide instruction through learning guides and on-line tutorials:* Finding quality information is the biggest challenge our faculty and students are faced in the research and instructional process. With the advent of distance delivery of instruction and web-based pages for libraries using the vast amounts of information available on the Internet, it is essential that independent learners are skilled in locating information. Students can access these tutorials and guides from home or from the computers in the library and walk through self-paced instruction on any topic from "What is the Internet? To How do I do research?"
- *Provide access to guides to recommended search engines for the Internet:* Using search engines effectively and choosing the best search engines for your specific needs may be the most challenging skill that learners need to master. Guides to recommend search engines that introduce and compare search engines in a standard format are an invaluable tool for independent learners. Students can readily compare the different features of several search engines and access the search engines directly from your library's page.
- *Provide instruction in the area of Information Literacy:* Teaching Information Literacy in the electronic environment is a new and exciting role for librarians. Creating courses and formal instruction in the discipline of information literacy with the purpose of encouraging independent learners and critical thinkers to meet the challenges of the new information age is the role of the future for librarians. In today's workplace, employees are not only expected to work well with others, communicate well, find creative solutions to problems; they will also be expected to use the Internet and electronic information effectively to solve problems and conduct business. More and more businesses are moving towards conducting business on the Web for advertising, delivering services and products as well as using the Internet as a communication tool. Librarians must be involved in

creating valuable employees with the current skills required to be successful on the job.

Librarians are the most appropriate professionals to lead the team of people in finding the answers to the challenges we are facing in the digital environments of electronic information and the Internet. They have always been the experts at teaching people how to use the tools to locate that information regardless of format. They are the most effective searchers and researchers and their basic role of teaching those skills has not changed. Thus, in this fast and ever-changing information environment, librarians need to make full use of information and multimedia technology to support a greatly expanded teaching venture. The technology and varied format of information is changing and making new demands on their profession. In this fast-paced world it is important that they change with the changing roles and challenges.

AS MANAGERS

Researcher address how change has affect everyone in the organisations from leaders to employees and clients—the needs to shift his or her mind-sets, seeing the organisation and their established and new roles sometimes highly threatening and unfamiliar activities. Thus he added, employees need emotional support to adapt to change; support in learning new ways of working and relating. Linda claimed that information technology has changed a librarian's jobs; they have to readjust to new situation and develop new skills of managing the investments of an organisation—in people, technologies, and collections. As managers, they need to look for outcomes rather than just thinking about managing a resource at the resource level. The human resource in any organisation is the key to its success or failure.

Changes in Library Management

We have seen that the major external force that is technology had affected libraries; that means the library managers must use new structures in their management. *Strategic planning—strategic thinking*—should be a fundamental concept that librarians incorporate into their daily activities. Overall they need to give greater attention to strategic planning at the organisation and departmental level, and then integrating these strategic plans into the goals and activities of individual professionals. With a shifting organisational environment and culture, managers should shift their responsibilities and approach to one that is more consultative and supportive rather than one of authority and control.

The role of the manager should focus on:

- Coaching and mentoring staff.
- Development of staff.
- Developing shared values and vision among staff.

- Providing resources within framework of cost-benefit assessment.
- Taking pride in the accomplishments of others,
- Providing incentives to team work.

Library staff who are struggling to keep up with the demands in today's work environment require, indeed deserve, new ways for accomplishing their work. The redesign of the library organisation is imperative if we are to move rapidly and with an entrepreneurial spirit in the delivery of services in the current interactive high- speed communication environment.

Thus to be successful, libraries must reshape the prevailing corporate culture and build into their organisational structures and their approaches to work.

As managers, researcher stress that they must possess:

- The ability to identify, anticipate, and quickly respond to constantly changing customer needs.
- Capable of leaps forward and breakthrough performance.
- Must be ready to abandon formerly successful approaches to work, strategies, processing systems and services.
- Good communication at all levels, staff participation and training.

The librarians in transition that want to consciously manage their change efforts need to help their staff understand the change process and how they can positively participate. Creating an overall framework that shows the considered changes are a natural evolution from current practices, assessing that the organisation has the expertise and climate to implement the proposed changes.

Instead of organising personnel around how librarians do their work, librarians must:

- Organise around customers and how they do their work.
- Reduce hierarchy, flatten the organisation, and eliminate redundancy in order to be more responsive to changing needs and new opportunities and developments.
- Give up their need for control and their desire to create stability.

We Live in a Time of Change

The information has change our profession and library managers today have to pick up new skills to adjust to changes and to be able to survive in the future.

AS INFORMATION RESOURCE MANAGER

The term Information Resource Manager refers to:

- "Individuals who are responsible for the provision of information resources—be they print or electronic or technical infrastructure—and the power of digital technology, which grows everyday. To provide the leadership to conceptualise and manage the broad array of information resources that are necessary to support its mission".

As an Information Resource Manager, the librarian would continually go through a ten-step process:

- *Step 1. Define the Customers:* Who are the library's primary customers?
- *Step 2. Understand the Customers Needs:* One of the best ways to help you analyse the needs of the workforce and effectiveness of your current information strategy, is to arrange an information audit examples:
  — Implementation of custom survey designed to take an inventory of products, services and personnel related to information activities
  — Interviews with key personnel
  — Understand the users needs
  — Analysis of surveys and interviews
  — Creation of 'information strategy' designed to help maximize investment in users and services
  — Recommendations
- *Step 3. Map Needs against Decisions and Sources:* This will list information originators and users; sources required and decision supported. It will also identify high pay-off opportunities, for example where certain information has multiple uses.
- *Step 4. Implement a Sourcing Strategy:* The source/needs map from step 3 will point to clusters of information needs that can give economies in purchasing. For example, purchasing a networked CD-ROM may be more cost-effective than doing multiple ad-hoc online searches.
- *Step 5. Define Information Policies and Standards:* Steps 1-4 will reveal, often to many people for the first time, the sheer wealth of information that is available. This step therefore involves:
  — Classification standards,
  — Ownership,
  — Life-cycle management standards
  — Agreed 'protocols and procedures' between owners and users.
- *Step 6. Select a Pilot Project:* Select a key decision process that involves people across several departments as a pilot.
- *Step 7. Select and Adapt Appropriate Technology:* With the selected pilot project acting as a focal point, now is the time to start detailed consideration example of the computer solution. The choices are bewildering, and are proliferating daily.
- Step 8. *Nurture the Intelligence Processes:* This requires encouraging interaction across departmental boundaries and subcultures. Therefore, the creation of events and forums to encourage this interchange is often a useful starting point.

- *Step 9. Focus Dissemination:* Issue weekly or monthly bulletins of key developments; it should be short and focused. They give organisation relevant and specific information that no external newsletter, with its generic coverage, can provide.
- *Step 10. Market the Capability:* Create two way interactions with library clients. Use all the techniques of marketing to reach the library's internal audience and consider carefully the incentives the library can offer to encourage the regular inflow of useful information.

AS TRAINER

Ben regard managing technological change is somewhat akin to the Queen's concept of progress in Through the Looking Glass. He claimed *"It takes all the running you can do, to keep in the same place. If you want to get somewhere else, you must run at least twice as that."* Thus to 'manage' this frenetic running pace, training is critically important. Trainers have to be very philosophical people, very adaptable, too. MacKellar claimed that two million anecdotes of unhappy and unavoidable crisis situations, however, do not replace the necessity of thorough preparation and competent training coverage, especially with basic tools such as Internet, CD-ROMs and other electronic sources.

He added, in the documentation manual for Folio VIEWS, the following four statements are listed, emphasising the fact that trainers have to train users to do more than simply be able to push the right buttons:

- *Information* does not equal knowledge.
- Use of *information* can lead to knowledge.
- If you can't find the *information* you need, gaining knowledge can be difficult.
- If you can't use the *information* once you find it, gaining knowledge can be impossible.

So, what can trainers do to move users from button pushing to knowledge gathering? They can be patient, teach some underlying technology, and explain some basic search rules. Erlendsdottir consider training in libraries as in other organisations, is divided into two main categories:

1. *Maintenance training*—that enables the library to maintain its existing procedures and include induction training for new entrants to the library system or particular parts.
2. *Basic updating and improvement training in identified areas*—whereby training should be concerned with the whole person, concepts, skills and behaviour patterns.

As suggested, the technological training needs of the librarians in libraries depend on the IT level of the particular level.

Thus, the librarian must:

- know the Art of the Search.
- know what the systems contain example how the shopping streets of information are laid out.
- know the back alleys as well as the main routes to the information example on the CD-ROMs.
- bargain with the system to get the 'best answers' in the cheapest, quickest way.
- consider using a greater range of visual and auditory challenges in the presentation.
- keep abreast of the ongoing and latest technological advancements.
- able to identify the body of core knowledge and skills required by them to run information and communication technology applications.
- improve and promote the existing and new library services to reach their clients.

Training library users to use these technological resources, and to understand the cultural rules and the new environment such as functional setup, linking, split screens, exporting, cutting and pasting) are the challenges. Trainers are similar in a way to personal shoppers for Westerners who land in Hong Kong and don't know the environment or culture. Thus the trainer's end goal is to see these clients finally doing their own shopping in the information marketplace, hopefully with enough expertise to be able to pick up a few bargains.

Why the Need for Training

The three major benefits are:

1. Appreciate the gaps that may exist between what is currently being done and what needs to be done.
2. Opportunity to make corrections in their systems within a safe environment.
3. Develop 'ownership' and reduce or eliminate staff and users resistance to change, thereby adding longevity to the system.

Training for trainers is regard a necessity in academic libraries and it is the library's responsibility to structure training so as to help librarians clarify both their own expectations and the expectations of their clients and the organisation itself.

AS RESEARCHER

In a complex and rapidly changing environment, higher education must help students to become information literate. Information literacy enables students to recognise the value of information and use it to make informed choices in their personal, professional and academic lives. An information literate student effectively accesses, evaluates, organises, synthesises and applies information from a variety of sources and formats in a variety of contexts. Information literacy requires an ongoing involvement in learning and in evaluating information so that life long learning is possible."

As research and teaching increasingly rely on global networks for the creation, storage and dissemination of knowledge, the need to educate information-literate students has become more widely recognised. Students often lack the skills necessary to succeed in this rapidly changing environment, and faculty need training and support to make use of new technologies for effective teaching and learning. The current environment provides an opportunity for librarians to playa key role in the evolution of an integrated information literacy curriculum, in contrast to past efforts which were sporadic and rarely programmatically based. Librarians have always played a key role in research activities in the academic environment.

They have conducted library instructional orientations sessions to assist students doing research. Thus, to assist clients in their research activities, the librarian must acquire the information skills to manage the overload of information available in many formats propelled by technological advancements.

The Search Strategy

The best strategy involves identifying "what type of information need and which library resources will best provide that information." The time spent developing a well-organised search strategy will reduce the overall time and effort required to assist and conduct research. Following the steps in the *flowchart* below will lead to a well organised research report:

Follow chart

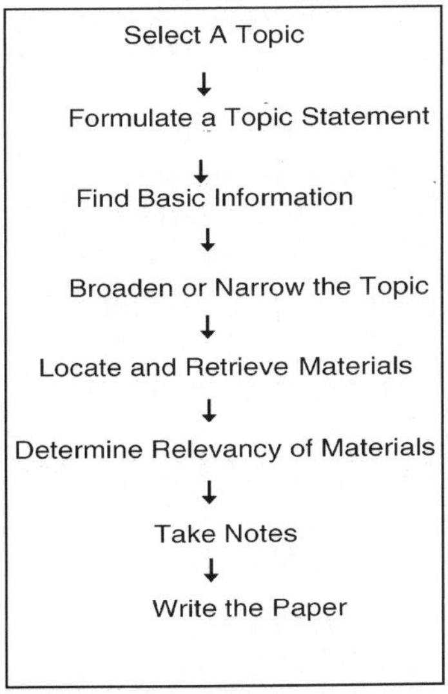

Select A Topic
↓
Formulate a Topic Statement
↓
Find Basic Information
↓
Broaden or Narrow the Topic
↓
Locate and Retrieve Materials
↓
Determine Relevancy of Materials
↓
Take Notes
↓
Write the Paper

Information Literacy Competencies

The impact on student who is information literate is able to:

- Identify and articulate needs which require information solutions:
  - — Recognise a specific information need.
  - — Focus and articulate the information need into a researchable question.
  - — Understand that the type and amount of infor-mation selected is determined in part by the parameters of the need, as well as by the information available.
- Identify and select appropriate information sources:
  - — Recognise the availability of a variety of sources and of assistance with using them.
  - — Identify types of information resources in a variety of formats and understand their characteristics.
  - — Select types of information resources appropriate to a specific information need.
- Formulate and efficiently execute search queries appropriate for the information resource:
  - — Understand that different information sources and formats require different searching techniques, including browsing.
  - — Select the search strategies appropriate to the topic and resource.
  - — Understand that various resources may use different controlled vocabularies to refer to the same topic.
  - — Use search language appropriate to the source, such as a controlled vocabulary, key words, natural language, author and title searches to locate relevant items in print and electronic resources.
  - — Use online search techniques and tools to locate relevant citations and to further refine the search.
- Interpret and analyse search results and select relevant sources:
  - — Understand that search results may be presented according to various ordering principles.
  - — Assess the number and relevance of sources cited to determine whether the search strategy must be refined.
  - — Recognise the components of a citation and differentiate between types of resources cited, such as a book, periodical, or government document, as well as the format.
  - — Use the components of a citation to choose those most suitable for the information need.
  - — Perceive gaps in information retrieved and determine whether the search should be refined.
- Locate and retrieve relevant sources in a variety of formats from the global information environment:

  - — Understand the organisation of materials in libraries and use locally produced location guides.
  - — Understand how to use classification systems and their rationale.
  - — Use location information in the bibliographic record to retrieve locally owned resources.
  - — Use local resources to locate information sources in the global information environment.
  - — Understand that libraries have developed methods for locating and sharing resources not owned locally and use the appropriate resource sharing system, such as interlibrary loan or document delivery, to retrieve information.
  - — Understand that the Internet may be a useful resource for locating, retrieving and transferring information electronically.
- Critically evaluate the information retrieved:
  - — Use a variety of criteria, such as author's credentials, peer review, and reputation of the publisher, to assess the authority of the source.
  - — Assess the relevancy of a source to an information need by examining publication date, purpose, and intended audience.
  - — Recognise omission in the coverage of a topic.
  - — Recognise and evaluate documentation for the information source, such as research methodology, bibliography or footnotes.
  - — Distinguish between primary and secondary sources in different disciplines and evaluate their appropriateness to the information need.
  - — Apply evaluation criteria to all information formats.
- Organise, synthesise, integrate and apply the information:
  - — Use appropriate documentation style to cite sources used.
  - — Summarise the information retrieved.
  - — Recognise and accept the ambiguity of multiple points of view.
  - — Organise the information in a logical and useful manner.
  - — Synthesise the ideas and concepts from the information sources collected.
  - — Determine the extent to which the information can be applied to the information need.
  - — Integrate the new information into existing body of knowlcdgc.
  - — Create a logical argument based on information retrieved.
- Self-assess the information-seeking processes used:
  - — Understand that information-seeking consists of evolving, non-linear processes that include making multiple decisions and choices.
  - — Describe the criteria used to make decisions and choices at each step of the particular process used.

- — Assess effectiveness of each step of the process and refine the search process in order to make it more effective.
- — Understand that many of the components of an information seeking process are transferable and, therefore, are applicable to a variety of information needs.

- Understand the structure of the information environment and the process by which both scholarly and popular information is produced, organised and disseminated:
  - — Understand that information structure, *e.g.*, how information is produced, organised, and disseminated, can vary from discipline to discipline.
  - — Understand that the value of a particular type of information resource may vary from discipline to discipline.
  - — Understand that the information structure in a particular discipline can change and modify search strategies to accommodate these changes.
- Understand public policy and the ethical issues affecting the access and use of information:
  - — Understand the ethics of information use, such as knowing how and when to give credit to information and ideas gleaned from others by appropriately citing sources in order to avoid plagiarism.
  - — Respect intellectual property rights by respecting copyright.
  - — Understand concepts and issues relating to censorship, intellectual freedom, and respect for differing points of view.
  - — Understand the social/political issues affecting information, such as:
    - — Privacy.
    - — Privatisation and access to government information.
    - — Electronic access to information.
    - — The exponential growth of information.
    - — Equal access to information.

CYBRARIANS

The word 'Cybrarian' was coined by Michel Bauwens, Information Officer at BP Nutrition in Antwerp, Belgium, to describe the staff in a virtual library. We may expand this definition to an Information Professional/Librarian who utilises digital and networked communications technologies to the fullest to retrieve, evaluate and disseminate information. While it is not currently possible to obtain a degree in 'cybrarianship', there are possibilities for advancing your knowledge of these technologies.

Characteristics of Cybrarians

So, what then are the characteristics of cybrarians. Keller commented:

- They remember the fundamental functions librarians perform: selection, description and intellectual access, interpretation, distribution, and preservation.
- They remember that they are present to serve the current, local population of readers first, but also perhaps remote readers as well, thanks to the networks.
- They remember also that they perform a vital role as custodians of culture, assuring that the records of man's investigations and creative works survive for those not yet born.
- Many of them are subject specialists, expert and educated in a discipline as well as prepared to 'teach' in structured and unstructured settings.
- Many of them are technical specialists, catalogers, circulation librarians, conservationists.
- Some of them were either subject specialists or technical specialists or both and then became managers or leaders.
- All of them are comfortable with the constant on-rush of LT. and realise their fundamental functions must be performed regardless of the media or format of the information carrier.
- All of them are acutely aware of the need to be as responsive as possible to individuals even while translating a cacophony of individual needs and requests to systems and services intended to serve whole populations, whole communities.
- All of them will be ready to work with their colleagues in the next building, the next city or town, the next country or continent by using the communications potential of the networks.
- None of them will need a lot of sleep, for there will be more and more for them to do.
- Many of them will have strong entrepreneurial spirit.

The IP is knowledge-based and service-oriented. In some form, the role of the IP has always been to assist others with a quest for knowledge. Information and the knowledge to which it leads have evolved through many forms-speech, writing, print, broadcast media and computer-based electronic media. Access to a high speed, national or international computer network will significantly alter the way in which professionals will work in the coming decade. He added tomorrow's cybrarian who is familiar with this multitude of information databases and services which can be searched, will possess a role that will emphasise on information-hunting strategy and provide a strategic advice for users with technologically literate background

Bibliography

Ajit Singh Siwatch: *Library and Information Science, Vols. I to III* , Shree Publishers, 2010.

Amjad Ali: *Ane's Library and Information Science*, Ane Books India, 2006.

Anil Parnami: *Library Information : System and E-Journal Archiving*, Cyber Tech, 2011.

B.S. Aggarwal: *Issues in Library Information Science* , Oxford Book Company, 2007.

Bhupendra Narayan Singh: *Library and Information Science in the Digital Age Vols. I to III*, Anmol Pub, 2011.

Bikika Laloo Tariang: *Library and Information Science Education*, Ess Ess Publications, 2012.

C K Sharma; Rakesh Kumar and Akhil Kumar Singh: *Library and Information Science (3 Vols-Set)*, Atlantic, 2008.

C Lal and K Kumar: *Library and Information Science*, Ess Ess Pub, 2010.

C Praveen Singh: *Library and Information Science*, Alfa, 2008.

D.B. Patil and M.M. Kooganuramath: *Library and Information Science*, APH, 2011.

D.C. Ojha and D.V. Kothari: *Library and Information Science : Vol. 5. Digital Libraries*, Scientific, 2005.

G. Devarajan: *Applied Research in Library and Information Science*, Ess Ess Pub, 2005.

G. Devarajan: *Research in Library and Information Science*, Ess Ess Pub, 2002.

K.L.M. Swaminathan: *Library and Information Science (3 Vols-Set)*, Sarup and Sons, 2001.

K.T. Dilli: *Library and Information Science in a Digital Era*, Atlantic, 2009.

Kanchan Kamila: *Library and Information Science*, Ess Ess Publications, 2012.

Khalid K. Faruqi and Mehtab Alam: *Library Information Systems and E-Journal Archiving*, Authorspress, 2005.

Khalid K. Faruqi and Mehtab Alam: *Library and Information Science*, Aakar Books, 2005.

Krishan Kumar And Jaideep Sharma: *Library And Information Science Education in India*, Har-anand Publications, 2009.

Kundan Godia: *Electronic Services in Library and Information Science*, Adhyayan, 2007.

Kusum Verma: *Library Information and Society*, Vista International, 2005.

Kusum Verma: *Library Information Services and Systems*, Vista International Pub, 2008.

Kusum Verma: *Modern Practices of Library Information Services*, Vista International, 2006.

L.B. Rakesh: *Library and Information Science in Digital Age*, Alfa Pub, 2006.

P K Singh: *Techniques in Library and Information Science*, Shree Pub, 2007.

P. Balasubramanian: *Advanced Computer Application in Library and Information Science*, Deep and Deep, 2011.

P.S.G. Kumar: *Foundations of Library and Information Science*, B.R. Publishing Corporation, 2012.

Punit Ralhan: *Advancement in Library and Information Science*, Oxford Book Company, 2009 .

Purushotham Tiwari and R.S. Kochar: *Library and Information Science*, APH, 2010.

Purushotham Tiwari: *Dictionary of Library and Information Science*, A.P.H. Pub, 2011.

R P Bajpai: *Current Trends in Library and Information Science*, Shree Pub, 2007.

Raghunath Pandey and M.N. Velayudhan Pillai: *Library and Information Science*, Jnanada Prakashan, 2011.

Ram Shobhit Singh: *Library Information Systems and E-Journal Archiving,* Anmol, Pub. 2008.

S.R. Das: *Managing Library Information Systems*, Arise Pub, 2008.

Sambhu Nath Halder and Sibsankar Jana: *Library and Information Science in Changing Paradigm*, Ess Ess Publications, 2013.

Santosh Patel: *Library Information : Preservation and Access*, Authors Press, 2003.

Shiv Ram Verma: *Foundations of Library and Information Science*, Shree, 2005.

Suryakant and O.S. Shekhar Singh: *Library and Information Science:*

Objective Questions Ability Tests For NET/SLET/JRF, Ess Ess

Pub, 2011.

T. Nasirudheen: *A Comprehensive Course in Library and Information Science*, Ess Ess Publications, 2012.

T. Saravanan: *Library and Information Science*, APH, 2008.

V.G. Choukhande: *Information Needs and Information Seeking Behaviour: Library and Information Science Research*, Shivneri Pub, 2008.

Vaishali Khaparde: *Advancement in Library and Information Science*, Ess Ess Publications, 2012.

Vrushali Dandavate: *Application of Six Sigma in Library and Information Science*, Ajay Khatri and Pradip Umdale, Ess Ess Publications, 2013.

Y.L. Chopra and Mamta Chopra: *Challenges Before Library and Information Science in New Millennium*, Ess Ess, 2001.

Index

A

Abstracts 108, 111, 113, 114, 115
Accommodate 80, 260, 298
Adequate 246
Adhocracy 266
Advantageous 195
Antiquarian 36
Appetites 81
Assumption 183

B

Barriers 68, 79, 277
Bureaucratic 54, 55, 266, 277

C

Cataloguing 93, 97
Centralized 94, 103
Cochrane 114, 115
Commercial 227
Comprehensive 220
Consortium 168, 187
Constellation 81, 268
Convergence 254, 268
Correspondence 103
Criteria 104

D

Data Acquisition 15
Description 107
Desideratum 36
Dictate 134, 281, 284
Diminish 82
Disparate 254, 260
Dissemination 68, 77, 270, 285, 293, 295
Distinctive 81
Distinguish 67, 80, 85, 297

E

Earmarked 264
Elementary 97
EMBASE 108, 113, 114
Embedded 259
Empathy 166
Encourage 219
Enhancing 192
European 90, 94, 99
Excavations 37

F

Facilitating 198
Familiarize 151
Feasibility 253

G

Geographical 89, 98, 103

H

Hierarchical 221
Hinayana 39
HyperCard 92, 93